Two Score and Ten

G.V. RAMAKRISHNA (b. 1930), started his career as a biochemist with the Rockefeller Foundation doing research in Haematology in the Bowring Hospital in Bangalore, his home town. He opted for the civil service and joined the Indian Administrative Service (IAS) in 1952.

He did his quota of service in the state of Andhra Pradesh for nearly 13 years, ending up as Chief Secretary in 1983. At the Centre he held positions at every level, including those of under, deputy, joint, additional secretaries and Secretary.

Early in his career he went to Harvard University for his MPA (Master in Public Administration), that included a business policy course at the Business School. He studied economics under Galbraith, Ed Mason and other notable economists of the late fifties.

In his diplomatic assignments, he was Minister of Economic Affairs at the Embassy in Washington in 1972 and was later India's Ambassador to the European Economic Community (European Union) in 1989.

In his varied career he worked for ten years with the Finance Ministry. He also worked in the Ministries of Industry, Steel, Coal and Petroleum. He was adviser in the Planning Commission in 1981 and Member in 1994. He was the first Chairman of SEBI and also of the Disinvestment Commission.

Two Score and Ten

My Experiences in Government

G V Ramakrishna

ACADEMIC FOUNDATION
NEW DELHI

First Published in 2004 by

ACADEMIC FOUNDATION

4772-73 / 23 Bharat Ram Road, (23 Ansari Road),
Darya Ganj, New Delhi - 110 002.
INDIA.

Phones : 23245001, 02, 03, 04.
Fax : +91-11-23245005.
e-mail : academic@vsnl.com
www : academicfoundation.com

Two Score and Ten : My Experiences in Government
by G.V. Ramakrishna

ISBN 81-7188-339-7

Designed and typeset by Italics India, New Delhi
and printed at Print Perfect, New Delhi.

Dedicated to my wife

Lalita Ramakrishna

who has been a source of inspiration for this book

Contents

Preface

A few months ago I completed fifty years in the service of Government. The normal period of service of a Government official is about thirty six years. I entered the IAS in 1952 and retired in 1988. Thereafter, I was appointed by four successive Prime Ministers to a number of posts. The range and variety of jobs was unusual and interesting.

The variety of assignments gave me an insight into the working of the Government, the capital market shenanigans and our diplomatic demands abroad. I wish to share these experiences with the readers in a frank and analytical manner.

For the last four years, after I left the Disinvestment Commission by the end of 1999, I continued as Chairman of the Construction Industry Development Council to which I had been nominated by the Deputy Chairman of the Planning Commission. With the approval of the Reserve Bank of India, I have been the Chairman of the Bank of America's Local Advisory Board for two years and also on the Board of Governors of HelpAge India. I am also chairing the Grading Committees of ICRA for construction companies and real estate developers.

As this book covers events spread over fifty years it would be useful to the reader to get some idea of contemporary responses to the events as they unfolded. I have presented extracts, wherever appropriate, of some of the leading articles and editorials of those times in the Press.

In order to elaborate my views on a number of subjects mostly connected with my work over all these years, a few selected articles and speeches are appended for reference.

Some photographs with notable personages are also provided to capture my interaction and meetings with them.

Since the book was written, a number of new developments have taken place in some of the areas covered in the book, particularly in disinvestment. I have tried to update the book by referring to some of them. I have also added, at appropriate places, some recent news reports which bring the subject up-to-date as far as possible.

Acknowledgements

I would like to record my gratitute to C.B. Bhave, Sucheta Dalal and Debashish Basu for their valuable contributions for the chapter on SEBI. I would like to thank my wife for making useful suggestions, patiently editing and correcting mistakes in typing. This book could not have been finished in time without her help. Finally, I would like to thank my publishers, Academic Foundation, for their meticulous and thorough effort in bringing out this book.

— GVR

List of Photographs / Illustrations

1

Early Days

Family History

THE earliest ancestor I know about is Venkateswara Yajwa, a Smartha Brahmin, who was a native of Sholavandi, a village now submerged under the Mettur Dam in Tamil Nadu. His grandson Annayyar, was a high official in the establishment of Dewan Purnaiya and was said to have been highly regarded by Tipu Sultan.

Annayyar took permission to demit service before his time, as he was unhappy with the politics of court life and wanted to live in peace. He wanted to settle in Gopichettipalayam, (the G in my name), then a part of Tipu's dominions. He purchased land there. The local residents were initially not in favour of an outsider settling in the village but the influence of the Dewan and the Sultan overcame the opposition. Later, the family became identified with that area.

Annayyar's great grandson was G. Srinivasa Iyer, my grandfather. He moved to Mysore, with his brother G.

Ramaswamy Sastrigal, who was older to him by nearly 20 years. The family travelled for two or three days by bullock carts carrying kerosene lanterns at night. At Mysore, the family was barely able to make a living. Ramaswamy Sastrigal was one of the foremost scholars in Vedanta and Nyaya in those days, but could only depend upon the Palace and Sringeri Mutt patronage. Later in life, he became Professor of Vedanta in the Maharaja's Sanskrit College in Mysore. My grandfather managed to continue his studies up to M.A., depending mainly on scholarships. He entered the Mysore Civil Service. He found service in the Revenue side incompatible with his ideas; he, therefore, took leave, went to Madras and completed his M.L., which gave him an entry into the judicial service of Mysore State as a district munsiff. He served as Judge of the Mysore High Court from 1927 till his retirement in 1932. He was known to be a strict judge, who would never be influenced wrongly. He was officiating Chief Justice, but was not confirmed before his retirement, as would have been done in the normal course, because Sir Mirza Ismail, the Dewan, was displeased that he did not toe the Government line in one or two cases at that time. Sir Mirza is said to have regretted his decision later on.

We continued to be a traditional family observing all the religious festivals and poojas. There was no dining table in our house and we all ate from plates lined up on the floor. These dinner sessions were interesting since we had discussions on many subjects including the Ramayana, the Freedom Movement and the World War.

Although women were not generally educated beyond middle school, some of them in my family were inclined to be more adventurous, at least in their thinking, than others. My paternal grandmother learnt English from a private tutor, Miss Lynn, and with her help translated Jane Eyre into Tamil in a book *Sasirekai* published in the thirties. In his autobiography, Madras High Court judge and Viceroy's Executive Counsellor Sir C. Sankaran Nair, writes as follows: 'While on the ridge at Delhi witnessing the procession of the King and Queen and the free movements of English women, the wife of Mr. Seshagiri Iyer, afterwards a Judge of the High Court, drew my wife's attention to the freedom of the English ladies and told her that she wished God would make her an English woman in her next life and not a Brahmin'. Seshagiri Iyer was my mother's maternal grandfather who came from an orthodox family of Trichinopoly in Tamil Nadu. In 1911, he was member of the Madras Legislative Assembly and went to Delhi for the Delhi Durbar of 1911. Perhaps his wife had a premonition of her bleak future. After her husband passed away in the twenties she had to have her head shaved and wear the traditional widow's dress which she must have detested.

When I was eight years and my sister and brother were six and four, our mother passed away. My brother, G.V. Viswanath joined the IAS in Karnataka state and retired as Additional Chief Secretary. Our father did not remarry and we all stayed with our grandparents. Our schooling was in Bangalore. My uncle was the Public Prosecutor and father G.S. Venkataramana Iyer joined the state government as Assistant Secretary and later served as the Secretary of the Mysore Legislature for over 25 years. My family had a strong predilection for government service.

My grandfather had a Fiat Ardita car, which he had bought from Sir Mirza Ismail, but it was rarely used by the family. My grandmother had a part time driver to take her to the ladies club for a game of cards. My father would take a bus to go to office and walk about three miles on the way back. I used to go to college by bicycle. Those days cycles had to have lamps at night. These were kerosene lamps till we got the dynamos. Those riding without lamps had to pay a fine of Rs. 5.

My schooling was in middle class schools. The Bangalore High School was started in 1941 by retired professors led by C.R. Narayana Rao. We had our classes in the rooms of a rented house and sometimes under a large tree. The teachers were dedicated and the students did well in their public exams. After intermediate college I joined the Chemistry Honours course at the Central College, Bangalore, one of the oldest colleges from where C. Rajagopalachari (Rajaji) had graduated years earlier. H.V.R. Iengar ICS, the right hand man of Sardar Patel, also passed out of this college with Honours in Chemistry.

After I graduated with an honours degree in Chemistry with a gold medal from the Mysore University (now called the Bangalore University) in 1949, I wanted to work in the subject as a scientist. I joined the Department of Chemical Technology in Bombay in the Dyeing section. After a few months I realized that my interests lay in medicine and biochemistry. I returned to Bangalore in time to join the Masters Degree course. When I graduated in 1950, I applied and got the job of Assistant brewer in the United Breweries on a salary of Rs. 700 per month When the appointment order came by mail, my grandfather was aghast at the idea. He asked me to decline the job and insisted that I take the civil services exam. As I could not take the exam before 1951, being under age, my professor recommended me for the post of chemist with the Rockefeller Foundation Team that was doing research on anaemias. The salary was Rs. 180 per month which was an improvement over Rs. 160 per month which I was offered as a demonstrator in the college. I joined the team of Dr. M.D. Anderson, which also had an Indian doctor. In those days research was being conducted on Vitamin B12 to test its efficacy in anaemias and also as a growth-promoting factor. The drug was brought to India with a FDA code number, as commercial use was not yet approved by the US FDA.

I was thrilled to work in the Bowring Hospital Bangalore where we were given ten beds for anaemia patients. Dr. Anderson wanted to examine the rural population for anaemias in pregnant women and also hook worm related anaemias. We had a van in which we would go into the villages around Bangalore and collect blood and stool samples. We would travel into the villages from 8 a.m. to 1 p.m. and collect samples, come back to the travellers' bungalow and analyse them till 6 p.m. After dinner our team would go to a village cinema or 'touring talkies', as they were called. I was also asked to test the growth promoting effects of Vit B12. We picked a hostel for boys and administered B12 to some boys and placebos to the control group and also analysed the nutrient content of the food that they were given.

I thoroughly enjoyed a year of this work. As I was nearing the age for applying for the UPSC exam for the IAS,

I asked Dr. Anderson whether I could get a scholarship to go the US for a Ph.D. in Biochemistry. He said that a doctor would be sent that year and that I had to wait for another year. My grandfather felt that I should enter the civil service. So I quit the job in March 1951 and sat down to serious study to take the IAS exam in September. When the results were declared after the interview in January 1952, I was set for a life in Government on a starting salary of Rs. 350 per month.

I was allotted to Hyderabad State but sent to Madras Presidency for training in the Telugu speaking district of Visakhapatnam. I first reported to the Chief Secretary Mr. Sathianathan ICS, in Fort. St. George Madras. I was surprised to see a very relaxed person sitting behind a vacant table with a book by P.G. Wodehouse. He was kind and said that I would like my training in Vizag as it had a senior Collector Mr. V.K. Rao. In those days many of the senior posts in the Secretariat, Board of Revenue and even in some big districts were held by ICS officers. Mr. V.K. Rao sent his jeep to the Railway station to take me to his residence to stay with him. When he went on tour to the hill station Araku he took me along with him in his jeep. Till the sixties, Collectors were given jeeps and not Ambassador cars for official duties.

In the Districts

A few months after I went to Vizag, the State of Andhra was formed and Mr. Rao was posted on special duty for sorting out the finances of the two States. The next Collector was Mr. Gwynn who was the last of the British ICS officers in Madras. He was a bachelor and a hard worker. His father had also been in the ICS in Madras and so he had a feeling for the State. Long after he retired, Mr. Gwynn compiled an English-Telugu dictionary which took him ten years to complete. He was given an award by the Andhra Pradesh Government in London where he had settled down after his marriage to an Indian lady. With the formation of Andhra, I was transferred and allotted to the Andhra Cadre.

Our training in the district was for a period of 14 months. It covered all the departments which operated at the district level and included revenue training. At that time the Zamindari Abolition Act had been passed a few years earlier, and was still under implementation. Many of the Zamindaris had no proper survey and settlement. Training in survey, involved field visits for long hours to measure and demarcate boundaries and to measure the areas and fix survey stones. The settlement process under Settlement officers of Collector's rank involved public hearings and determination of wet (irrigated) and dry (unirrigated) lands and fixing the fertility of the lands for the purpose of settling or fixing the land revenue and water charges. Then pattas or title deeds were issued in the names of tenants of the zamindar. Part of the revenue training was to study the work of the village accountant who had to maintain about 25 registers and the village headman who had about 10 registers. Then came the work of the Revenue Inspector and the Tahsildar which involved various types of reports after field enquiries. Other areas of training were forests, agriculture, police and treasury. The last was a complicated process at the level of district treasuries which were, at that time divided into banking and non banking treasuries. All revenue and stamp duty collections and all payments made throughout the district passed through the district treasury. For some period we were asked to act as District treasury officers. This was a difficult and responsible part of the training. Then there was magisterial work starting with Third class powers and moving on to Second class and First class powers depending on the recommendations of the District judge who would peruse the judgments of the trainees. There were tests to be passed in revenue, which were codified in the Boards Standing Orders or BSOs, as they were called in official jargon, and also in the local language.

After I got the powers of a First Class Magistrate, the district judge gave me a case involving a murder where the committal proceedings were done at the first class magistrate's level. This case was about the paramour of a village woman killing her husband with a long stick used for pounding paddy. After examining the evidence which essentially involved long standing enmity between the paramour and the husband and no eye witnesses, I had to discharge the accused after examining legal precedents. There was consternation in the prosecution and they decided to go in revision to the High Court. After several months the High Court concurred with my order. The district judge rang up to congratulate me.

During my village training I was posted to a Sub Collector's division in Narasipatnam. There was no electricity, and water had to be fetched from a nearby well and there was only dry sanitation. I stayed in a godown with a tiled roof. In the summer the temperature was 43 to 46 degrees Centigrate. The godown became an oven during daytime. I had court work in the verandah and in the evenings I would sit in the verandah and my cook would tend the petromax light which added to the heat. Coming from Bangalore with its salubrious climate, this was quite an experience. One day while priming the lamp, the tank burst and my cook became a flaming candle. He ran and doused himself with water from the well but not before he was badly burnt. While he was in the local hospital for a month I had to get my meals from the local karnam or patwari a on payment of Rs. 50 per month for two meals a day for myself and my cook.

After training in various Departments at the district level I was posted in independent charge as Subcollector of Vizianagaram. Unlike Narsipatnam, this place had electricity but no wet sanitation. State elections were announced in 1994 and I was Returning Officer (RO) for two constituencies, where the main candidates were the Rajah of Vizianagaram and his wife. Those days balloting was cumbersome. There were separate boxes for each candidate and the ballot paper was like a one rupee note, which had to be put in the box of the candidate of choice. When counting started around 6 p.m. it was found that there were about 4000 invalid votes, because the voters had used haldi, kumkum, and writings like good luck, om, etc. in English or Telugu. The RO had to personally sign each of the invalid papers. As this was a daunting task I sought instructions whether a facsimile of my signature could be affixed and the State Electoral Officer was Mr. Gwynn my former Collector. After checking with Delhi he said the facsimile could not be used. I sat up all night signing all the invalid votes. The Rajah and his wife were elected by a large majority because of traditional loyalty to the family.

Vijayawada

When, in 1955, I was transferred as Joint Magistrate to Vijayawada, work was significantly different. There was no separation of the judiciary from the executive. I had judicial work, hearing appeals from 2nd and 3rd class magistrates and trying 1st class cases myself. There were some interesting cases, which came up for trial before me. One was the spurious gold case. The *modus operandi* was as follows.

The crooks would hang around the Railway station and locate a villager who had just alighted from a train and was going outside on the road. One of the partners would walk a little ahead of the victim and drop a small packet wrapped in pink paper on the road and walk ahead fast. The villager would come across the packet when the accomplice would catch up with him and ask him what he had found. They would open the packet and find a piece of 'gold'. The accomplice would tell him that they could share it and took him to a goldsmith nearby who was also an accomplice. The goldsmith would tell the finders that the gold was valuable but he could not cut the piece into two as he had no implements. The accomplice would then tell the villager that he could keep the whole piece by paying him half the value of the piece. The villager would part with his money and the accomplice would vanish after wishing him good luck. Later when the victim located another goldsmith he was told that the 'gold' was spurious. I had a number of pink packets in my court as material objects in cases that came to me. I was amused to note several years later that a similar story was brought to the screen in the Hollywood film *Sting*.

The 'itching powder case' was another specialty of Vijayawada. The quarry would be an unsuspecting villager just coming out of the railway station. The first crook would go behind him and sprinkle some powder on the back of his neck and run away. The victim would be in agony with acute itching and run to the nearest public tap to wash his neck, leaving his bag away from the tap. The second crook would quickly walk away with the bag. Such cases also came to my court.

The new state of Andhra was formed by breaking away a large area with a majority Telugu speaking population and the capital of the State was Kurnool.

The formation of the new State was the result of extended agitation culminating in the fast unto death of Potti Sriramulu. It used to be said that even when he begged for food, his supporters saw the new State coming and kept him away from any form of nourishment, till he actually passed away a few days before the State was born. The truth of this story has not been verified.

Ministers had to pass through Vijayawada to go to the circar or coastal districts from the capital Kurnool and change from meter gauge to broad gauge or vice versa. The senior minister Kala Venkata Rao was in charge of revenue in the Prakasam ministry. I had to go to the railway station frequently around 11 p.m. to receive him. While waiting for the train I used the room of the Police Inspector to do some work. After a few times Venkata Rao said that I need not go to the station and the station police would look after him. He was always courteous to all officers. In fact, politicians those days were generally more courteous to officers than they are today. While I was in Vijayawada, the state of Andhra Pradesh was formed in 1956.

There was an incident while I was in Vijayawada which is interesting in more senses than one.

In the districts, there was the practice of annual Settlement of Revenue for each village, called the Jamabandi. The Sub Collector would conduct Jamabandi for all the villages in each of the Taluks in his Division, every year except the Taluk chosen by the District Collector for his inspection for that year. This was also the occasion for the public to attend and present their petitions called Jamabandi petitions which may be for individual problems or general issues. These were disposed of by orders issued on the spot after hearing the petitioner and the revenue officials.

In order to examine the 30 odd registers of each village for about 30 villages in the Taluk, village officers would be summoned to the taluk headquarters with all the registers for their villages. An Inspection Team would go from the Sub Collector's or the Collector's office and camp there for about a week to prepare the inspection reports and to finalise the revenue for each of the villages. This event was something like the bridegroom's barat going to the bride's place for the wedding. When I went for Jamabandi of one of the taluks I took my cook with me along with the provisions for cooking my meals. The fresh vegetables and milk would be bought locally with the money I had given to my cook as imprest. I heard through the grapevine that the Head Clerk and the others were being fed by the village officers who would raise money for the purpose. When I confronted the Head Clerk with this, he admitted that, while it was against the rules to accept any consideration from the officers whose work was being inspected, this was the customary practice. I suspended him and framed charges for removal from service. He came and wept before me and further enquiries showed that this was indeed the practice for the good reason that there were no hotels and food had to be prepared by the village officers who considered it an insult to accept any payment. The staff, who got daily allowance, pocketed it.

On further consideration I thought I had been unduly harsh in my punishment. I went to the Collector, N. Ramesan, who was the appellate authority and told him about the case and said he may wish to consider the appeal sympathetically and reduce the punishment. He smiled and said, "you have been in service for only three years and it is good that have begun to climb down from the ivory tower." I learnt with some relief, that the Collector had reduced the punishment to one of stoppage of increment for three months, a rather mild punishment without any effect on his prospects. The Head Clerk was one of the best in my office, and his notes and drafts were of a high order. I later ran into him several years later and he came and greeted me and I sheepishly asked him how he was. He said he was all right. He then said, "you were so strict those days, if you see what happens today you will be aghast"! How true he was. I suspect he was polite enough not to say I would be turning in my grave.

Ramesan had a razor sharp mind and would dispose of files with great speed and then settle down with his other pursuits like Sanskrit, archaelogy, temple architecture for which he later won recognition with a Doctorate. For him and some others, official work was only a part of life which could become full only with other pursuits which one can carry past retirement. In later years in Delhi I worked with similar officers like Bhoothalingam and L.K. Jha who were a great inspiration for younger officers.

After Ramesan left on transfer P.V. Ratnam came. He was a very different person. Every file became a project on which he would work for hours and write an erudite thesis on the origin of the problem and the philosophy of the solution. He would work till midnight and get up at 4 a.m. to continue his work. He became a good friend and would expound his theories of life. He was a man of principles who did not let anyone forget that fact.

During the early years after independence the country was fortunate to have gentlemen politicians and cultured ministers with a history of sacrifice, and dedicated civil servants. What we see today is a far cry from those days. Nostalgia leads to a certain sadness. Perhaps there is no escape from the *zeitgeist* whether one likes it or not. One hopes that a new generation of educated voters will bring about a change.

Move to Delhi

In those days, officers were deputed to the Centre early in their service. After about 14 months in Vijayawada I was sent on deputation to Delhi in January 1957 as Under Secretary in the Ministry of Heavy Industry. Mr. L.K. Jha was the Secretary. This was the first of several assignments that I had under him. I was given the subjects of steel and cement. In those days of control of production and distribution, industrial licensing, import and export there was quite a bit to do in the Ministry. A few months later, in 1998, the Ministry of Steel was formed and I was shifted there under Mr. Bhoothalingam who was the Secretary. Working under ICS secretaries like Jha and Bhoothalingam was a valuable experience. They were brilliant men with a quick grasp of the essentials of any issue and with considerable writing skills. In the Steel Ministry there was no special secretary or even a joint secretary. The Ministry which dealt with Iron and Steel control, including steel imports and distribution, and the construction of the three steel plants at Durgapur, Bhilai and Rourkela, was run by the Secretary, two deputy secretaries K.S. Raghupathi (who was the son in law of K.M. Munshi) and G. Ramanathan, and three under secretaries of which, I was one. There was a lot of pressure on the secretary to take at least one joint secretary but he said that he would not have a joint secretary till one of his deputy secretaries became ripe for promotion. Later they both became joint secretaries and a few deputy secretaries were taken.

There was considerable trust and delegation of powers. In fact, I could pass bills for several crores of rupees with the concurrence of the under secretary in finance, something that even joint secretaries could not do in the seventies and later. Both Jha and Bhoothalingam were particular about quick dispatch of official work and they wanted notes to be clear and concise. They also wanted junior officers to express their views freely and never influenced their notings. They would never make suggestions as to what should be written or that notes should be taken back and re written. They would point out the lacunae in the notes and would give reasons while overruling a junior officer on the file.

These features of work in the Central Secretariat at an early stage in my career influenced my approach to work even in later years. I also learnt to deal with big business men with courtesy and firmness. They would quickly size up the officer and treat him with respect.

Harvard

In 1959, selections were on for fellowships for study at Harvard University in the US for MPA (Master of Public Administration). My secretary recommended me strongly and I got the fellowship. This was my first trip abroad and I decided to make the most of this opportunity. I travelled by sea from Hong Kong to San Francisco in a large sea liner of American President Lines. The ship stopped at Tokyo and Yokohama. I got off the ship and saw both these places during my trip to the US. The ship was full of students, mostly Chinese and some Indians, going to various universities in the US. I then took the land route from San Francisco to Boston traveling by Greyhound bus and train, stopping on the way to see places like Los Angeles, San Diego, Grand Canyon, an opportunity that I did not get later when I visited the US several times on work.

Studies at Harvard were interesting at the Littauer Centre where we had eminent economists like Galbraith, Haberler and Ed Mason. I thought that, apart from development economics, it would be useful to have a taste of US business, and so I asked for permission to do a full course at the Harvard Business School (B School). The authorities said that, since I was from the Government, it would not be possible to accommodate me and, in any case, no one from the course for government officials had been to the Business School. I went up to the Dean and after some persuasion he agreed. The Business School being across the Charles river, I acquired a bicycle to go to the B. School for the next class in Business policy after a class at Littauer Centre (later called the Kennedy School of Government). The case method of study being followed was known the world over and IIM Ahmedabad later adopted it in collaboration with Harvard University.

The experience at Harvard was interesting and useful. Being a student of science, this was my first exposure to economics and business policy and this stood me in good stead later in my various assignments.

On the way back to India, I stopped over at various places in Europe and saw places which I never got an opportunity of seeing later.

On my return to India in 1960, I was posted as Collector and District Magistrate of Nellore, the southern most district of Andhra Pradesh (A.P.). This was a large district with very dry areas and also very productive irrigated and prosperous areas. These were the early days of Panchayati Raj and A.P. was one of the earliest states to implement it. In Panchayati Raj the district was divided into Blocks with Block Development Officers servicing the Panchayat Samithis consisting of elected persons with reservations for the weaker sections. Within the allotted Block budgets, they could decide on the distribution of funds between irrigation, housing, public health centres, and other social and economic activities. The Zilla Parishad was the district level body to make the allocations blockwise and undertake district level works. This was headed by an elected president. However, the collector who was a member of the Parishad was the chairman of the standing committees which took the final decisions. This was a sort of guided democracy in operation at that time, but people were getting used to running their own development projects and programmes. Later the scheme underwent several changes.

The year went by uneventfully, except for a heavy rain and storm which entailed rescue and relief work.

Hyderabad

Andhra Pradesh was known for its agricultural wealth and enterprising farmers but had little to show in industry except for some sugar and rice mills.

The new State was keen to develop its mineral resources and also set up industries to balance the predominantly agricultural orientation of the State. The A.P. Mining Corporation (APMC) was set up and I was posted to Hyderabad as the first Managing Director. The Chairman was Mr. P.M. Nayak ICS. When I reported to him he handed the registration papers of APMC and said I should start from scratch. I located a personal assistant, an office room, and a peon. Furniture was hired and then we got to work. I familiarized myself with the relevant legislation and the procedures application for prospecting licences for iron ore, barytes, limestone, silica and mica. The Barium Chemicals factory was being established in the private sector and we wanted to supply the raw material to the company. The

Mining and Mineral Trading Corporation (MMTC) of the Government of India was exporting iron ore to Japan and we became suppliers to them.

After a year, during which I recruited a geologist, a mining engineer and other staff for starting the work of APMC, I was given additional charge of the A.P. Industrial Development Corporation (APIDC). This was set up to assist private industry by giving loans and equity and by generally helping out with government approvals.

Joint Ventures

An important development was the concept of joint ventures between Government and Private sector. Sanjeeva Reddy was the Chief Minister and I explained that we could not get very far by investing the meager resources of the State to promote industries with the funds solely coming from the State plan. We could leverage our funds by forming joint ventures with 26 per cent from Government, 25 per cent from the private entrepreneur and the balance from the public, towards equity. The management would be in the hands of the private sector partner and the chairman would be a nominee of APIDC. We could thus approach financial institutions for loans. They were at first reluctant to extend loans to joint ventures as the whole concept was new. I went to Delhi to meet the finance secretary who was none other than my former steel secretary Bhoothalingam. After I explained the position and the need for encouraging industries through the joint venture mode, he agreed and a policy decision was taken to allow financial institutions to extend loans and also underwrite public issues by the joint ventures. This was the origin of joint ventures and the Chief Minister was very pleased with my initiative in this matter. Other states followed this method and my colleague P.C. Nayak visited Hyderabad to discuss details for adopting this method in Maharashtra. We became good friends and later had occasion to work together in Delhi in the Ministry of Industry. Nayak was hard working, practical, jovial and very popular with colleagues.

Foreign Collaboration

In order to put into practice the concept of joint ventures, I got project reports prepared for a bearings project and a glass project. I had my first experience in applying for industrial and capital goods licensing, and in foreign collaboration negotiations. For the bearings factory, the field was already occupied by world leaders like SKF, FAG and other foreign companies. So we selected the well known Japanese company Koyo Seiko. I went to Japan and negotiated the foreign collaboration agreement which had to be approved by the government. Negotiations with the Japanese were interesting. Because of the English language being new to many of their executives, every proposal of mine was translated into Japanese and then there would be extended discussion among eight or nine people and the response would come after five minutes during which time I would doodle on my pad and observe the expressions on the faces across the table which yielded little, as they would be poker faced like seasoned players. However, I managed to get them to invest in the company at least 10 per cent of the capital. This was one of the first instances of a Japanese company investing in an Indian company, although they had been giving technical collaboration.

My earlier stint in Delhi had put me in touch with several deputy and joint secretaries and this helped when I went to them as an applicant on the other side of the table. For the glass factory, we selected a Hungarian glass company, which was a government owned company, as foreign collaborator. I went to Hungary with the joint venture partner to negotiate the agreement. The Chairman of APIDC was Mr. A.V. Bhanoji Rao, an aristocratic gentleman from Vizag, who had been in politics for some years. He was in the Indian delegation for the Second Round Table in London. Although advanced in years he was quite active and fully supportive of my efforts.

My grandfather G. Srinivasa Iyer, Judge of Mysore High Court, Mysore Durbar, 1944

My father Sri G.S. Venkataramana Iyer receiving the Maharaja of Mysore at the legislature, Bangalore Legislature 1958

▲

With Pandit Nehru and General Cariappa — Republic Day Parade, 1953

Receiving Panditji at Vijaywada, 1955

▼

▲
With Shri C.M. Trivedi, Governor, Andhra – at the Mission Memorial Vijaywada, 1955

With President of Koyo Seiko after signing the
Collaboration Agreement for the bearings project, 1963
▼

With Finance Secretary Bhoothalingam, 1958

With Y.B. Chavan, Finance Minister; and Secretary, I.G. Patel at the IMF annual meeting, Copenhagen, 1969

2

Finance Ministry

IN 1966, I was sent on deputation to Delhi for the second time, as deputy secretary in the Department of Economic Affairs (DEA) which was a coveted post. My secretary was Bhoothalingam. A few days after I joined, there was a flutter in the corridors with whispered conversation. The rupee had been devalued.

The six years I spent in DEA were the most interesting in the tenure of my career. I dealt with the United Nations Development Programme (UNDP) for a year and then moved to the World Bank, International Monetary Fund (IMF) and Asian Development Bank desk. When I joined the Fund Bank division, one of the first tasks entrusted to me was to receive Mc Namara, the new President, on his first official visit to India in September 1968. He and his team had come in a special plane from Geneva with only the pilot and a teenaged *garcon* who doubled up as helper, cabin attendant, mechanic and the pilot's odd job man. After his visit to places in India, Mc Namara and his team were to leave for Kathmandu one morning around 7 a.m. When we were in the VIP waiting room the *garcon* came and announced with gesticulations that the plane had problems and could not fly till it got some spare parts from abroad. Mc Namara was agitated but could not blame any one. The commercial flights had taken off. As the host in charge I had a problem on my hands. Here was an opportunity to show how India could react to situations. I called up my colleague Krishnaswamy who had earlier worked in the Defence Ministry and asked him if he could talk to the Air Force officers and arrange a plane to take the World Bank President to Kathmandu at the earliest. The costs would be borne by the Department of Economic Affairs. I assumed that my Secretary would support me in the decision. After fifteen minutes S.K. called back to say that the Air Force would lay on a plane within half an hour. Mc Namara was relieved and impressed. I had to keep him engaged in conversation and I raised the question of urban decay and referred to the potential of Calcutta and suggested the Bank may like to have a look at it. Mc Namara thought it was a good idea and instructed his officers to send a team to Calcutta for reconnaissance. This was the fortuitous origin of the Calcutta urban project which fructified after about six months.

The International Bank for Reconstruction and Development (World Bank) and International Monetary Fund (IMF)

These two institutions came into being in 1944 after the Bretton Woods Conference in a place called Bretton Woods in New Hampshire in the US. Earlier, the Agenda Committee had met in Atlantic City in New Jersey. All the developed countries, India and some developing countries participated. The two institutions were called the Bretton Woods twins.

The International Bank for Reconstruction and Development, also called the World Bank, had three institutions under its umbrella. The International Development Association (IDA), formed in 1960 and the International Finance Corporation (IFC) created in 1956 are part of the World Bank Group. IDA was the soft lending affiliate that gave loans to governments of developing countries. The IFC was for making equity contributions and loans to the private sector.

While the Bank made loans for about seven years out of funds that it raised in the market, and charged interest at going rates, IDA gave 'credits' which carried a nominal interest of 0.75 per cent and a 50 year repayment period, with a 10 year grace period. Funds for IDA came from grants from the richer countries through 'replenishments'.

The World Bank gave its first reconstruction loans to France, the Netherlands and Luxembourg, which had suffered extensive destruction during the war. Later, the Marshall Plan was announced and there were no more reconstruction loans from the Bank. The emphasis shifted exclusively to development loans to the developing countries. The first loan in Asia was a loan of $ 34 million for Railway Reconstruction and Development given to India in August in 1949.

The first five years, after Mc Namara took over as the President of the World Bank, saw a great deal of enthusiasm in the Bank for development assistance. India was the biggest beneficiary of both the Bank and IDA (International

Development Association) its soft lending affiliate. The resources of IDA were replenished substantially, largely because of Mc Namara's support and influence among the other donors.

In order to absorb all this assistance the Government of India in the Department of Economic Affairs selected a team led by C.S. Swaminathan, a competent and amiable officer of the audit service, who had been working in the Department for a few years under C.S. Krishnamoorthi the joint secretary. I started as Director under Swaminathan and later succeeded him. The work involved working closely with various ministries and also the state governments. Projects had to be prepared in accordance with the Bank's requirements, projecting cost estimates, Government of India share, details of the implementing agency and time schedule. There were several stages in the processing of the project proposals. A reconnaissance visit by the Bank team, with experts and consultants to give ideas as to how the proposal should be prepared, was followed by a pre appraisal team and an appraisal team. This was the yellow cover stage in Bank jargon. The final proposal to the Board of Directors was in a green cover. Our Executive Director to the Bank, Dr. S.R. Sen was closely following up the progress in the Bank.

With a view to improving the performance of the sector to which the project belonged, there were a series of general, sectoral and project specific conditionalities, which had to be built into the Loan Agreement before presentation to the Board. The conditionalities also related to policy issues, organizational structure and implementation procedures. This was a crucial part of the negotiations and the common link for all the projects was the Department of Economic Affairs. As director in DEA, I had to liaise with the concerned ministry and the Bank staff. After internal clearances had been obtained, a negotiating team consisting of the ministry and state government representatives (wherever states were involved), and invariably a representative of DEA would go to Washington for final negotiations on the details, particularly the conditionalities. Frequently, we had to seek directions from Delhi during negotiations. I was the DEA representative for nearly 12 or 13 negotiations over a period of three years. This entailed hard preparatory work and long hours of negotiations in Washington. With some give and take, most of the negotiations were concluded successfully. The only negotiation that fell through was the one relating to the Food Corporation in 1972.

Another important area of work related to the India Consortium was set up in 1958 under the leadership of the World Bank. The consortium consisted of about ten countries who would provide bilateral assistance directly to India. Pledges of assistance were made by the countries at the meetings with the Bank and IDA indicating their own contributions. Most of the assistance was tied to purchases from the donor countries. Apart from the Bank and IDA, the Scandinavian countries were the first to 'untie' their aid which meant that we could procure equipment from the cheapest source and not necessarily from the donor country. There was considerable variation in the composition and terms of aid from the different countries.

There was a further classification into project and programme assistance. The latter was given for free imports of raw materials and finished capital goods not linked to any project. The assistance was broken into loans and grants and the period of repayment and the interest also varied. The utilization of the assistance was a topic of frequent discussion. The concerned officers in the Finance Ministry dealing with bilateral aid would allocate and monitor the utilization and keep the Fund Bank division informed. The whole thing was quite complex with the DEA being the sole repository of the esoteric system of foreign aid gathering, allocation to various ministries, utilization and reporting to the Consortium.

On the IMF side, there was the Annual consultation on the economic situation, fiscal and monetary policies. In the IMF, members made their subscriptions in gold (20 per cent) and in the local currency (80 per cent). Subscriptions were equated to quotas, which in turn determined the votes and the drawing rights to which the members were eligible. These drawing rights could be exercised in any foreign currency required for meeting the deficits in balance of payments. When a member drew these currencies it would give the equivalent amount in the local currency to the Fund. This was known as 'purchase' of the foreign currency. When the loan was repaid, the process was called 'repurchase' as the rupees were returned to the borrowing country. There were different tranches of drawing rights, each of 25 per cent, to which a country was entitled. After the first two tranches, the conditionalities became more strict and negotiations more complex. Economic compulsion of getting foreign exchange had to be balanced with the political consequences of implementing some of the conditions. It is believed in many quarters that the devaluation of 1966 and the more recent liberalisation measures taken after 1991 were dictated by the Fund and the Bank in return for assistance. Surveillance has gone down now because our foreign exchange reserves have become healthy and we do not owe any money to the IMF.

During 1968, IMF introduced the Special Drawing Rights (SDRs) which were in addition to the normal drawing rights. The basic idea was to increase the liquidity of funds of all the members. These SDRs provided members with additional credit facilities with the IMF. In spite of our best efforts, no special treatment was given to developing countries by linking SDRs to additional development assistance.

3

Washington

AFTER nearly six years in DEA, there was a vacancy in Washington when our alternate Executive Director (ED), Manu Shroff was due to return to India. Dr. I.G. Patel felt that with the large borrowing programme we had developed with the Bank Group, my experience would be useful at the other end. I was accordingly sent as Minister Economic in the Embassy since we had to share the post of alternate ED, (earlier filled by Manu Shroff), with Sri Lanka. The previous incumbent in the post of Minister Economic was M.G. Kaul, who later became Economic Secretary when I.G. Patel went to UNDP.

I got a second opportunity, though a short one, of working with L.K. Jha who was the ambassador in Washington. He returned to India a few months after I went there, and most of my tenure was with T.N. Kaul who succeeded L.K. Jha.

The period in Washington gave me the first taste of diplomatic life. However, my field was economic and financial. I established contact with senior officials in the

World Bank and IMF and the US Department of Treasury. I had to meet people in the Agriculture Department when I signed the agreement for the last shipment of wheat, which had started in the early sixties. I had also made friends in the various committees of the US Congress and Senate, dealing with economic matters. In all these contacts the role of Ganju who was engaged for liaison in the early sixties, was very helpful. He had been in the US for over twenty-five years and had wide contacts in Washington, which successive Ambassadors had found useful.

An Indian observer in the US would have noticed that the average American was quite ignorant of India and even less interested. There was a popular serial *All in the family* in which the main character was Archie Bunker, a construction worker, who typified the middle class. His main interests were football and baseball. If India was mentioned he would react by saying 'never heard of it'. The better educated had an impression of India as a poor country living on foreign doles and a land of snake charmers and sadhus. In more sophisticated circles there was a great deal of interest in India and its religions. The topic of conversation would invariably turn to the caste system. The picture has only changed slightly now with the better educated recognizing the scientific and technological advances particularly in the software field.

As we had been importing large quantities of wheat as aid from the US, one of the topics was the food shortage in India. I was asked why we could not slaughter the large number of cows for food as the US was doing. I was then impelled to write a paper entitled "Why Not Kill the Cow?"

which was published in the UN Journal in 1974. This article has been updated till 1980.[1]

The Bangladesh war and its after effects on Indo US relations were still persisting. I had accompanied Ambassador Kaul on his visits to meet Kissinger and other senior officers of the US Governments and I got a taste of high level diplomacy. Ambassador Kaul was generally a blunt talker, and he conveyed to Kissinger our concern and anger at the US tilt towards Pakistan in very forthright terms. Kissinger was conciliatory and diplomatic, while refuting the allegation. Later when both the Ambassador and the political minister Gonsalves were out of the US, I acted as *Charge d'Affaires* for about a month and this exposed me to all aspects of work in the Embassy and to wider contacts outside.

Two local topics of great importance at that time were the Vietnam war and the impeachment of Nixon in the Watergate matter. The order, discipline and decorum observed in the Senate hearings was impressive and a contrast to our Parliamentary proceedings. We saw on television the surprising spectacle of the US Ambassador Ellsworth Bunker wrap up the American flag and run to the helicopter to leave Saigon before the Viet Cong arrived.

The nuclear implosion, as we called it at that time, also brought a lot of criticism from the US administration and academic groups. But we had enough material and it was easy to defend and justify the Pokhran experiment. At that time our brief was to say that it was for peaceful purposes.

---

1. See page 335 for the appended article "Why Not Kill the Cow?"

When this was accepted with a pinch of salt, we left it at that.

Even after coming to Washington I continued to be a member of the Indian delegation for the India Consortium, which was usually held in Paris. In June 1975, when we were walking to a restaurant for dinner we got information about the imposition of the Emergency. On return to Washington, all of us in the Embassy got a number of calls from Indians about the Emergency. We had to give diplomatic replies. Indian associations protested and wrote to the Ambassador. We had to deal with the situation carefully. While it was difficult to justify the action we also could not criticize it but had to explain it. Defending the indefensible is one of the burdens of Indian diplomats.

The Pittsburgh Temple

One Saturday in May or June 1975 (I cannot recall the exact date), when I was in my office in the Chancery, I got a phone call from an American who said he was from the Pittsburgh police, and as the Ambassador was not in Washington, he was told to call me. He said that at a meeting of Indians in Pittsburgh there was a lot of shouting, and two groups were fighting for the microphone and about to come to blows. Before arresting them, he wanted to keep the Embassy in the picture. I asked him to hold action and to put me in touch on the telephone, with some of the Indians at the meeting. He called one of them and I asked him what the problem was. It appears that there was a meeting of Indians to discuss the construction of the Lord Venkateswara temple. They had acquired an old church building which was going cheap, and also was situated on seven small undulations which was auspicious for the 'Lord of Seven Hills' as Lord Venkateswara is referred to in India. The foundation stone had been laid, along with the offering of nine gems, at a ceremony attended by Anna Rao the chief executive of the Tirumala temple in India. An Indian group had been formed to plan the details of the building to be put up for the temple. There was a difference of opinion as to whether the temple should be exclusively for Lord Venkateswara or whether it should provide for worshippers of Lord Siva. During the meeting these differences came to the fore and hot words were exchanged. I told this gentleman that I would go Pittsburgh on the following day, which was a Sunday, and the two groups could meet me. In the meanwhile there should be no occasion for the police to intervene. I then informed the Ambassador, who was in the West Coast, about the problem and he agreed that I should visit Pittsburgh.

When I went to Pittsburgh next afternoon, the two groups met me at the airport. They had reserved a room for me, and also two rooms for themselves. The groups were broadly divided between the Tamil and the Telugu speaking persons. Both groups had highly qualified and affluent professionals working in the US. Since I had served in Andhra Pradesh, and visited the temple at Tirumala, and also knew both languages, they were at ease talking to me, but not between themselves. After I discussed the issues with one group, they would go back to their room and the other group would come in. This exercise went on till night, and there was no compromise. I then told them that they should think of having separate associations and two temples.

Next morning I visited the temple site, and returned to Washington and reported the matter to the Ambassador who agreed with me. A few days later there was a message from the External Affairs Ministry transmitting a question in the Andhra Pradesh Assembly about the temple coming up on a church land. There was also a photograph of the cross on top of the building and the question was raised about the appropriateness of the temple coming up under the cross. I had not noticed this when I visited the site. When I enquired from the group leaders in Pittsburgh, they said that there was the cross on the old church, but as it was expensive to remove the heavy cross it was thought prudent to leave it in place till the construction started, when cranes would be available. I conveyed this to Delhi and to Hyderabad and there was no further query.

That evening, an interesting incident at a party, reflected the divisions among the Indian community in the US in 1975. As I moved among the guests, I spoke in Tamil with the Tamilians, they invited me to their T.V. interview and I accepted. After a while, I met a Telugu gentleman, whose invitation to meet their association, I accepted. Later I met a Kannada person, who spoke of Bangalore my hometown, and invited me to their meeting, (which invitation also I accepted), at a different time. A little while later, when all the three were together, I joined them. The first gentleman said that I was going to their function, the second repeated the same, looking at me quizzically. The third person also said that I was going to the Kannada function. There was dismay among all the three. A few minutes later, they came to me separately, and said that they had made a mistake about the timing of my meeting, that they had some other programme and therefore regretted that the engagement with me had to be cancelled. I got the message. Things have got worse since then. On a visit to Washington in 1993, I was told that there were 35 Indian associations in the greater Washington area, one for each state and sometimes one for each subdivision of the state.

After a three and a half year stint in Washington, I returned to India, which was still under the Emergency in April 1976.

With US Secretary of State, Henry Kissinger and Ambassador Kaul, Washington, 1974

Signing a World Bank loan agreement, Washington, 1974
(Dr. S.R. Sen, Indian Executive Director is also present)

▲ With Witteveen, Managing Director, IMF, Washington, 1974

With Finance Minister C. Subramanian, New York, 1974 ▼

54c

▲
Patrick Moynihan (US Ambassador to India)
with the author and Mrs. Ramakrishna, Washington, 1974

Signing the last wheat agreement with USAID, Washington, 1974

Brides of India — with Mrs. L.K. Jha, Indian Embassy, Washington, 1973

With Ambassador L.K. Jha, Washington, 1973

With Satyajit Ray and Ambassador Kaul, Washington, 1975

With R.K. Narayan, Washington, 1974

4

Hyderabad

ON my return to India the atmosphere of the Emergency was palpable. In the corridors of Delhi everyone would walk close to the wall with a touch of stealth as if someone was following them. Centres of power were clearly known at all levels. I was happy to get out of Delhi to return once again to my state. I reported in Hyderabad and was given the posting of Secretary, Municipal Administration, far removed from my experience of the last ten years in finance. The elections of 1977 had thrown up the new Janata Government under Morarji Desai. The only state under Congress rule was in Andhra Pradesh with Vengala Rao as the Chief Minister. The feeling in Hyderabad was that I would not stay long in the state. Although I had been away from the state for ten years I had old friends who were kind and supportive. The chief secretary A. Krishnaswami and the secretary to the chief minister Krishnaswami Rao Sahib, who later became secretary to the P.M. and the cabinet secretary, were particularly kind to me. They were fine officers who represented the best in the service and they earned the respect of every officer by their affability, competence and rectitude.

The Chief Minister was Vengala Rao who was arguably the best Chief Minister the state had. He was accessible to all senior officers. Even if there were a large number of visitors and petitioners, his office had instructions to let in an officer without delay by holding back the other visitors. He was businesslike and decisive. You had to state the issues and your suggestions in about three minutes and after thinking and asking questions he would give his decision in the next two minutes. It was a real pleasure to work with him.

With Vengala Rao (Chief Minister, Andhra Pradesh) in 1978

While I was municipal secretary, the Minister was Subbarayudu who had a simple unsophisticated demeanor which masked a very shrewd mind. He knew a great deal as out municipal administration and in fact guided me, who was new to the subject. He had simple habits and was strict in dealing with corrupt officials about whom he would get information from the field. The maximum favour he would accept from a known visitor would be a cigarette which was superior to his own brand.

The highlight of my short stay in Hyderabad was the new scheme of property tax assessment on which I worked for about three months. This was in essence based on plinth area of the building with extras for variables like age, type of construction, purpose of use, location etc. I discussed it with Rao Sahib and the finance secretary B.P.R. Vithal, another shining star of the A.P. cadre. They agreed reluctantly and warned me that I should be prepared for opposition from municipal staff who had opportunities of making money in the subjective system of determining Annual Rental Value for the purpose of fixing the tax payable. However, they agreed that I could take a paper to the Cabinet after having a word with the Chief Minister. When I explained that my system would reduce corruption and make the system more objective and transparent, he agreed that I could take the paper to one of the meetings of the cabinet.

In the meanwhile elections were held in January 1977 and the Janata Government was formed in Delhi. There was a great deal of shuffling of officers. I was asked for the post of Additional Secretary in the Department of Industrial Development. I had not completed my three year cooling-off period and I had just returned to the state for the second time after ten years with the Government of India from 1966. There was opposition from the establishment in Delhi and this was supported by Morarji Desai the P.M. After several efforts to get a waiver in the new context, where several officers had been tainted in the Emergency and were not acceptable to the new Government, the P.M. agreed. So I packed up again to go to Delhi. I had worked as Under Secretary in 1957, Deputy Secretary, Director and Joint Secretary from 1966 to 1976. Now I was going to Delhi, for the third time, as Additional Secretary in an economic ministry.

My paper on municipal property tax was ignored in Hyderabad.[1] The Urban Development Journal 'Nagarlok', had published the paper which provoked discussion and some criticism. Some years later the Patna Municipal Corporation had implemented my proposal and the matter went to court. After twenty two years, in 1998 the matter went before the Supreme Court in an appeal against the Patna High Court which had upheld my proposal and the Supreme Court upheld the High Court decision. In fact very few people remembered my proposal after such a long gap in time. Now this proposal is being followed in several states on the recommendation of the Central Government following the Supreme Court decision. Just recently, it has been introduced (with simplifications) by the Delhi Municipal Corporation.

1. Paper attached < Facing page >.

< Municipal Property Tax >

Municipal Property Tax
A New Approach

G.V. Ramakrishna*

The Levy and assessment of property tax by municipal bodies has given rise to widespread complaints from the public. In this paper an attempt is made to analyse the basis of the present system, and causes for complaints, and to suggest a new approach which may meet most of the legitimate objections against the existing practices.

In the state of Andhra Pradesh, as in many other states, property tax is at present levied with reference to the 'annual rental value' (ARV) of buildings. In actual practice the fixation of the ARV is beset with numerous difficulties. The ARV is theoretically expected to reflect the rent that a particular building will fetch in a free market where tenant and landlord are able to arrive at a mutually acceptable rent under competitive conditions. However, the determination of ARV for actually rented buildings has several snags. It is even more complicated in the case of owner occupied buildings.

Rented buildings can be classified into three categories:

(i) those for which fair rent has actually been fixed under the Rent Control Act.

(ii) those that are within the purview of the Rent Control Act but fair rent has not actually been fixed under the Act; and

(iii) those that are outside the purview of the Rent Control Act.

For buildings in the first category, the ARV will be the actual fair rent fixed for the building in accordance with a recent decision of the Supreme Court.

For buildings in the second category, the Supreme Court decision would have the effect of having the ARV fixed with reference to the fair rent fixable under the Rent Control Act. However, it is possible to take the view consistent with the above decision that where the actual rent received exceeds the notional fair rent fixable under the Rent Control Act, such actual rent may be taken into account for arriving at the ARV.

For the third category of buildings the ARV will be based on the declared rent as evidenced by lease deeds or declarations of tenant and landlord. It is, however, open for the Valuation Officer to disregard the declared rent and adopt an estimated rent if in his opinion there is suppression of facts or collusion between the tenant and landlord for declaring a lower rent than what

* Additional Secretary, Ministry of Industry (Department of Industrial Development), Government of India, New Delhi.

Contd...

...Contd...

would be the market. In the fixation of estimated rent there is considerable discretion and hence discrepancy in the rent fixed by different Valuation Officers. In theory the market rent prevailing in the area for similar buildings is supposed to be taken as the estimated rent. In actual practice it is difficult to arrive at a truly representative and accurate market rent as no two buildings are completely alike and the rents for similar buildings are themselves highly variable owing to various non-economic factors. Moreover, the sampling of rents for similar buildings will vary with different Valuation Officers. Hence, even with the most conscientious effort, it is not possible to fix the ARV in such cases on a demonstrably objective basis. It is this situation that has been the main cause of complaints of arbitrariness in the assessment of property tax.

In the case of buildings, wholly or partly occupied by the owner, the task of fixing the ARV is somewhat more difficult. If such buildings come within the purview of the Rent Control Act then the fair rent fixable under the Act has to be arrived at. If they are outside the purview of the Act, the market rent that the building fetches will be the basis for arriving at the ARV. While legally there is no specific relief or concession in property tax payable on owner occupied buildings, in practice, Valuation Officers fix the ARV of such buildings 10 to 50 per cent below the market rent. There is again scope for discretionary variations.

It will be noticed from the above narration of the theory and practice of fixing the ARV of buildings that the assessment of property tax lays itself open to the charge that it is at best discretionary to a large extent and at the worst arbitrary to an unacceptable degree.

There are two other factors that are relevant for an understanding of the current situation. Municipalities are increasingly faced with the problem of having to meet the rising demand for civic services owing to growth of urban population without any increase in the available sources of revenue. With the abolition of octroi and the withdrawal of the right of motor vehicle taxation without any corresponding compensation, municipalities have been forced to rely increasingly on property tax as an expanding source of revenue. They have sought to raise additional revenues by revising and rectifying the under-assessment of property tax on a systematic basis, by raising the rate of taxation and by improving the collection of arrear and current taxes.

The absence of elected councils during the last few years and the administration of municipalities by Special Officers has enabled this progress to take place without the deliberative processes of local government.

The combined result of the system of assessing property tax, with its built-in element of discretion, and its enthusiastic application in circumstances of compelling financial need, has been the widespread dissatisfaction among tax payers.

The municipal authorities explain that in most cases the assessments prevailing earlier were well below legally appropriate levels, and if, in the process of correcting under-assessments, higher taxes and demanded that tax payers should count the blessings of earlier under-assessments and lower taxes rather than complain about the loss of the earlier irregular benefits. They also point

Contd...

...*Contd*...

out that in the case of rented buildings the assessments are made on firm evidence of increasing rents. With less assurance they point out that there are not many cases of correction or increase in the case of owner-occupied buildings.

A careful consideration of the nature of complaints from tax payers and the response of the municipal authorities shows that the problem has to be dealt with in two distinct parts.

First, the degree of discretion and possible arbitrariness in the present system has to be reduced, if not eliminated altogether. Whether it is possible to devise a new and practical basis for assessment of property tax in a manner that can be demonstrably objective has to be examined. This is dealt with in the latter part of this paper.

Second, whether the taxation can be made more progressive by giving relief to the lower middle classes, who depend on rents as the main source of income and to owner-occupied residential buildings, without affecting the overall revenues of the municipalities in any significant manner.

A New Basis for Property Tax

The basic idea is to move away from the concept of property tax, levied with reference to ARV, to the levy of property tax with reference to objective criteria related to the building. Although attempts have been made to levy property tax with reference to the plinth area of buildings, such measures have not been able to stand the test of judicial scrutiny mainly on the ground that plinth area alone cannot be a sufficient criterion but other attendant factors should also be taken into account. The Kerala Buildings Tax Act (19 of 1961) sought to levy the tax on buildings on the basis of plinth area alone and in State of Kerala *versus* Haji K. Kutty Naha (AIR 1969 SC 378) the Supreme Court held that the charging section violated the equality clause of the Constitution and the main grounds for judgment were that no attempt was made for rational classification of buildings and the Legislature had not taken into consideration other factors, like, the nature of the construction, the location, the class to which the building belongs and the purpose for which it is used.

While in the light of the Supreme Court judgment, the levy of property tax on the basis of plinth area alone would not be constitutionally valid and perhaps also not be sufficiently scientific, it would also be imprudent to give up the whole concept altogether. On the other hand, attempts should be made to have a rational classification on the basis of the factors referred to in the Supreme Court judgment and other relevant factors. Under the new system now proposed, there will be a basic tax related to the plinth area or carpet area. For buildings with appurtenant land exceeding three times the built-up area, there will be a surcharge on the excess appurtenant land. On the basic tax and surcharge there will be extras based on the location of the building, the type of construction, the nature of its use, and the age of the building. Under each of these variables, there will be five or six categories into one of which the building will be classified. Thus, a building can be classified for purposes of taxation, according to six variables which are all capable of being determined objectively. The statements and examples of calculations bring out the details

Contd...

...*Contd*...

of the scheme on an illustrative basis. The advantages of the new system will be:

(a) once the rates of basic tax, surcharge and extras are published, it will be possible for a property owner himself to assess the tax payable and to pay tax on a self-assessment basis.

(b) the scope for discretion now exercised by Valuation Officers will be greatly reduced. Where there can be variations in assessments made by the owner and the VO, as in determining the type of construction, the difference in tax will not be very large and the matter can be easily resolved in revision.

(c) the computerization of tax system will be made easier and more scientific.

(d) the effort and expense in quinquennial revision of property tax can be saved and the staff used for intensive verification of the property characteristics of buildings with higher taxes.

(e) the variation of taxes can be made by municipalities by altering the rates of basic rate and extras.

(f) progression in taxation can be brought about by fixation of extras in a manner that gives relief to the weaker sections of society.

The question may be asked, if with a more scientific and objective system such as the one described above, the benefit can extend beyond the mere elimination of arbitrariness to the introduction of an element of progression in property taxation. From what has been stated earlier it can be seen that the system lends itself to achieving the second objective also. The fixation of the basic rates and the extras can be done in a carefully controlled manner to provide relief to the weaker sections of society without any significant effect on municipal revenues. It would also be possible to give specific relief to owners occupying their own buildings for residential purposes. The examples, worked out in the statements bring this out clearly.

While in the new system described above, it would be possible and indeed necessary to remove the restraining influence of the Rent Control Act on the levy of property tax, it is also recognised that suitable adjustments may have to be made in the fair rent on account of any likely increases in property tax in certain types and categories of buildings. Some provisions to this effect are already there in the Rent Control Act and perhaps they may have to be amplified further.

The far-reaching and fundamental changes in the system of levying and assessing property tax will also require suitable amendments to the existing legal provisions in the various municipal Acts.

The above proposals are being made mainly to elicit comments and to provoke a meaningful discussion on the subject. It may be emphasised that no decision of the Government has been taken on these proposals so far.

Contd...

...Contd...

SCHEDULE

Rates of Basic Tax, Surcharge and Extras Applicable for Calculating Property Tax on Buildings under Rule 8 of the Municipal Corporation of Hyderabad Property Tax Rule, 1977

1. Basic Tax:

(a) Per square meter of carpet area. Rs.

(b) Surcharge for appurtenant land in excess of 3 times the built up area. Rs.

2. Extras: As percentage of Basic tax and surcharge

(a) Location

I	II	III	IV	V
10%	20%	30%	40%	50%

(b) Type of construction:

I	II	III	IV	V	VI
10%	20%	50%	75%	100%	Special Rates.

(c) Nature of Use:

I	II	III	IV	V	VI
10%	20%	30%	50%	75%	Special Rates

(d) Age of the Buildings:

I	II	III	IV	V
Nil	10%	20%	30%	50%

The rates of extras are purely illustrative.

3. Explanation:

(a) Location:

			Circle No.	Ward No.
I	:	(A)		
		(B)		"
II	:	(A)	"	"
		(B)		
		(C)		
III	:	(A)		
		(B)		
		(C)		
IV	:	(A)	"	"
		(B)		
V	:	(A)	"	"
		(B)		

Contd...

...*Contd...*

(b) Type of Construction:

I.	Roof	:	A.C. Sheet or metal sheet or thatch.
	Floor	:	Mud, rough stone without base course.
	Walls	:	Brick in mud with or without plastering.
II	Roof	:	Mangalore or other tile.
	Floor	:	Rough stone with base course or cement.
	Walls	:	Brick in lime or cement mortar with lime plaster.
	Others	:	Less than 2 toilets, common or attached.
III	Roof	:	R.C.C. or jack arch.
	Floor	:	Polished stone, ordinary mosaic.
	Walls	:	Brick in lime or cement with plaster.
	Others	:	Two or more attached bath-rooms, panel doors or common.
IV	Roof	:	R.C.C.
	Floor	:	Superior mosaic or marble over at least 60 per cent of carpet area.
	Others	:	Two or more attached bath-rooms, concealed wiring, mosaic or tiled dado in bath-rooms, flush doors.
V	Roof	:	R.C.C.
	Floor	:	Superior mosaic, marble over at least 50 per cent of carpet area of cement mortar with lime or cement plaster.
	Walls	:	Bricks in lime.
	Others	:	Bath-rooms, etc., as in IV, plus wood panelled walls, air-conditioning ducts, false ceilings, substantial use of ornamental stone facing.
VI			Industrial sheds with sheet roof erected on pillars but without walls.

Note: The type of construction of a building will be determined with reference to the features given above. The preponderance of features of a given category will determine the classification of the building in that category.

Contd...

...Contd...

Examples for calculating property tax on objective criteria:

Basic Tax 50 paise per sq. ft.

Surcharge 10 paise per sq. yd. on excess appurtenant land.

Example I

Carpet Area		*Rs.*	
1,000 sq. ft.	Basic Tax:	500	
Extras:	L-II 20%	100	
	C-III 50%	250	
	U-I 10%	50	
	B-III 20%	100	
		1000	Per year
Owner occupied-rebate for residential building 25%		250	
		750	Per year

Example II

Carpet Area		*Rs.*	
10,000 sq. ft.	Basic Tax:	5,000	
Extras:	L-I 10%	500	
	C-II 20%	1,000	
	U-V 100%	5,000	
	B-II 10%	500	
		12,000	Per year

Example III

Carpet Area		*Rs.*	
9,000 sq. ft.	Basic Tax:	450	
	Surcharge	90	
		540	
appurtenant land of 1200 sq. yds. (Excess of 900 sq. yards.)			
Extras:	L-II 20%	108	
	C-III 50%	270	
	U-I 10%	54	
	B-III 20%	108	
		1,080	Per year

Note: L- Location Category. C- Type of Construction.
U- Nature of Use. B- Age of Building.

Contd...

...*Contd*...

The basic rate, surcharge and the extras are purely illustrative.

(C) Nature of Use

I Residential – Residences, Hostels, Guest Houses.

II Public Utility – Water Works, Electricity, Government Offices, etc.

III Recreation – Clubs, Associations.

IV Commerical – Shops, Restaurants, Warehouses, Godowns.

V Industrial – Manufacturing, Processing, packing operations.

VI Cinema Theaters

Airconditioned Rs. – per seat capacity.

Non-Airconditioned Rs. – per seat capacity.

Hotels – Special rates based on room tariffs and area of common facilities like restaurants, shops, etc.

(D) Age of building

I Above 40 years.

II Above 30-40 years.

III Above 20-30 years.

IV Above 10-20 years.

V 10 years and below.

Plinth area: Covered verandahs, corridors and balconies will be included in the plinth area. Open courtyard, verandahs, sit-outs will be excluded from plinth area.

COMMENTS

Nirmala Banerjee*

Ramakrishna is entirely justified in saying that the present-procedure on the basis of a notional fair rent is indeed arbitrary; it does leave too much discretion in the hands of the assessors who become susceptible to corruption. One has all sympathy in his quest for an 'objective' basis for the tax. I feel, however, that he has been altogether unsuccessful in providing an acceptable alternative for the 'rental value'. He has started with a measure objective enough, *viz.*, the square-feet plinth area of each housing unit; but he immediately modifies his criterion by devising a set of surcharges based on qualities such as location, type of construction, age of building, etc. He is perfectly right in doing so because plinth area catches only a small aspect of the desirability of a housing unit. If we were to ignore other aspects, this would lead to serious distortions. A tax based on area alone will put the same burden on housing units which are otherwise totally unequal. By adding these further considerations, one is aiming at reaching a kind of grouping of housing units into some kind of 'equal' categories. Equal in respect of what? An equal set should, on the one hand, roughly include people of similar abilities to pay and,

* Fellow in Economics, Centre for Studies in Social Science, Kolkata.

Contd...

...*Contd*...

on the other, provide similar levels of satisfaction. Then alone it would be an alternative to a rental basis of property tax.

To elaborate, firstly, there is no reason to believe that any list of such criteria will either exhaust the possibilities that affect the desirability of a property or together manage to rank housing units according to their relative attractions. There is no simple way, in natura, to rank between locations, facilities, design and fittings or the airiness or lightiness of different apartments in a large city growing over a long period. It may at best be possible only in a totally planned, officially built city, like Chandigarh, but never in a metro, like Kolkata or Mumbai, where land use and associations have developed over time as per a complex of variables. Secondly, given that any method of categorising properties by a given criterion can at best be a very broad approximation, then such system of discrete surcharge rates cannot but be regressive. For each criterion, it can only refer to the basic minimum level of a certain characteristic for inclusion in each category. It cannot take into account the possible variations within a range. For example, in considering the type of construction, all properties with polished floors would be in one category regardless of whether the floor is black marble of just plain cement tiles. Similarly, for location and so on. Therefore, within each category the rate would be regressive till it reaches the next slab where it will suddenly jump up to a higher level again to become increasingly regressive within that next range. This point is highly relevant in any society where incomes can be as widely skewed as in India and there is reliable evidence that real estate is very much a deposit of black money.

Thirdly, – and this is the most important criticism of Ramakrishna's attempt – there is the basic problem of a composite criterion. Whenever we have to take account of several aspects, the resultant criterion is an index, arrived at by weighting those several aspects to give a single measure. Even if Ramakrishna does not suggest such a single measure, his method would ultimately give us for each housing unit a unique rate. To be at all sensible, the ranking by these rates should mirror the relative desirability of all housing units. If now the relative rates for each category of each criterion are altered somewhat – and there is no special sanctity about one such set rather than another – then the new ranking of rates would implicity define a new ranking in order of desirability. In an attempt to locate a set of objective criteria, we are necessarily thrown back to an arbitrary valuation of the relative desirability of housing. For example, suppose we are comparing a new but badly-built house with an old but well-built house. At Ramakrishna's rates they will be ranked in a certain order. A slight change in the surcharge rates in respect of age can reverse this ranking although the relative desirability for the occupants remains unaltered. The arbitrariness is inherent in this procedure unless we have a cross-check, *i.e.*, the rates correspond in some sense to an independent criterion of desirability, such as the relative rents they would fetch on the market.

Moreover, for any system of progressive taxation the rate of progression must be related to some clearly measureable aspect, such as, income, wealth or consumption. In the housing market, no such measure is available except for their rental or capital values. For example, suppose we assume that given Ramakrishna's various criteria, a property superior in one aspect is also supe-

Contd...

...Contd...

rior in all other aspects, *i.e.*, the better-built house is in a more desirable area and is newer. Even then the problem remains; and by what numerical amount is this superior to the one next in rank? What 'objective' criterion could supply the answer, unless it is the potential rent that such a housing unit would fetch in the market.

Insofar as Ramakrishna's rates are not obviously outrageous, they are, I suspect, founded on a set of implict rental values. To pose such a system as an alternative to the rental value basis is misleading, hiding its arbitrariness under a cloak of objectivity. But there is merit in his proposal – provided his various criteria are used not to supplant but to supplement the existing system of assessment on rental value. The defects of this system are many and obvious and some criteria as suggested by Ramakrishna can be used from time to time to lay down guidelines for assessing officers in order to temper these defects; but it is no use denying that these guidelines for each city can only be arrived at by familiarity with the rental market there, however, imperfect it may be.

In conclusion, it is easy to find objective criteria, but it is very difficult to find appropriate ones. Moreover, a multiplicity of criteria in such a context has to be resolved by the construction of a single criterion which takes account of the multiple aspects. The rental value provides such a construction of the various aspects relevant to the issues; where it fails to do so because of market imperfections, it is easier to correct by taking into account specific aspects rather than trying to replace it by another.

5

Industry

WHEN I went to Delhi, the atmosphere was one of relief and freedom after the hard days of the emergency. Officers were talking freely and people in general were celebrating every festival with enthusiasm. There was also a degree of indiscipline creeping in as we went into 1978.

In the Ministry of Industry there were three departments – Industrial Development, Heavy Industries and Technical Development. I was taken in the department of Industrial Development as additional secretary. The minister was George Fernandes, who had acquired a larger than life image as a firebrand leader who had come out of the Baroda Dynamite case. He was one of the best ministers with whom I had worked. He was polite to all the officers and allowed them to express their views freely. The secretary was Sharad Marathe whom I had known earlier in Washington. He was to a large extent responsible for getting me to Delhi by getting the rules waived. Soon after I joined, a new industrial policy was framed by the new Government.

Although, traditionally, the two important committees on industrial licensing and capital goods imports were chaired by the secretary, Marathe entrusted the task to me with the minister's approval. All the decisions of the two committees had to be approved by the minister. During the two and a half years when I was chairing the committees the minister approved all our recommendations. On a few occasions he would ask for clarifications. Earlier, imports above a limit of Rs. 150 crores had to go to the cabinet committee, but the new Government delegated this to the minister. The result was that, whereas, earlier the decisions would take two to four weeks, now they would be taken in a week at the most.

There was a feeling that government licensing had to be relaxed and a committee under my chairmanship was appointed. We made modest recommendations for relaxing of licensing for new projects and for expansions up to Rs. 5 crores and this was accepted. Sentiment in Government was not for complete decontrol and this continued with several governments till 1991.

An important recommendation I made was to encourage small industries in the states for expansion of employment. The scheme for setting up District Industries Centres (DICs) was enthusiastically welcomed by the minister and he convened a meeting of the state ministers and extended financial support, and the states took to the idea enthusiastically. New DIC buildings were set up in all the states and district industries officers were appointed. The scheme was a success in some of the states but enthusiasm flagged after a new government was formed in 1980. The scheme, however, still continues in some of the states.

Sanjay Gandhi and his friends were influential in the new Government. In Industry, the minister of state was Chanana, an economist from Punjab and a protégé of Sanjay. When cabinet minister R. Venkataraman first came to the ministry to take charge, Chanana showed him scant respect. When I was asked to propose work allocation, which I did on the basis of past precedents, the cabinet minister approved it and the order was issued. Chanana went into a rage when he saw the order and rejected it outright. He almost threw the paper into the waste paper basket. He, in a way, held it against me for proposing the work distribution and took a general dislike to me, one of the reasons being, that I had been brought into the ministry by the Janata Government. He wanted me to alter some of the recommendations of the capital goods committee and when I said that it could not be done under the rules, but that he was free to over rule the committee, he was angry. One day he called me, offered me a cup of tea and asked me whether I would like to get a promotion as secretary. I said that my turn had not yet come and there were seniors in the queue. He said I did not know what was good for me.

After Marathe's retirement in October 1980, S.M. Ghosh took over as secretary. One day he called me and said that the minister wanted me to go on leave or else he would spoil my record. I asked Ghosh if I could ask the minister himself and he agreed. I walked into the minister's room and asked him if what Ghosh said was true. He denied it and said that I was one of the best officers and how could he spoil my record and said he would ask Ghosh why he said it. I said he could do so straight away. He made a movement to pick up the phone and put the instrument down. He knew the game was up but continued to deny Ghosh's statement.

I thought it was time to keep the cabinet secretary in the picture. I met S.S. Grewal who said that he knew about the problem and said that in my own interest he would shift me out of the ministry. I agreed and said that I had not asked for an appointment in a particular ministry. After a month I was shifted to the Planning Commission as Adviser. The deputy chairman was N.D. Tewari and later S.B. Chavan took over.

Planning Commision

At the Planning Commission, I was given charge of the state plans for UP, Gujarat, Madhya Pradesh and Punjab, apart from the subject of rural development in all the States.

My days in the Planning Commission were interesting and I got into the job with enthusiasm. I visited all the four States at least once in connection with their plans in all the departments and also looked at their rural development projects. I led a team to survey the flood damage in UP. I was the convener of the interstate committee on the construction works for sharing of the river waters between UP and MP in the Bundelkhand area for which the Planning Commission had given assistance. In Punjab, I visited a number of places and also visited the Thein Dam site and made recommendations for funding it. My visits to Gujarat were interesting, particularly in the field of rural development. A feature of the bureaucracy in Gujarat was the forward looking, business friendly and entrepreneurial approach of most of the officers. It was almost a seamless relationship between the Government and the business community. This probably explains the progress made in Gujarat during those days.

In connection with rural development, I visited Assam, Meghalaya and Nagaland apart from other states. In Nagaland the commissioner was Achyut Gokhale, a dedicated officer who was popular with the local people. I visited the interior places and saw the forest border with Burma. The forest there is pristine and natural, unlike the shrubbery and cultivated trees that pass for forests elsewhere. It was somewhat like seeing a tiger in its natural habitat as against seeing it in a zoo. The Gokhales were hospitable and continue to be good friends.

In January 1983, when I was in my office, there was a call from the Deputy Chairman's office that I was wanted. When I went there S.B. Chavan was in a meeting with some of the members. He smiled at me and congratulated me and said that I had been promoted as Secretary to the Government of India in the Department of coal and that I would be relieved in a day or two.

6

Coal and Energy

SIVA Shankar was the Minister of Energy (consisting of coal and petroleum). He was an Andhra politician, whom I had known earlier in my days in the state. Under Coal India Ltd there were four companies Central, Eastern, Bharat Coking Coal and Western Coal Fields. After some days the Minister called me for a chat and asked about the systems and procedures for procurement by the coal companies. The annual purchases by the companies were over Rs. 2000 crores. I said that these were left to the companies and there were committees for the purpose. The Ministry did not get involved except for broad project approvals. The minister asked that such cases should be seen by me and him. I demurred and did not take action to change the existing procedures.

When he found that I was not cooperating, the minister got in direct touch with the coal company chiefs and asked for the purchase papers. They were unhappy but could do nothing. There was a case of procurement of copper cables for pumping of water in underground mines which needed dewatering during monsoon in order to maintain production. The minister wanted an enquiry into the matter. I said after a detailed examination that there was no wrong doing and in fact some money had been saved by timely procurement before copper prices went up. The minister was angry and said that it was difficult to get on with me. He spoke to the cabinet secretary Rao Sahib who was an officer of A.P. cadre who knew me quite well. When he spoke to me I said that I would be glad for a change instead of daily friction with the minister whose wishes I could not meet. After four months, I moved out of the coal department to the advisory board of energy, which had just been formed with Lovraj Kumar as the first secretary. He then moved as Secretary Steel and there was a vacancy in the advisory board.

The chairman of the Board was K.C. Pant who had joined the Indira Gandhi government but had no cabinet post vacant. It was pleasant working with him. Lovraj Kumar was functioning for a while from the petroleum department where he was Secretary. When I took over, there was no office for the Board. We were given three rooms in Patel Bhavan. I was given two bright officers Jairam Ramesh and E.A.S. Sarma. We found the rooms bare. There was no cooling although it was mid summer. I had to hire some furniture and an air cooler and start work. The furnishing of the room for the chairman who held a cabinet rank took some time. K.C. Pant was patient and we finally settled down to a plan of action.

In late July 1983, one morning I got a phone call at my residence at about 5.30 a.m. from the A.P. House that the new Chief Minister wanted to talk to me. The new Chief Minster was N.T. Rama Rao who had won a big electoral victory for the Telugu Desam Party against the Congress. He asked me on the phone whether I could see him at 6.30 a.m. and said that he would send a car to my residence. I was somewhat perplexed but hastily got ready and went to see him. He was cordial and warm, and said that he wanted to do a lot of good to the state and needed the assistance of good officers. He asked me whether I would go as Chief Secretary. I said that I wanted time to think about the matter. I also said that he did not know me and I did not know him and asked why he had selected me when there were officers senior to me in the state. He said he had made enquiries and was satisfied that I was the man he wanted. He wanted a quick decision and had also spoken to the Cabinet Secretary.

I then called the Cabinet Secretary on the phone after I went to office and he said that indeed the Chief Minister had spoken to him about me. He said that the convention was that when an officer was asked for the post of Chief Secretary the request would be honored as the state had first claim on its officers for its top post. I said that I had already changed jobs frequently. I was holding a Secretary's post and the posting in Hyderabad was not a promotion. In any case I did not know Rama Rao and how I would get on with him. I said it would help if he got orders of the P.M. that since I was not keen on going, and the Centre wanted to keep up the tradition, if there was any problem of my continuance as Chief Secretary, I would be accommodated in the Centre. Rao Saheb was amused but thought I was cautious and wise to seek this assurance and he eventually got it from the P.M. So I packed up and moved to Andhra for the third time.

In an underground coalmine of Eastern Coal Fields, West Bengal, 1983

With N.T. Rama Rao, (Chief Minister, Andhra Pradesh), Hyderabad 1983

7

Andhra Pradesh

WHEN I landed in Hyderabad to take over as Chief Secretary I was received by officials including the police. The entire government staff had been on strike for the last 10 days. I had to travel in a police vehicle to the guest house as the staff drivers were on strike. There was no service at the guest house because of the strike. The police asked their staff to clean a room for me. I ordered breakfast from a private hotel and settled down to work. When I called on the Chief Minister, he was warm and said that together we could do a lot of good to the state. The first priority was to settle the strike. One of the main grievances was the reduction in the retirement age back to the original 55 years from the recently revised age of 58 years. The matter was in the courts and we agreed to wait for the result. There were a number of issues raised by the staff with varying financial implications. I sat with the principal finance secretary Sankara Guruswamy, a sharp and competent officer, and worked out the details of how far we could go with minimum financial burden on the state. Earlier, when I was municipal secretary in 1976, I had known some of the workers' leaders and it was easier to deal with them. After intensive negotiations for about seven days, during which I kept the secretary to the C.M. informed, I asked him to get the C.M.'s approval for the settlement. Finally, when the strike was settled I took the leaders to the C.M.'s residence for a meeting to thank him and to give him a chance to praise the cooperative attitude of the staff. On the whole the matter ended on an amicable note. The press, however, highlighted my role in the successful negotiations and I learnt that the C.M. was not very pleased. It was perhaps his sense of insecurity and his earlier high profile career in movies that made him seek credit in the press. This trait surfaced once again in the Singareni coalfield affair dealt with later.

The C.M. usually wanted to meet officers at 6.30 in the morning. The secretaries would come for the meeting and go home for breakfast and come to the office at 11 a.m. I persuaded NTR to have the meetings a little later and he started them around 7.30 a.m. During these meetings he would hold forth like a soliloquy with his well known flair for dramatics. The officers would listen with amusement. After a few minutes, he would realize the situation, smile sheepishly and try to go back to normal conversation.

In October 1983, the Queen of England and the Duke were to visit Hyderabad for a few days to celebrate their wedding anniversary. I took charge of the arrangements and went into all the details. The police commissioner Vijayarama Rao, an able officer, extended full cooperation with the traffic and other arrangements. One of the events of the visit was the Governor's banquet for the Queen. The guest list sent from Delhi to Governor Ram Lal was imbalanced and omitted important local persons like the Speaker of the Assembly, the Chief Justice, the Director General of Police and others. On the other hand, it was weighted heavily in favour of Congress politicians, ex-ministers and others. I drew the attention of the C.M. to this and said that the banquet was a government affair and the Governor should go by the protocol. As the feeling was that Ram Lal was appointed in AP to keep an eye on the C.M., he readily agreed with me and said that he would go to see the Governor and wanted me to go with him. When the matter was explained to the Governor, he said that I could speak to the Prime Minister's Office and sort it out and he would go by their decision. I spoke to PMO and R.K. Dhawan was nice about it. He readily saw the point and said that I could rearrange the invitation list but include at least some of the prominent Congressmen. So the list was recast. At the banquet the politicians turned up in different coloured clothes. The Queen was amused and asked me if there was no standard formal dress for such occasions. I said there was, but politicians had the freedom to wear the colours of their party. For Telugu Desam it was orange, while for the Congress it was white and, others came in colours of their choice. The banquet passed off without any further incident.

During the visit of the Queen, I presented to her a large woodwork piece from Kondapalli, which was well known for its wood crafts. She liked it and during my visit to the National Museum in London some years later I was surprised to see the piece displayed with the caption 'Presented to H.M. the Queen by the Chief Secretary A.P.'

On the occasion of the Republic Day the Army departed from past practice and decided that its contingents would not present a salute to the C.M. After consultations with Delhi, a compromise was worked out by which the army contingent would participate in the march past but not in the subsequent proceedings.

In January there was a proposal for film stars and former friends of the C.M. to collect money for the poor by performing in the stadium. The C.M. wanted me to ask all the officials of the Sales Tax and other departments, to sell tickets by approaching the shopkeepers. I told the C.M. that it was not proper and would result in increased corruption. He was angry but eventually agreed with me.

In March 1984, there was a strike in the Singareni collieries, which went on for quite some days affecting coal production for power generation. The C.M. went to Bombay for a meeting. The Managing Director was Ahmed, a competent and firm officer, who was in daily touch with me on the negotiations and I would relay the information to the C.M. in Bombay. After negotiations, Ahmed said the time was ripe to strike a deal and get the workers back to work without too much of a burden on the company. I asked him to go ahead. When the C.M. returned to Hyderabad he was angry that the strike had been settled without his getting any credit. He went to Kothagudem by helicopter along with a minister, his secretary and me. He wanted to address a large gathering. At 12 noon it was very hot. The night shift workers were resting and the others were in the pits. A group of school children and some women had been gathered. The C.M. was furious and after addressing them for some time he was sweating a lot. I called the doctor who advised that the meeting be adjourned and the C.M. be taken to the circuit house for some rest. We then adjourned to the guesthouse. The C.M. called in the M.D. Ahmed, and talked rudely to him for settling the strike without waiting for his return from Bombay. I said that I had asked the M.D. to settle with the workers, as production was affected and we would have missed the settlement if we had waited. I said that the C.M. was aware of this position and there was no reason for him to berate the M.D. unless he wanted to show his displeasure against me.

On my return to Hyderabad the next morning, I met the C.M. at his residence and said that his harsh words against an honest and good officer like Ahmed were not justified. He flared up and said that he was justified and he would do it again if the situation warranted.

After a few days I met the C.M. and handed in my leave application. He took it and said that he would let me know. Nothing happened for a few weeks and I found it difficult to function. In the meanwhile a number of his friends met me and tried to persuade me to withdraw my application and stay on in the State. I politely declined. After a few days the C.M. sent for me. When I went to see him he was most courteous and talked about my family and invited me to have breakfast with him. Afterwards, he took me to his room and handed over my leave application sanctioning two months leave. He said he was sorry to lose me, wished me well and came to the car to see me off. That was Mr. N.T. Rama Rao. Generous, impetuous and whimsical.

When I contacted Rao Sahib he said that it was difficult to find a job for me in Delhi at short notice and asked me to be patient. Eventually, he found a new post of secretary of a committee to review the financial year under the chairmanship of L.K. Jha. For the third time I joined Mr. Jha. After a few months of organizing the work, Dr. P.C. Alexander called me and said that I should see Justice Sarkaria who was heading the Commission on Centre-State relations. The judge said that the secretary of the Commission was retiring and he wanted a replacement and asked if I would join. I said that if the PMO wanted me to join him I would do so. I joined the Commission. The work was interesting and I organized the preparation of a number of status papers on various aspects of our work. This was appreciated by the judge who wanted to prepare his report without delay. I began to draft the report.

In October 1984, when I was in my office I got a call that the P.M. had been shot several times by her own body guard. What happened in Delhi thereafter is well documented. After Rajiv Gandhi was sworn in as the new P.M. there was a reshuffle of secretaries and I was asked whether I preferred the Planning Commission or the Petroleum Ministry. I had been in the Planning Commission and knew that one could not be action-oriented there. I, therefore opted for Petroleum. Justice Sarkaria would not relieve me unless I recommended a suitable replacement for myself who could carry on the work in the Commission. I suggested my colleague Sankara Guruswamy who was interviewed and accepted. I promptly moved to Petroleum in February 1985.

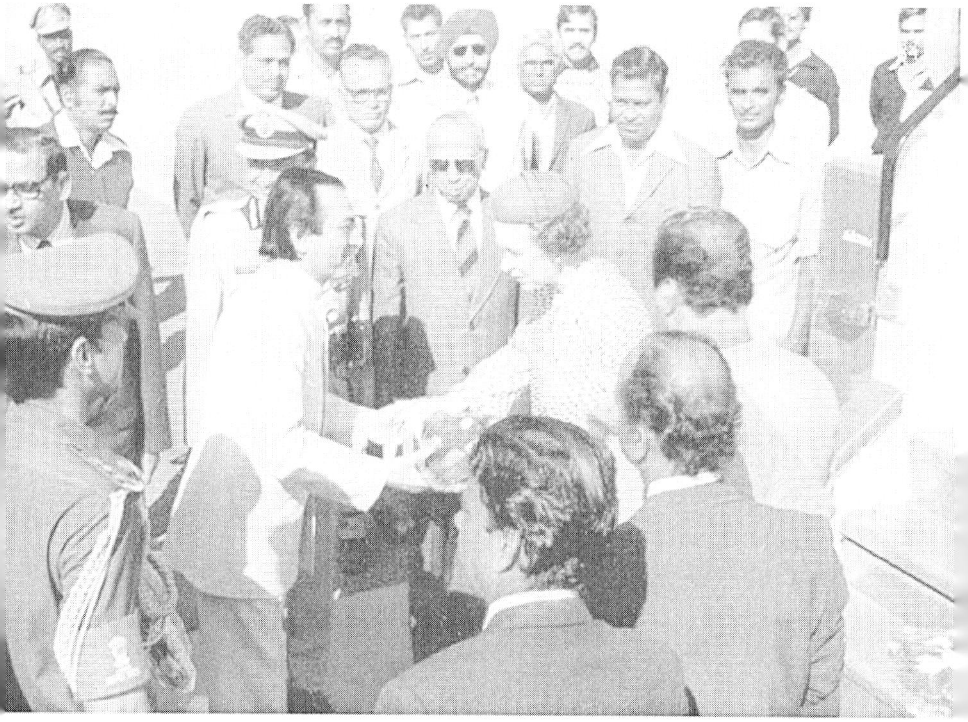

▲
Queen Elizabeth being received by Governor Ramlal — Hyderabad, 1983

The Queen and the Duke of Edinburgh in Hyderabad, 1983
▼

Five Petroleum Secretaries, New Delhi, 2000
From left to right : Vijay Kelkar (1994 - 1997), G.V. Ramakrishna (1985 - 1988), P.K. Dave (1971 - 1975), Probir Sen Gupta (1997 - 1998), A.S. Gill (1983 - 1985) along with M.A. Pathan, Chairman, Indian Oil Corporation

Inaugurating the Annual IOC Golf Championship, Bangalore, 1997

8

Petroleum Ministry

WHEN I joined the Petroleum Ministry in February 1985 my friends told me that it was a 'hot' place and I had to watch my step. At that time the Ministry was very large with petroleum, natural gas and petrochemicals coming within its purview. All the public sector companies in these fields were large with huge projects worth several thousand crores of rupees investment. The scope for corruption was enormous depending on the officials and the minister.

At that time the HBJ (Hazipur Bijaipur Jagdishpur) gas pipeline project had been sanctioned and the procurement of pipes had commenced before I joined the Ministry but most of the work remained to be done. The first lot of pipes had been ordered from Sumitomo, a Japanese company, and had been delivered. Orders were also placed for some more pipes from Brazil. The smaller diameter pipes were to be ordered from the Rourkela steel plant in India. The coating of all these pipes was to be done in India. The biggest component was the welding, coating and laying of the pipes over a distance of 1700 kilometers. This was a specialized job involving special welding to withstand high pressure. The pipeline had to cross major rivers, canals and roads in four states – Gujarat, Rajasthan, UP and MP. There were compressors at intervals to maintain pressure and other anti-corrosion and signalling equipment to be installed.

A few days after I joined, there was a meeting in the office of the Finance Minister V.P. Singh on the Hazira-Bijaipur Jagdishpur (HBJ) pipeline. The total cost of the project was over Rs. 1700 crores. The natural gas from the Oil and Natural Gas Commission (ONGC) fields in South Bassein was to be transported over a distance of 1700 kilometres through three sizes of pipes of 36 inches, 24 inches and 18 inches in diameter. Pipes were to be procured separately by Government. The larger pipes had already been procured from Sumitomo of Japan, and others ordered from Brazil. The smaller pipes were to be procured locally from the Rourkela steel plant. The subject for discussion was whether the welding, testing and laying of the pipeline with ancillaries, was to be broken up or given to a single contractor with responsibility for coordination and final quality certification. Those present included the finance secretary Venkitaramanan, the P.M's additional secretary, Gopi Arora and others. After some discussion, everyone agreed that the best course would be to entrust the whole job to a single reputable contractor with single point responsibility for timely completion and quality control. The gas in the pipeline was to support three power plants and three fertilizer factories along the way. As these projects had already started construction, I was given the responsibility of getting the project completed on time to be able to supply gas to all of them.

After the meeting, I met the senior officers of Engineers India Ltd (EIL) who had been associated with the project preparation from the beginning. Tender papers were prepared in record time and I personally went through them with the EIL officers. Pre-qualification conditions were laid down carefully so as to get the most experienced firms in the field. Provision for the financing of the project was also built into the tender terms. This was also to be taken into account while evaluating the bids. Specifications were laid down in stringent terms in accordance with international standards. A special full time project team was constituted within EIL under the leadership of Grover, Director Projects, to deal with all aspects of the project till completion.

The parties that had qualified to bid with reference to their experience and track record were Snam Progetti of Italy; a Consortium of three consisting of Spie Capag (France), Toyo Engineering and NKK (of Japan); and a Canadian firm. The bids were opened in the presence of the bidders and their signatures were obtained on all the tenders, along with those of the EIL team members. The lowest was the bid of the Spie Capag consortium followed by the Italian firm and the Canadians. The difference between the lowest and the next higher bid was about Rs. 120 crores as against the total value of work of about Rs. 700 crores. The choice was made after one or two meetings with the EIL project team. When the respective bids were known to all the bidders, the Canadians withdrew from the contest, but not before making an effort to see if they could 'swing' the project in their favour. The Snam representative in India was Quattrochi who had been in India for several years. Snam had won several contracts in India for offshore work for ONGC and also in fertilizer projects. The Snam representative met me several times to urge that his was the lowest after taking into account their financing terms. However, it was found that the French and Japanese had also offered financing and this had been taken into account. I had to tell Quattrochi that there was no point in meeting me again and again and he was not getting the contract, as he was much higher than the lowest. He brought his chief to India and when he called on me, I told the chief that his was a worldwide company that had done some work in India also. He should tell his India representative that in tenders he should be prepared to lose some without making a fuss about it. He agreed and looked meaningfully at Quattrochi who was squirming in his seat.

This was not the end of it. One winter morning in 1986, I was asked to go to the minister Naval Kishore Sharma's house with the HBJ file. When I went there he offered me a cup of coffee, and asked me to wait and went out of his house with the file. He came back after about half an hour. (It was later revealed that he had been to see Arun Nehru who was then Power Minister.) Sharma pulled out a slip of paper and copied from it on to the file and handed it to me with a wry smile. He had noted that the evaluation made by the EIL team and endorsed by me had to be reviewed by an official group under the cabinet secretary, including the defence adviser Arunachalam, the expenditure secretary Ganapati and myself. The secretary of the group was Kamlesh Sharma, a foreign service officer who was at that time working in the finance ministry. I took the file and returned to my office and rang up cabinet secretary P.K. Kaul with whom I had worked when we were both directors in the Department of Economic Affairs in the sixties. I met him and showed the minister's note. He called a meeting of the review committee in the next few days. I attended the meeting and explained how the tender procedures had been followed in a transparent manner and asked how they would like go about the matter. After some discussion they wanted to meet the head of the EIL team and I took him for the next meeting. Grover, Director Projects GAIL, came along with the books and international codes for high-pressure pipelines and explained the procedures followed in pre-qualifying the bidders, and in the evaluation process. As the views of the committee had not crystallized, I met Kaul later and told him, that if the committee was inclined to disregard the evaluation, I would either have to give a note of dissent or go on leave to enable them to appoint someone else in my place. I could then give my defence later if necessary. I explained that if I did not defend the evaluation of the EIL team or my support for it, I could be hauled up by the Government which was showing signs of anger against me for not going in favour of Snam. Kaul was nice about it and said that there was no reason for me to feel apprehensive about the matter. At this stage a further matter was raised by Quattrochi with the chairman of the committee about the eligibility of the consortium partner NKK with reference to their experience. More evidence was given about their experience with certificates from Japan and the committee was satisfied. Thereafter, the committee discussed the matter further, agreed with me and asked the secretary Kamlesh Sharma to draft the report. He wanted some assistance from my officers about the background and details of the project. In the final report approved by Kaul it was stated that the committee was 'one hundred per cent satisfied with the evaluation'. This vindicated my stand. In about a fortnight Kaul was sent as Ambassador to the US and it was generally believed that this sudden change had something to do with his support for my ministry's handling of the matter.

A little while later minister Sharma signed my note after seeing the Kaul committee report and the file went to the Finance ministry. Naval Kishore Sharma was soon shifted from the ministry and went as Congress president to Rajasthan. He was upset and angry. When he left the ministry he told me, 'I am going now, I don't know how long you will be here'. I said that I would gladly go whenever I was ordered.

Chandrasekhar Singh from Bihar came as the next minister. He was a mild man and a gentleman, and easy to deal with. At this stage an attempt was made to get the contract split between the French consortium and Snam. I objected to this by pointing out in a four page note on the file that this was contrary to the original decision taken at the Finance Minister's meeting. I noted that tenders were invited for a complete turnkey job. If the contract was to be split now it would be against the terms of the bid and in the implementation there would be several complications. There would be rivalry between the parties and the work would be delayed. It was then agreed not to split the contract.

There was a lot of drama before the agreement was finally signed. The draft of the contract came to me with the legal opinion of the Gas Authority of India. (GAIL) Some instinct told me that it would be better to get the opinion of the Solicitor General and I asked GAIL to get this. It was cleared by him with some modifications. Then I asked GAIL to get the contract vetted by the Attorney General (AG) also. They expressed surprise but got the contract further seen by the AG. At this stage I did not know how valuable these opinions of the two top law officers of the Government would be later.

There were a series of successive queries from the PMO about details like liquidated damages etc. These were answered. Then there was a query as to who had vetted the contract. I said that the top law officers had vetted the contract. Then some days later the question of financial evaluation was raised to find out whether the package offered by the Italians was not superior to that of the lowest bidder to off set the higher bid. The matter went to the Finance Ministry and the additional secretary, Geethakrishnan, personally handled the case, made a thorough evaluation, and came up with the conclusion that the petroleum ministry had correctly evaluated the bids in favour of the lowest bidder. The F.M. later approved the contract. Later when the F.M. went to Washington to attend the Annual Meetings of the Bank and the Fund, he was complimented for the clean manner in which the contract had been awarded.

The final contract was drawn up and the date was fixed. The top officials of the Spie consortium came for the signing ceremony for one of the largest international contracts. The press had been invited for refreshments after the signing ceremony. At this stage the file was called by the PMO and I was instructed to await its return before the actual signing. I met the minister who was busy preparing to go to London for the road show for the Third Round of oil exploration contracts. I told him this was not the time for him to go abroad and he should go to the P.M. to extricate the file and get orders to sign the contract, which had been cleared by all concerned. He cancelled his flight on my insistence but would not go to the P.M. and asked me to deal with Serla Grewal, the P.M.'s secretary. I said that the matter was not in her hands. He asked me to talk to Satish Sharma and I declined. By this time it was nearly 6'o clock and the signing ceremony was at 6.30 p.m. The Gas Authority of India (GAIL) chairman was calling me, in my office, every ten minutes saying all the foreign parties had arrived at the hotel for the signing. I asked him to put them off for sometime. The minister pleaded helplessness. Around 8 p.m. the Press was getting restless and so were the foreigners. I asked the GAIL chairman to say that there were some last minute legal matters and the signing would be held later. This came as a shock to all the foreigners. The French grumbled and left for the airport. The Japanese refused food and drink and waited at the table saying, "we came to sign and we will stay till signing". Finally, when it became clear that there would be no signing they left around 11 p.m. for the airport. The whole episode left a bad taste in everybody's mouth.

After a week or so the file was returned and a quiet signing ceremony was held.

Just before this, a strange event took place. On a Saturday morning a Vice President of Spie wanted to see me urgently and I called him. He came in and said they were very happy that the whole contract had been handled in a very clean manner without even a cup of coffee being taken from them. He said it was their practice in such contracts to give five per cent of the contract value, which at that time amounted for some Rs. 34 crores, to the persons who had dealt with the contract, and this amount was at my disposal to do what I wanted with it. I could keep it in India, or they would deposit it in a foreign account, or I could give it to anybody I wanted.

I was taken aback and sent for the Financial Adviser Balachandran and the concerned director Srinivasan, who were in the office. When they came, I asked the Frenchman to repeat what he had said. The officers were also taken aback. I asked them what we should do. They thought we should not touch it. I said that was not the solution. The huge amount was offered to me to do what I liked with it. I would not touch it, I would not give it to anybody, nor would I return the money to the Frenchman.

I told the Frenchman that I wanted the money to go to the Government and the amount should be given as a reduction in the contract value. He was stunned and said that it would not be possible at this stage. I said I wanted a letter from him to that effect by the evening or else there would be no contract. He said that he had to contact his bosses who were away from Paris, for the weekend. I said that he should trace out his bosses and come back with their okay for my proposal by 5 p.m. I then went for my usual Saturday round of golf. We all came back to the office around 5.15 p.m. and the Frenchman brought his blank letterhead. I asked him to type his offer of price reduction on the typewriter of the financial adviser. This was done and he signed the letter which stated that 'as a gesture of goodwill' his company had decided to give a reduction in the contract value to the extent of

Rs. 34 crores. I asked the director to place it on the file, which the financial adviser and I signed. The director was asked to send a copy of the letter to the chairman of GAIL so that he could reduce the contract value. I did not mention the incident to the minister. These facts were little known to anyone at that time, except to the officers concerned and the GAIL officials. The file will speak for itself.

The efforts of Quattrochi to thwart the contract did not end. He complained that the contract was not being executed according to international standards. Fortunately, we had engaged independent, well-known Dutch consultants for supervising the technical aspects of the work and they had certified the quality of the work at every stage. Thereafter, the P.M. wanted to review the progress of the project and we got ready on eight different occasions, to make the presentation and each time the review was postponed at very short notice.

Around this time there were problems in getting qualified welders for the pipeline. As the work was falling slightly behind schedule, I spoke to the senior vice president of Spie, the main contractor, and he agreed to airlift, at their own expense, welders from Turkey and other places. He was cooperative because of the clean manner in which the contract was awarded despite the efforts of Quattrochi to swing the contract in Snam's favour. Visas were arranged for the welders on an urgent basis through our embassies and work was on track once again.

There was a problem of getting certain specialised items of equipment for rust prevention of the pipeline. The supplier chosen by the engineers implementing the project was an Israeli company. There was a ban imposed by the Government at that time that there should be no trade with Israel. I spoke to my good friend, the foreign secretary, A.P. Venkateswaran, explained the problem and said that the important project needed a waiver of the rule. After we thought the matter through, we agreed that the Israeli company could send equipment to their US counterpart company who in turn could supply the items. It was agreed that no searching questions would be asked about the origin of the equipment.

One day Aditya Birla came to see the minister and I was called in. Birla said that his fertilizer plant at Jagdishpur was dependent on the HBJ gas and he had heard that the gas transport pipeline was going slow. I had by this time my own intelligence about the progress of the downstream projects using HBJ gas. I told Birla that the HBJ project was going on well and we would pay him a penalty of Rs. 10 lakhs for every day of delay and similarly he should pay GAIL Rs. 10 lakh a day if he was not ready to take the gas under the 'take or pay' contract. He backed out and said the he merely wanted to draw the attention of the minister to his anxiety about the project and he was satisfied that we were watching the progress.

Eventually the project was completed in time and the gas was taken first to the Bijaipur fertilizer plant of Indian Farmers Fertiliser Cooperative (IFFCO) four days before they were ready. The Minister went for the inauguration. By this time I was rather fed up with the whole project and declined to go, pleading indisposition, so as not to embarrass the minister.

As gas supplies began through the HBJ pipeline, the question of pricing the gas for various consumers came up. A committee was appointed under the adviser Vijay Kelkar to make a techno-economic study and make recommendations. Kelkar produced a very good report and most of the recommendations were accepted, and for the first time , the policy of pricing natural gas including the transportation costs was laid down by Government.

In 1986, the Third Round of bidding for the exploration of offshore oil fields was opened. 16 blocks were offered all-round the Indian coastline. The sentiment was low, as oil prices had crashed to around $10 per barrel. Road shows were held in London and PMO turned down the ministry proposal that I should go with the team, which was being led by minister Chandrasekhar Singh. This was generally believed to be their way of showing displeasure at the way I had handled the HBJ contract. However, for the road show in Houston, I went and made a presentation and told the oil companies that contrary to conventional wisdom this was the time to explore. With oil prices being low no production wells were being drilled. Exploration costs were low as a large number of drilling rigs were idle. They saw the point. After negotiations with several parties, we had agreements with seven of the big international oil companies for exploration costing several million dollars. Companies like Shell, Chevron,Texaco, Amoco, Mobil, BHP and others started exploration. These complex negotiations with the oil companies were conducted most competently by C.B. Bhave, director in the ministry, ably assisted by Vikram Mehta, adviser Oil India. Bhave later joined me in Securities and Exchange Board of India (SEBI) and has since been responsible for building up the National Securities Depository Ltd (NSDL). Vikram Mehta later left the public sector oil company, and is now the Chairman of the Shell Group of companies in India. I later heard that exploration was done in a number of blocks with 19 or 20 wells being drilled at a cost of over $100 million but without any results. One or two large companies wanted to continue exploration on the same terms but the ministry turned down the proposal and advised them to apply afresh in the next round.

No major oil company has come to explore in India thereafter. However, other smaller foreign companies, large Indian companies, and ONGC have had success in some of the off shore areas. Only now the Fourth Round has been opened for bidding for a number of off shore blocks.

We had long term contracts for the purchase of crude oil from Kuwait, Iraq, USSR and Saudi Arabia. I went to Kuwait and Saudi Arabia in 1986, to renew contacts. In Kuwait we entered into a mutual cooperation agreement with the Organisation of Arab Petroleum Exporting Countries (OAPEC). The Secretary General was Mr. Attiga Kuwaiti, a soft spoken man with pleasant manners. I visited their oil refinery and ports of Mina Abdulla and Mina Ahmadi. We agreed that there should be cooperation between the two countries in oil exploration and refining. Our Ambassador in Kuwait was N.N. Jha, a seasoned and able foreign service officer, who made all the arrangements for our visit. It was agreed that a conference would be held in India later in the year.

I then went to Riyadh mainly to meet the Petroleum Minister, the redoubtable Shaikh Yamani who, as representative of the largest producer, had a great deal of influence in OPEC, in setting production levels and price ranges. His every word was watched by the media and the market as signal for a rise or fall in oil prices. In fact the British privatization of Britoil got into a lot of trouble because of a statement of Yamani which was interpreted to signal a fall in prices. The share prices of Britoil fell. Nigel Lawson, the British Chancellor of the Exchequer, recalls in his book *The view from number 11*, how he was hauled over the coals because he had ventured on a fixed price sale of the shares of Britoil but because of Yamani's statement the market fell and there were no takers at the price quoted by the British. When I asked our Ambassador to fix up an appointment for me to meet Yamani, he was diffident and said that he would try. After some effort he managed to get an appointment for about fifteen minutes, for me to see the Minister.

When I went to meet Yamani I found him to be a rather informal man and he talked freely. In the course of our conversation, when I told him that I had been to Harvard University for my Masters in 1959, he said he had been there a year earlier, and we chatted about a number of our common friends at Harvard. He then said that his hobby was to make *ittars* (perfumes) according to his own recipes. He showed me a row of seven or eight bottles on his table as his personal concoctions. I said that scents and *ittars* are quite popular in India. He then opened his bottles of perfume one after the other and insisted on placing a drop of each perfume on the back of both my hands! I had to smell each one and pronounce my judgment. I began to smell like a perfume factory. Not being an expert, or even a user of *ittars,* I had to make polite comments. At the end of the meeting, he shook hands and said that they would have an evergreen contract for the supply of two million tones of oil per year and the prices would be related to international prices with some discount for India. The meeting lasted about 40 minutes. When I came out of the meeting, the Ambassador, who was waiting outside, showed surprise and asked how I was able to stay inside for such a long time when they had given me only fifteen minutes. I held out my hand for him to smell. Later over dinner I told him the full story.

I was to retire in March 1988. Tamil Nadu had come under President's Rule in January and Dr. P.C. Alexander was appointed Governor while he was still in London as the High Commissioner. During a dinner at my place for some of my close friends, the discussion turned on the subject of officers going as Adviser to the Governor. The talk was that the PMO was looking at senior secretaries due to retire shortly. The story was that when my name was included in the list, it had been struck off with a red pencil at 'higher levels'. S.S. Sidhu was appointed along with a Tamil Nadu cadre officer, A. Padmanabhan, who was earlier Chief Secretary before retiring.

I went to some of the refineries on a farewell visit. I went to Cochin and stopped on the way back at Hyderabad for a day or two. One night, when I was about to retire for the night, there was a call from Dr. Alexander. He said that he had taken over in Madras and asked me if I would like to go as his adviser. I said that my name had already been suggested but turned down and two others were appointed. He said that I should leave all that to him as the P.M. had promised to give him anyone he wanted as adviser and that this was the condition on which he had accepted the job. He was somewhat peeved that the advisers had been appointed without consulting him. He wanted me to merely say whether I would be prepared to work with him in Madras. I readily agreed as I had earlier met him in Delhi in various capacities and had high regard for him. After I returned to Delhi and was winding up matters like writing confidential reports etc., Dr. Alexander rang up from Madras asking me when I was joining. I said that I had not received any orders. After a few days he rang up again and I repeated the same story to him. He was impatient and asked me speak to Serla Grewal, P.M.'s secretary. I suggested that it was better he spoke to the P.M., if, as he said, he had been promised the person of his choice as adviser. Eventually he spoke to the P.M. and orders were issued. I left for Madras within a day or two thereafter.

▲ With Attiga, Secretary General, OAPEC, Kuwait, 1986

With Petroleum Minister, Chandrasekhar Singh, Houston, 1986 ▼

With Energy Minister Vasant Sathe and Petroleum Minister Brahm Dutt at OAPEC Conference, 198

9

Tamil Nadu

I had not studied or worked in Madras. My allotted cadre was Andhra Pradesh. There is a convention that officers belonging to a cadre are not appointed as Advisers during President's Rule in the same State, and I had met this condition. When I reached Madras (as it was then called) because of the political turmoil of the past few months, work had come to a standstill. Thousands of files were lying unattended and things were in a bad shape. The Governor was keen that we should all get down to clearing the backlog. This was my first experience of working with the T.N. bureaucracy. The officers at secretary level were competent and hardworking and I was able to establish a good rapport with all of them. We were able to clear most of the backlog in about ten days.

While we were settling down to normal work, Government staff in the district was restless and presented a number of demands. Eventually they went on strike towards the end of June along with all the teachers. They were followed by the secretariat staff on the 3rd June 1988.

All work came to a standstill throughout the state and the public was greatly inconvenienced. Initially the strike was handled by the chief secretary under the guidance of the other Adviser. The strike got into its 3rd week. Sidhu was due to leave on appointment to the prestigious post of Director General of ICAO (International Civil Aviation Organisation), and the Governor asked me to take direct charge of negotiations. After some hectic activity, and give and take on both sides, the two strikes were settled by the end of July, and we were able to get down to work. It was a coincidence that I started my term as Chief Secretary A.P. with a strike and now in T.N. also I had a similar experience.

The subjects entrusted to me were Finance, Planning, Industries, Agriculture, Commercial Taxes, Forests, Co-operation, Excise, Elections and Rural Development. Later in July, after one of the advisers, Sidhu, left for ICAO, I was also given the subjects of Police, Law and Order. All this meant working about 12 to 14 hours a day apart from fulfilling public functions that a Minister would normally do.

One of the contentious matters was the way in which the retailing of liquor was handled. I found that there was huge leakage of revenue to the tune of several hundreds of crores. Government sold liquor at low prices to an individual and allowed him to retail it at higher prices with high mark up. I was treading on the toes of many people including politicians. Efforts were made to get me shifted out of Madras or at least to take the subject away from me. The Governor gave me full backing and even went to Delhi to ask the Central Government to keep off.

There was the case of the fodder machine promoted by an American with the support of a prominent person from Delhi. The Governor was under considerable pressure to buy the machines for T.N. He passed on the foreigner to me and said I could do whatever was right. The gentleman met me and I told him the machine had to be tested in the Agricultural University and asked him to provide an experimental machine. He backed out. Later when the popular government took over, the matter was raised in the Legislature and the C.M. had to read from the file to say that nothing wrong had been done during President's rule or thereafter.

There is much talk these days about water shortage for irrigation and for drinking. I am reminded of a pilot project that I initiated. In the Thanjavur delta there is excessive rainfall in a normal year but only for a short period between late November and late January. A good part of the rainfall goes into the sea. A few weeks later the paddy crop needs a second wetting. When I discussed the matter with engineers and agricultural experts they said that as there were no hills in the area it would not be possible to build dams as in the other States. What about underground storage, I asked. We then worked on a pilot project for digging an underground storage of water. A pit would be dug in the ground for which the dimensions were worked out. The fisheries departments were then brought into the picture. They were quite enthusiastic and said that quick growing fish could be stocked in the ponds. Then, I had meetings in two villages with the farmers, the banks and the concerned others. The land for the pond would be given by one of the farmers for which he would be compensated and income from the fish would be shared by the participants. The project was called Farm Pond Scheme (Pannai Kuttai Tittam) and the banks agreed to finance it, provided the National Bank for Agricultural and Rural Development (NABARD) agreed to re-finance it. I then sent the proposal to NABARD who turned it down at first. I wrote to P.R. Nayak, the Deputy Governor of the Reserve Bank of India (RBI), who was the Chairman of NABARD and after a lot of pursuasion he agreed to re-finance the proposal. Soon thereafter I left Madras. Two years later when I was in SEBI, I got a letter from NABARD, who, because of my earlier interest in the project, sent me a copy of the evaluation report prepared by them after studying the project for two full seasons. I was pleasantly surprised to find the project was a huge success. Apart from stabilizing the paddy crop, the fish, the bananas and vegetables grown around the ponds gave a handsome income. The farmers' income had gone up by 60 per cent. I moved from one post to another and lost track of further developments. My latest enquiries in Chennai show that there was no follow up to proliferate the pond scheme in other villages. Even now it is not too late to revive the project. Will the efficient T.N. bureaucracy wake up now?

There was another interesting episode prior to elections. Rajiv Gandhi used to visit Madras and surrounding places to meet the people. His party had advised him that if the Congress went alone without any alliance it would sweep the polls. I was asked for my informal opinion. I said that this was a political matter and it would not be proper for me to express any opinion. Being pressed by Chidambaram, one of the ministers from T.N., to express my personal views, I met him, but took the home secretary with me. I said that if the Congress did not have a seat sharing arrangement with the AIADMK, the party may not enter Fort St. George, the seat of the government, for the next several years. The minister then asked me how I could say this as there were huge crowds to see Rajiv wherever he went. I said this is no indication, as the crowds are in fact sent by other parties to give a wrong impression to the Congress. The minister disagreed with me but said he would convey to Rajiv my informal views. In the event, there was no seat sharing arrangement and the results were as I had predicted. Later when I met the minister he showed chagrin and said that they should have taken my assessment seriously.

When elections were being conducted I welcomed the appointment of external observers and arranged facilities for them to visit places of their choice. Efforts were made at high levels to see if I could manage to ensure that certain parties got more votes. I firmly put my foot down and said that my instructions were that all officials should conduct themselves in a fair and impartial manner. The elections went off well and observers were satisfied.

I left Madras a day after the elected Government was sworn in.

▲
Convocation of Agriculture University, Tamil Nadu — 1988

With Jacques Delors, Chairman, EEC, Brussels, 1988

10

Brussels

DURING the course of my assignment in Madras, I had retired (in March 1988) and continued on re-employment, which I preferred to extension of service.

When I returned to Delhi I was a free man and prepared to wind up and plan my real retirement. I got a call from the Prime Minister's Office asking me whether I would be interested in going as Ambassador to the European Economic Community (now the European Union) in Brussels. I took a few days' time and consulted my wife. We had earlier in 1972 done a diplomatic stint in Washington where I was minister for economic affairs. After some hesitation my wife agreed and I accepted the assignment.

When I called on Prime Minister, Rajiv Gandhi, he said that he appreciated my work in Tamil Nadu and wanted me to go to Brussels for a three-year stint to take up economic matters with the European Community (EC). I then called on P.V. Narasimha Rao, the external affairs minister in his office. He was pleased to see me and took me home in his car and we had a cordial chat over tea. He said that the posting was for three years and there was a substantial economic content to the job which I should like. After about half an hour he saw me to the door and wished me well.

Brussels was an interesting assignment. Apart from the EEC, I was accredited to Belgium and Luxembourg. After I presented my credentials to the President of EC, Jacques Delors, the King of the Belgians and the Crown Prince of Luxembourg, I settled down to serious work.

As was customary I called on the ambassadors of some of the important countries. As the Western countries had separate ambassadors to the EEC, I called on them also. Not all of them were warm. I became friendly with the Japanese Ambassador because of our common interest in golf and I played a few rounds with him and some former Ambassadors in the Royal Belgian Golf Club.

When the Tianenman Square incident happened, there was a lot of criticism in the press and demonstrations on the streets of Brussels. As I had earlier fixed my appointment to call on the Chinese Ambassador, I consulted my senior colleagues in the embassy and decided to keep the appointment. The riot police posted outside the Chinese embassy were informed and they cleared the way for my car to go into the building. The Ambassador was cordial and appreciated my going to see him.

Thereafter, when we met at several functions, he would make it a point to come and greet me. I was not sure about the reaction of our Government to my visit, and was amused to read in the press that a few days after the incident in Beijing, the chief security adviser to the US President had paid a secret visit to the Chinese capital.

I then learnt that public criticism and private cordiality was part of the diplomatic game.

Negotiations for the new World Trade Organisation (WTO) Agreements were on in Geneva and the EC was an important participant representing twelve countries of Europe. There were a number of issues that were of vital importance to developing countries. The agreements on Intellectual Property Rights, on investment measures and services, were added on at Punta Del Este against the wishes of the developing countries. Assurances were given that the special needs of the developing countries would be kept in view. These were accepted with skepticism by the developing countries. Many of the clauses in the draft papers for discussion were one sided. After accessing all these papers and studying the Indian position, I introduced the subject to all the officers in the embassy in a number of meetings. I had introduced the system of weekly meetings at which one officer, by rotation, would make a detailed presentation of a single topic, and this would be followed by discussion. In this way all the officers became quite familiar with the issues and also the position of the GoI. The next step was to meet the embassy officials of the developing countries of Asia, Africa and Latin America on a one to one basis over lunch. Indian embassy officials were to meet their counterparts in other embassies. I also met ambassadors in groups. After about three months of these efforts the developing world was aware of the implications to their own countries of the various proposals.

The Pakistani and the Egyptian ambassadors were quite active and did their bit by meeting other envoys. It was generally accepted that the Indian embassy team was taking the lead.

We assembled the ambassadors of eighteen developing countries for an official meeting in the Indian Chancery. The meeting lasted two hours and was followed by lunch. It was agreed at the meeting that we should send a request to meet the Vice President of the EC (in charge of WTO matters), Andreissen, who was earlier Finance Minister of Netherlands. A written communication was prepared and signed by about eighteen ambassadors and sent to the EC.[1] I had met Andreissen a few times and after I spoke to him about the wishes of the developing countries he agreed to meet us over lunch at the international club. At this stage I thought it wise to take a back seat and requested the ambassadors of Pakistan, Brazil and Egypt to make their sectoral presentations and I wound up with a broader speech. The EC officials who had accompanied Andreissen kept elaborate notes and the senior commissioner responded in a guarded manner. I had sent a number of letters to the secretaries in Delhi warning them of the impending WTO agreements and suggested steps to avert or mitigate the adverse effects on us. I got very few responses.[2] This apathy cost us later in matters like technical standards, health and safety measures which affected our exports of marine products and other items like jute carpet backing. These exports to the European Community were rejected on the ground that they did not meet their health standards. We took time to upgrade the standards in our processing and packing units for marine products and get them approved by the EU authorities. We lost exports during this period.

---

1. Letter to Andreissen 5.1.1990 < Appended on page 118 >.
2. Letter to Industry Secretary 9.1.1990 < Appended on page 120 >.

For jute carpet backing we had to use different chemicals in processing them so as to meet the EU standards.

During this period there were a number of industry and trade delegations from India that visited Europe but they had very little interest in, and much less understanding of, the issues that were of vital importance for their growth and indeed, survival, that were being discussed in the WTO negotiations. The Government of India also did not take industry into confidence or discuss the pros and cons of the various issues and agreements that were discussed in Geneva. Even after the WTO agreements were signed, very few industry associations took the trouble of getting them for dissemination and discussion. In meetings that I addressed there was a surprising level of ignorance about the various agreements and their implications for our industry and exports.

On the other hand, it was well known that, during the negotiations, the official delegations of developed countries were in close touch with US and European industry, particularly in regard to standards, drugs, duties etc. These industries advised their officials how to negotiate keeping their business interests in view.

I visited Strasbourg from where the European Parliament functioned and met some of the members. Through the good offices of some friends it was arranged that I could meet the economic committee of the European Parliament. About twenty members were present and I made a presentation for about half an hour. There were a number of questions on the economy, Kashmir and other subjects and we answered them according to our official line with some elaboration. As a result of our close interaction with the members and staff of the European Parliament we were able to avert some resolutions against India. The first secretary Das Gupta played a valuable role in this and other matters. He was a highly intelligent and enthusiastic member of our team and very effective in conveying our point of view to others.

The Commerce Ministry had an India Trade Centre in Brussels set up about ten years ago under the India-EC trade promotion programme. This was placed under the trade wing of the embassy. There were officers from various organizations in India deputed to the Centre. The feed back from these officers went to India through long and tortuous procedures and was of little use to our companies. A proper data base was established for all our exports to Belgium and the EC countries. Lists of importers in these countries were prepared and made available to our Industry associations. A system of receiving and transmitting business enquiries to our exporters was put in place. The officers of the Trade Centre worked with a new enthusiasm. The term, India Inc was coined during our discussion to indicate a private sector orientation. We also recommended that Trade promotion offices should be opened in Prague and Budapest. Many Indian delegations from different industry associations, would visit Brussels in the summer, but with little advance preparation. It was suggested that each of the companies represented in the delegations should send advance information about their companies to the Embassy so as to enable meetings to be arranged at high levels. It was also suggested that delegations should not come at frequent intervals and ask for appointments with the same European companies or organizations. Frequent visits brought down the level at which the delegations were received. I suggested that the commerce ministry should coordinate the visits and draw up a roster of delegations and the time table of their visits to various countries.

There were over 300 Indian children who had been adopted by Belgian families some years ago. They were generally well disposed to India but had no contact with the embassy. I first got a complete list of all the families and their addresses, the number of children adopted etc. The embassy ladies arranged a party with small gifts for the first batch of children. A map of India was put up to enable parents to point out the places from which the children had come. The parents and the children were thrilled that they had been recognized and wanted to visit the places in India from where the adopted children came.

Another major event was the attendance of the King and the Queen at a function of the Indian embassy. On the occasion of the Belgian National Day, my wife and I had the opportunity of talking to both of them and found that they were interested in Indian culture and particularly Indian dance. When the leading exponent of Bharatanatyam, Malavika Sarukkai came to Europe we got her over to Brussels for a performance. We invited the King and Queen for the performance but they sent a negative reply. However, they were curious to see Indian dance and asked whether Malavika could go for an hour to the palace and give a private recital. She agreed and we took her to the palace. Malavika, with her mother handling the taped music, danced a padam. The King was engrossed and sat with a note pad jotting down terms and meanings. After a lengthy explanatory session with the dancer the King and Queen decided to attend the performance the next day. Last minute security arrangements were made and the front row was vacated for the Royal couple. The prestigious Beaux Arts theatre was filled to capacity by local Indians and some Belgians. The Royal couple originally came with the intention of staying only till the interval but they found the performance so good that they stayed till the end. We were proud to see the interest and admiration that the Royal couple showed for one of our ancient traditions. The next day they invited us for tea at the palace and were most hospitable and chatted informally with all of us.

A little known fact was the link between India and Belgium during the Second World War. When the Germans overran Belgium after a heroic defence by the Belgians, the poet Subramanya Bharati, composed a poem in Tamil in 1940, in honour of the brave Belgians. This was translated into English, French and Flemish with the title *Hail to Belgium* and was circulated and also presented to the King who was surprised and touched by the bonds that existed with India in those days. Bharati compared the Belgians to a village girl in a folktale in which she was brave enough to fight a tiger with the only weapon she had – a winnowing pan made of bamboo![3]

My wife and I felt it was important to observe the important festivals of all our religions and instituted a new practice of observing the important events of all the

3. Hail to Belgium < Appended on page 124 >.

religions. A special place was prepared in the lobby of the Chancery where decorated exhibits were kept to mark particular occasions. We had the picture of Guru Gobind Singh to mark his birthday, the Nativity Scene to mark Christmas and so on. On the occasion of Republic Day we had a large lighted map of India prepared by the ladies. In a secluded corner of the entrance hall of the Chancery the ladies had drawn a five-foot square rangoli pattern with lovely colours. In the center they had placed a traditional brass lamp with 72 wicks. When this was lit it attracted a great deal of admiration. A map of India made with different grains and pulses-rice, *urad*, *black urad*, *rajma* and *masoor dhal* etc. was put up on the entrance wall. The show was a commendable effort since the ladies had problems like getting round mud pots for decoration-items that are so common in our country. The idea was to bring an Indian flavour to the embassy and make the staff proud of being Indians.

The Dalai Lama visited Brussels and I called on him along with first secretary Amit Dasgupta. His Holiness was warm in welcoming us and was appreciative of the hospitality of India. He invited us to his talk the next day. The meeting was well attended. He spoke of world peace and tolerance.

When general elections were held at the end of 1989, the new Government under V.P. Singh wanted all retired persons appointed by the previous Government to resign. Apart from me the other two were Rasgotra in London and Karan Singh in Washington. I responded immediately and sent my resignation. Foreign Secretary S.K. Singh called me and asked what was the hurry! I said I had only complied with his request. At first I was informed that my resignation was not accepted and I could continue. After a fortnight the Foreign Secretary said he was sorry but I had to return. When I was in the midst of my packing, a Parliamentary delegation visited Belgium and I was asked to stay back for a month to make the necessary arrangements.

The delegation had senior leaders from all parties, including Shri A.B. Vajpayee, Ms. Margaret Alva and others. I found that it was not easy to handle such a large delegation with the sensitivities of the members being in inverse proportion to their seniority. However, with the help of all the embassy officials we managed. At Luxembourg we had arranged a lunch for their Prime Minister in a local restaurant. At the end of the lunch when everyone was waiting for the P.M. to go in a car, he picked up his umbrella and started walking on the street towards his office without even an escort! Our protocol conscious delegates were watching with a measure of surprise, but not with any intention of emulating the P.M. of Luxembourg.

I came to know that, when the termination of my three-year term in Belgium within a year was noticed, the attention of the P.M. was drawn to the fact that I was the Petroleum Secretary when he was the Finance Minister in 1986 when the controversial HBJ pipeline was handled by me. He appears to have felt that I should be utilized by Government in some other capacity in India. In May 1990 Finance Secretary Bimal Jalan called up to say that I was selected for the job of Chairman SEBI. At first I was reluctant. Neither Jalan nor I knew very much about the new job. After thinking about it for a fortnight, and a few reminders from Jalan, I accepted the job. Orders were promptly issued before I left Brussels. After reaching India, I took a month's leave and joined SEBI in August 1990 in what was to be one of my high profile jobs.

An article by a senior correspondent in Brussels summed up my work in an interesting article.[4]

4. Economic Times "Indo EC Ties" < Appended on page 126 >.

APPENDED REFERENCES

< Letter to Andreissen 5.1.1990 >

January 5, 1990

Your Excellency,

The Multilateral Trade Negotiations of the Uruguay Round in Geneva have reached a crucial stage. We have followed with interest the submissions of the European Communities on the various issues and the discussions thereon. As Heads of Delegations accredited to the European Communities, we wish to have an opportunity of conveying to you the views and concerns of our Governments on the issues of the Uruguay Round with particular reference to the approach taken by the EC so far.

We would accordingly be grateful if you could kindly accept this invitation to join us for Luncheon on any day of your convenience between the 22nd and 31st of January, 1990.

Accept, Excellency, our best wishes for a Happy New Year, and assurances of our highest consideration.

<u>Heads of Delegations and Ambassadors of:</u>

Algeria ....

Brazil ....

China ....

Colombia ....

Cuba ....

Egypt ....

India ....

Contd. ...

...Contd. ...

: 2 :

<u>Heads of Delegations and Ambassadors of:</u>

Pakistan ....

Sri Lanka ....

Trinidad & Tobago ....

Tunisia ....

Tanzania ....

Venezuela ....

Yugoslavia ....

Zambia ....

Zimbabwe ....

PERU

H.E. Mr. Frans Andriessen,
Vice-President,
Commission of the European Communities,
<u>Brussels.</u>

< Letter to Industry Secretary 9.1.1990 >

No. BRU/AMB/45/90 January 09, 1990

I am writing this letter on a matter of great importance for the promotion of our exports to EEC in the context of the emerging Single Market of 1992. I have already written a few letters to Commerce and Industry Secretaries regarding technical standards and specifications. A number of papers from the EEC have also been sent to BIS and other organizations. Senior officers of BIS have also visited Brussels for discussions. However, from the recent set of proposals sent by BIS and forwarded by the Ministry of Industries, it would appear that there is some gap in communication and lack of understanding of the major issues involved and there is too great a reliance being placed on assistance from the EEC for taking care of our problems. I am, therefore, conveying to you in this letter the basic structure within which we should operate and the steps that we should take urgently to ensure that our exports have access to European market after 1992.

2. There are three basic concepts relating to the sale of products in the Single Market. These are:

i) Regulations relating to safety environment, etc. These are statutory and have the force of law.

ii) Standard: These are voluntary industry standards which have to be accepted by producers, importers, retailers and consumers.

iii) Quality assurance: This is over and above the minimum standards and are intended to provide commercial advantage for products having special quality certification.

3. All these three aspects have to be dealt with by two categories of institutions and organizations. These are:

a) Producers who should be able to understand the regulations, standards and quality assurances that they will have to meet in order to get access to the Single Market.

b) Testing and certifying institutions who have to test the products submitted by the producers according to the regulations and standards and issue certificates. In order to get recognition of these certificates, the institutions will have to equip themselves with the buildings, equipment and trained staff to follow the testing procedures prescribed by higher bodies.

Contd...

...Contd. ...

4. Our approach to producers on the one hand, and testing and certifying institutions, on the other, will have to be somewhat different.

5. As regards the producers, we have already made the proposal for having sectoral seminars, for different product groups such as machine tools, auto parts, electrical equipment, electronics, marine products, etc. In these sectoral seminars, the common European regulations, standards and quality requirements should be explained to the producers. They should also be informed of the in-house testing facilities that should be set up by them and the procedures to be followed for carrying out such in-house tests. They should also be informed of the manner in which they can obtain test certificates from approved institutions which will be recognised in Europe. For conducting these seminars, we should have experts in particular fields, with knowledge of the regulations and standards and the testing procedures. We should look for these experts not only from the EEC but also from other sources. Our experience is that EEC experts are of mediocre quality and lack the knowledge or interest in studying the regulations and specifications and conveying them to our producers. The EEC also does not give us the opportunity of selecting consultants. Therefore, we should look at the following sources for getting experts for conducting the sectoral seminars:-

i) EEC, in one or two limited areas where preliminary work has already been done by EEC experts, such as, auto parts and food processing.

ii) Experts funded by bilateral technical assistance from countries like UK, FRG, France, etc. The selection of experts be made in consultation with the major industries in these countries who have investments in India or with the assistance of the national governments who will be financing the costs of the seminars.

iii) Commonwealth Secretariat: In the case of UK institutions or other Commonwealth institutions who can organize these seminars. The expenses can be covered under Commonwealth assistance. My soundings show that this would be quite feasible.

iv) Our own financing. We should be prepared in some cases to get Indian industry to provide the Rupees against release of foreign exchange to engage high quality experts in certain fields.

6. In sum, in this area of sectoral seminars, it would be useful to consult industry organizations in India and get their views and suggestions regarding experts that may be known to them and their agreement to funding cost of seminars against release of foreign exchange where external assistance is not readily available. In Brussels, we have already begun to list out consultants with estimate of costs for holding seminars in a few sectors and this information will be sent on to your Ministry shortly.

Contd...

...Contd. ...

7. As regards testing and certifying institutions, the EEC's latest paper of 15th June, 1989, which follows their earlier paper of 7th May, 1985, is enclosed for careful study. It would be clear from this paper that the Community is trying to provide clear and objective means of assessing the competence and responsibilities of testing, certification, and inspection bodies and would enter into bilateral agreements on the mutual recognition of test reports or certificates. Such bilateral agreement is being negotiated by the Community with OECD member countries (other than EEC members). Under Community law, any product, including one originating in a third country, which has been lawfully marketed in one member-state, will be able to circulate freely within the Community as a whole. We may, therefore, explore two avenues simultaneously. One, to get prepared to negotiate a bilateral agreement with the Community and for mutual recognition of test reports etc., and secondly, to establish institution-to-institution linkages between Indian testing institutions and European testing bodies.

8. As regards the bilateral agreement with EEC, it is stipulated that the technical competence of the known Community partner should be adequate and the Community will be concerned to ensure that tests or inspections carried out by a known Community body will offer the same guarantees as those located within the Community. There should be equivalent safeguards with regard to continued technical competence of the testing, certification and inspection bodies. In our approach to the Community for the bilateral agreement, we should start by identifying our best institutions either within BIS or elsewhere, as designated bodies for particular product groups. We should then seek an understanding with the EEC that when these bodies achieve the technical competence on par with similar European bodies, they should be recognised for issue of test certificates.

9. The most important part of the exercise relates to the upgradation of our testing and certification bodies. Almost all of them would require upgradation in terms of civil works, up to date equipment and trained manpower. For each designated institution, we should seek to establish linkage with an appropriate institution in one of the EEC countries and that institution should provide technical assistance and guidance and training for bringing our institution on par with theirs. This matching of institutions should be undertaken immediately and the concerned body in the EEC country should be approached through our Missions for entering into inter-institutional arrangements. Bilateral technical assistance funds could be sought, if feasible. Concerned officials from Indian institutions should, after adequate preparation through our Missions, visit the European institutions to discuss the details of the arrangements.

10. I would, therefore, suggest that the proposals made in this letter are considered urgently and necessary action taken in consultation with industry, BIS and other organizations. If

Contd...

...*Contd.* ...

any further clarifications are required, we would always be prepared to furnish them.

Yours sincerely,

(G.V. Ramakrishna)

Shri A.N. Varma,

Secretary,

Department of Industrial Development,

Ministry of Industries,

New Delhi.

Copy to:

1. Shri S. P. Shukla, Commerce Secretary, New Delhi.
2. Shri A. Madhavan, Ambassador of India, Bonn.
3. Shri M. K. Rasgotra, High Commissioner of India, London.
4. Smt. S. Kochar, Ambassador of India, Paris.

S/C (G. V. Ramakrishna)
Ambassador of India

Copy also to:

1. Shri R. Rajamani, Secretary, Department of Electronics, Lok Nayak Bhawan, New Delhi.
2. Shri M. Dubey, Secretary (ER), Ministry of External Affairs, New Delhi.

(G. V. Ramakrishna)
Ambassador of India

< Hail to Belgium >

HAIL TO BELGIUM

This poem was written in Tamil by Subramania Bharati (1882-1921) during the German invasion of Belgium in 1914. (English Translation by Lalita Ramakrishna)

You fell in the cause of the righteous;
When the enemy attacked with evil force
You would not suffer it;
Like the young girl who fended a tiger
With a kitchen sieve, like her
You defied the offending intruders;
You succumbed because of your principles
Thus you stood tall through your deeds. ...

... That which enters the sacrificial fire
Rises resplendent with fame and courage
And returns to vivify the world of men
This have the Holy Vedas decreed.
When men stoop low to evil deeds
There are those who perish upholding the right
And hearing of their glorious sacrifice
New hope in life and goodness prevails.

HOMMAGE A LA BELGIQUE

Ce poème, écrit en langue tamoule par Subramania Bharati (1882-1921). fût rédigé an cours de l'occupation allemande de la Belgique, en 1914.

C'est en défendant la cause des justes que vous êtes tombés;
Lorsque l'ennemi, armé de toute la puissance du mal, a passé à l'attaque,
Vous ne l'avez pas toléré.
Comme une enfant, essayant de détourner un tigre avec une petite passoire,
C'est comme cette enfant que vous avez défié l'occupant malfaiteur;
C'est à cause de vos principes que vous êtes tombés;
Voilà pourquoi vos actes vous rendent grands! ...

... Tout ce qui entre le bûcher ardent du sacrifice,
En sort transformé, resplendissant d'honneur et de courage,
Et retourne vers la terre des hommes, pour la vivifier de sa grâce :
Les Védas sácrés ont décrété cela.
Lorsque les hommes s'abaissent à faire le mal,
Certains meurent en défendant la cause du bien.
Et c'est leur glorieux sacrifice
Qui engendre à nouveau l'espoir et la bonté.

< Economic Times "Indo EC Ties" >

ECONOMIC TIMES *June 1990*

Indo-EC ties: diplomacy at its best

From Malcolm Subhan

Brussels: Businessmen, visiting foreign parts tend to keep well away from their own embassies as a general rule. And not without good reasons in many cases: diplomats usually look down their noses at "boxwallahs."

Indian businessmen, industrialists and bankers would do well, however, to start their European trip with a visit to the country's diplomatic mission to the European Community in Brussels. Here they will be able to talk to experts on virtually every aspect of the single European market of concern to them, including such highly technical, if basic, issues as industrial standards.

A five minute taxi ride will bring them to the India Trade Centre (ITC), a mine of commercial information for the exporter, much of it now contained on an expanding database, on the European market for agricultural products; textiles and clothing; engineering goods; electronic products and software.

This transformation is largely the work of the out-going Ambassador, Shri G.V. Ramakrishna, who took a number of initiatives on arriving here a year ago. He required each diplomat to become an expert on one or two aspects of the single European market.

To this end they not only had to keep up with all the relevant EC documents on the subject but also keep in touch with EC officials dealing with it. And having mastered their subject, they were expected to lecture on it to their colleagues, thus ensuring that everyone had a basic knowledge of the single market.

At the same time Ambassador Ramakrishna undertook to revitalize the India Trade Centre, which has been run as the commercial wing of the diplomatic mission since it was established here under the Indo-EC trade promotion programme just over 10 years ago. He told the half dozen advisors their role was that of international marketing managers of India Inc.

The fact is that each advisor has a wealth of commercial information on the sector he is responsible for; he also has contacts with both trade bodies and individual companies, often established at European trade fairs. But this information is relayed to Indian companies through cumbersome official channels, probably reaching its ultimate beneficiaries in diluted form.

Ambassador Ramakrishna decided to short-circuit the process. He told each advisor at the ITC to become operational. This involved establishing direct contacts with anywhere up to 20 Indian companies in each sector, and inaugurating a two-way flow of information.

Contd. ...

...Contd. ...

The Ambassador also speeded up the implementation of the plan to install a database at the ITC, to be linked electronically to the major Indian embassies in Europe. The database, which is regularly updated, contains information on both Indian and European companies.

One of Ambassador Ramakrishna's last tasks was to updated the report on Indian exports, his predecessor had drawn up just over a year ago with the cooperation of his colleagues in four other EC capitals. The result is a text of some 200 pages containing hard commercial information on the European market for 25 to 30 products, together with information on the relevant EC policies (on technical standards, for example).

The report also contains recommendations for up-dating India's export promotion arrangements in both Eastern and Western Europe. The fact is that with barriers between the two halves of Europe crumbling, Ambassador Ramakrishna recommended last September that trade promotion offices be opened in Prague and Budapest.

He wants to see the trade promotion programme in Western Europe rationalized and given a strongly commercial bias. To this end he favours strong links with Indian exporters, who would be expected also to contribute to the programme. In order to secure the best marketing talent, the Ambassador would not limit recruitment to government officials.

As Ambassdor to Belgium also, Mr. Ramakrishna established good relations with not only with the country's foreign trade officials, but also its leading industrialists and bankers. This has enabled him to secure high level meetings for commercial and industrial delegations visiting Belgium, such as the recent Assocham Delegation, led by TIL Chairman, Mr Avijit Mazumadar.

Such visits obviously mobilize the full resources of the Indian institution here. But they also make heavy demands on the top management of Belgian companies. Surprising as it may seem to Indian businessmen, who tend to write off the Belgian market and industry as too small to merit attention, their Belgian counterparts must play host each week to delegations from the world over.

If visits from Indian industrialists and businessmen are to be successful, Ambassador Ramakrishna has maintained, they must be carefully planned and spaced out. To this end he has insisted that his embassy be provided detailed information on both the company and its objectives in joining the delegation.

The ground rules for trade with Belgium, and other EC countries, are set by the European Community, acting through the Brussels-based European Commission, Ambassador Ramakrishna quickly established a close relationship with the EC Commissioner for external trade, Frans Andriessen.

The relationship proved especially helpful when the Indian Ambassador undertook the unprecedented task of persuading some 30 of his colleagues from Asia, Africa and Latin America to organise a joint representation to Mr Andriessen on the Uruguay Round of GATT-sponsored trade negotiations. The success of Ambassador Ramakrishna's venture, the first of its kind, prompted both his colleagues in Geneva and the commerce ministry in New Delhi to launch similar undertakings.

The EC's relations with India itself are handled by one of Mr. Andriessen's colleagues, Commissioner Abel Matutes, who is responsible for relations

Contd. ...

...Contd. ...

with all Latin America and South and South-East Asia. A Spanish business-men and banker, Mr Matures has given priority to Central America, his only visits to Asia being in connection with ASEAN.

Among Ambassador Ramakrishna's initiatives in the cultural field the most unexpected had to do with the children of Indian origin who have been adopted by some 450 Belgian families over the years. Although this is a community that can be expected to be friendlly to India, it has been ignored by the country's diplomatic representatives.

This unexpected recognition of their existence by the embassy bas released a fund of goodwill towards India. Many of the parents who attended are now planning to visit India, in many cases for the first time. By maintaining the links he has established, Ambassador Ramakrishna hopes it will be able to build up a pro-India constituency in the long run.

Presentation of Credentials to Crown Prince of Luxembourg, 1989

With King and Queen of the Belgians, Brussels, 1989

128b

With Shri I.K. Gujral and Mr. Andreissen, Brussels, 1989

With Dalai Lama, Brussels, 1990

Alpana exhibit by the Embassy ladies at Brussels, 1990

Rangoli demonstration by the Embassy ladies, Asia Pacific Ladies Group, Brussels, 1989

Odissi dance at Brussels, 1990

The lighted map of India, New Year's Eve, Brussels, 1989

Adopted Indian children get together at Indian Embassy, Brussels, 1989

The grain map of India, Brussels, 1990

With the Leader of the Parliamentary Delegation, Shri A.B. Vajpayee, Brussels, 1990

18 Ambassadors discuss WTO at the Indian Chancery, Brussels, 1990

■ Two-and-a-half years after inception, we are still without powers. Some call us a toothless tiger, but we keep smiling.

Securities & Exchange Board of India chief G.V. Ramakrishna, quoted in *Business Standard*.

Cartoon : *Business World,* Volume 10, Issue 21, 30 January - 12 February, 1991

Business Standard

CALCUTTA MONDAY 14 JANUARY 1991

Sebi burning bright

There is a tiger roaring in Bombay, and we are not talking here of the Shiv Sena's fierce election symbol. The Securities and Exchange Board of India (Sebi) is yet to acquire powers, but it is making enough noise to warn the *dalals* of Dalal Street of the shape of things to come. However, even grounds are not enough for the Sebi chief, who can't wait to get his hands on the real powerstrings.

Two and a half years after inception, we are still without powers. Some call us a toothless tiger, but we keep smiling," Mr. G. V. Ramakrishna said the other day. Asked how Sebi would function after getting the much-awaited powers, he says, Wait and see with a clever, smile on his face. Which makes us paraphrase an old limerick:

A wily old broker from Raigarh
went to ride on this tiger
They came back from the ride
With the broker inside
and a smile on the face of the tiger

11

SEBI

THE Indian capital market and the Bombay Stock Exchange are among the oldest in the world. Over the years a number of old habits and malpractices became ingrained in the system. While from the eighties, markets in the developed world grew at a rapid pace and regulatory bodies were established, in India the only statutory regulation came during the Second World War in the form of the Capital Issues (Control) Act 1948 (CCI Act). This was brought into being mainly to control the new issues by companies so as to release savings for the war effort. The regulation of the secondary market was left largely to the Stock Exchanges. These exchanges were run by boards, which consisted of influential brokers. The exchanges were run like private clubs. Several types of malpractices crept in, with members of the boards themselves becoming the main breakers of the rules.

Both in the CCI Act and the SCR Act, (Securities Contracts Regulation Act) investor protection had no place

A Glossary of Stock Market Terms is appended at the end of this chapter, page 217.

at all. In the early years after the war, public issues were small and also few and far between. After the liberalization process began in the early nineties, public issues got a new impetus. As new companies came into existence, and more of them got listed with the Exchanges, both the primary and the secondary markets grew. Yet there was no effort at protecting the small investor.

My post retirement appointment to SEBI by V.P. Singh was the second, the first being the posting in Brussels made by Rajiv Gandhi. My friends wondered how I was selected for this job. I said it was sheer destiny.

Earlier my only acquaintance with the capital market was when I had heard P.D. Kasbekar, the Controller of capital issues, discuss with I.G. Patel the new capital issues in our weekly meetings in the Department of Economic Affairs. An issue of Rs. 2 crores was considered very large and there were extended discussions on allowing it or not.

Before I joined in Bombay, SEBI had been formed by an administrative order in April 1988, and S.A. Dave from Industrial Development Bank of India (IDBI) was appointed Chairman. There were a few officials taken on deputation from the banks and financial institutions. Dave was later appointed Chairman of Unit Trust of India (UTI) and he continued to hold additional charge of SEBI.

When I reached Bombay (Mumbai now), no one in the capital markets had heard about me. The financial circles showed an amused curiosity. So I was accepted on probation. At one of the early meetings with the Press I was asked whether I had dealt in shares. When I replied in the negative I was asked how I was qualified to handle SEBI. I asked in return, whether, when they went to a cardiologist would they ask if he had undergone a bypass operation! The Press gradually began to warm up to me thereafter. I made it a point to meet the Press at frequent intervals.

I tried hard to understand the complexities of the capital market. I knew that this could not be got only from books but also by talking and listening to people with experience. So my doors were kept open although some measure of discipline was brought by Ragini, who proved to be an excellent secretary, in organizing papers, keeping appointments and in handling visitors with tact and firmness.

In the early days, I devoted my time to studying books and journals and meeting visitors to understand the theory and practice in the capital market.

I was assisted by a band of able and dedicated officers, particularly, C.B. Bhave, Vijay Ranjan, Pratip Kar, Pandya and Patel, the executive directors, and Dharmishta Raval and Murthy, the legal advisers.

The Capital Markets

The decade of the eighties was a period of extraordinary growth for the capital market in our country. For the first time, the capital market had come to be integrated with the financial system of the country and had demonstrated its potential to mobilize substantial resources. By the end of the decade, it was vying with intermediation by the traditional purveyors of long-term finance, (the financial institutions), in catalyzing industrial development through a process of disintermediation. This term was used to denote that savings were channeled directly to companies without the institutions raising the money first and then lending or investing in companies.

There were also structural and institutional changes in the financial services sector with the emergence of merchant bankers, mutual funds and venture capital funds, which, provided services in the areas of issue management, corporate counselling, capital restructuring, venture capital, loan syndications etc. The mutual funds, who were recent entrants, increased in number and began to assume an important role in extending the benefits of the capital market to small and medium investors, through expert advice, and risk-sharing in collective schemes. The evolution of these new institutions emphasized the need to reduce the scope for malpractices and for strong regulation to offer adequate protection to the investors.

Towards the end of the eighties, there was an increase in the number of takeovers and the Government had to revise the guidelines for takeovers. We have yet to evolve a satisfactory Takeover Code, which harmonises corporate democracy with equity and stability.

An efficient capital market must be efficient both in mobilizing resources and also in allocating it. The first efficiency is tested through the primary market, and the second, through the secondary market though both are interrelated. However, on account of market imperfections, which still prevail in the secondary markets, its allocative efficiency is yet to be tested. Secondary markets have not become efficient monitors of corporate performance, as the prices of scrips do not, often, bear a relationship with the fundamentals, indicating that the speculative element is dominant in the secondary market and there are ample opportunities for price manipulation. A small number of market participants can still influence the market substantially. Besides, the disclosure requirements are often not adequate and dissemination of market related information is still poor. Our markets are thinly traded despite substantial increase in the turnover. According to the data available on reported transactions on the Bombay Stock Exchange for 1989-90, not more than five per cent to six per cent of the turnover in specified shares had resulted in deliveries. In a thinly traded market like ours, even a limited amount of speculative trading can exert an upward or downward pressure of prices.

We stepped into the 1990s in a dichotomous situation. On the one hand, we had a potent capital market, waiting to grow while on the other hand, was a market full of fundamental deficiencies. An expanding market, with imperfections growing at an equal speed, spells danger for the investor. The investor, caught in this conflicting situation, is always likely to be at the losing end, and once investor confidence in the market is impaired, the capital market may not grow to levels desirable for the economy. Unless all these basic conflicts are resolved, the market will be prone to frequent cyclical movements, bringing about payment crises, as was witnessed in our stock markets in recent times.

The stock exchanges must provide facilities and services through which investors can efficiently accumulate, liquidate, reallocate and value their holdings at competitively determined prices. Issuers can then raise additional capital at the lowest practical cost. This process must be fair and equitable with market facilities, trading procedures, disclosures (that assure maintenance of investor confidence) and maximization of market liquidity.

Experience from the industrial and developing world suggests that capital markets develop in a healthy manner only with effective market regulation in terms of listing, disclosure and transparency, trading rules, liquidity and margin requirements, timely settlements, frequent auditing and accounting of brokerage operations in listed securities. Effective regulation encourages and supports the market's own needs for better information on macroeconomic conditions. It also provides microeconomic signals on corporate health, performance and management, through improved research and reporting ability.

Protecting the integrity of the market is a way of promoting another objective of regulation particularly relevant to a growing market like ours, namely the development and growth of the securities market.

The investor has to face two kinds of risks. One, relating to the market, the economy, and the individual company's performance, which are all collectively called commercial and market risk. The other risk relates to the integrity and efficiency of the market, called systemic risk. The investor takes the commercial and market risk. It should be the duty of the regulatory and self-regulatory bodies to minimize the systemic risk. The Indian capital market was beset with a number of problems mostly affecting investor interests and the integrity of the market.

The market is broadly divided into primary and secondary segments. The primary market means the direct sale of shares by the issuing company to the investor. The secondary market provides for the resale of those shares to other buyers in the stock exchanges through stockbrokers.

The Primary Market

In the primary market a number of problems were encountered by the investors. When a company wants to raise capital, it issues a prospectus which is supposed to inform the investor about all the relevant details of the company, the industry, the risks – economic, technical and commercial, that are likely to be encountered in its business. The investor is then expected to use his judgment whether to buy the shares or not, keeping in view the price at which the shares are being offered. The companies use the services of merchant bankers to prepare the prospectuses and to bring out all the relevant facts and risk factors. Then, there are the underwriters who agree to take up the shares that are not sold directly by the issuer to the investors. These are the intermediaries between the issuer and the investors. There are other agencies such as registrars and share transfer agents which will be referred to later.

After the issue opens and all the investors apply for shares, a situation may arise where more people apply for shares than are available, and the allotment of shares is made according to rules of the stock exchange. The successful applicants will then be sent letters of allotment, while the unsuccessful or partially successful ones will get their money back. In this arrangement a number of problems arose.

One of the interesting features of allotment was the way in which the so-called promoter's quota was being used to favour friends and government officials. When we investigated the allotment of promoters' quota by a few companies we found that in the list a number of VIPs' names figured. I took this list and showed it to the F.M. in Delhi. He had one glance at the list and threw it back at me, like a hot potato, and said that I could do whatever I liked.

The prospectuses gave very little information and the merchant bankers did not do their job with due diligence. Companies took a lot of time to make allotments and to issue letters which are marketable in the hands of the holders. The unsuccessful applicants did not get their money back for a long time. The companies used this float money for their own purposes for as long as six months to one year as interest free money. In 1992 this amounted to Rs. 1600 cores. The Companies Act provides for time limits for these steps but there was no enforcement.

Stock Invest

SEBI took the initiative to devise a new financial instrument to avoid the problem of refunds. The Stock Invest scheme was introduced after a great deal of effort, by SEBI officials, to persuade banks and the RBI to support it. Under the scheme, the investor will have a bank account in which his money will gather interest. The bank, on application by the account holder, issues a Stock Invest certificate for the amount specified and 'escrows' the amount in his account. The certificate can then be used to apply for shares in a company. If the applicant is successful in getting the full allotment, the bank will encash the certificate. If he is partially successful the Stock Invest can be encashed partially. If the applicant does not get any allotment, the Stock Invest will be returned for cancellation, and meanwhile, the amount will remain in the bank account, earning interest.

There were several complaints of delays in issuing shares certificates and in refund of money to unsuccessful applicants, and in share transfers in the name of the purchasers. The Companies Act had provisions for these also, but there was no enforcement. SEBI took up these matters also with the companies. The intermediaries in the secondary market were the brokers and the share transfer agents. Regulations were framed for them. Companies were asked to pay interest on delayed transfers.

We set up a procedure to receive investor complaints against companies and to classify and publicise them regularly in the Press. After sometime, this began to bite and companies would come to SEBI to explain how they had redressed the grievances. Things improved somewhat, but not enough, as SEBI still did not have any statutory powers.

Investor Grievances

In 1990, only a small number of investor complaints were being received, as people did not expect SEBI to do any thing. These complaints related both to the primary market and the secondary market. Since SEBI did not have any powers, I thought one way of dealing with the errant companies would be to publicise the complaints about them as this would adversely impact their capacity to raise funds. So we started issuing press releases giving the names of the companies and the number of complaints of different kinds received against them. We also wrote to the companies asking them to redress these grievances. All this encouraged more investors to bring to SEBI's attention all their complaints. As the flood of complaints increased we had to appoint special agents to process them, acknowledge them and thereafter SEBI would write to the companies. The compliance by the companies went up after we got statutory powers. In 1992 the redressal of complaints was 27,000 out of 1,29,111 complaints (21 per cent), and in 1993, 366,000 grievances were redressed out of 713,000 complaints (51 per cent).[1]

SEBI next took up the task of providing better information in the prospectuses. The companies raised various objections including cost of bigger size paper. According to the Companies Act the prospectus has to accompany the application form as a perforated attachment. In order to comply with SEBI's requirement they would print a few applications with the prospectus and the remaining application forms would have only perforations intended to show that the applicant had torn off the prospectus. This loophole was plugged by asking the prospectus to be printed on the reverse of the application form itself. The issuers retaliated by printing in miniscule letters and this had to be dealt with.

From the beginning of my tenure, till May 1992, I had no statutory powers. I had to improvise and make do with what I had. There was a circular of the Department of Economic Affairs that merchant bankers, who were involved in public issues, had to be cleared by the Government. I got this power transferred to SEBI. With this SEBI could ask

1. JPC Report on Capital Market, p 333 para 14.45.

The cover page of the magazine *Capital Market,* issue dated December 19, 1993

The cover page of the magazine *Capital Market* (Hindi edition), issue dated December 19, 1993

them to get the prospectuses vetted by it. This gave some sort of handle, though tenuous, to enforce better disclosures to the public.

The merchant bankers were also brought in line by registering them in three categories. By the end of 1993, there were 350 registered merchant bankers. SEBI began by telling them where their due diligence was lacking and if there was no improvement, gave them penalty points for each transgression. After eight penalty points the merchant banker was liable to have his registration suspended or cancelled. The merchant bankers were asked to have an MoU with the promoters of companies so that the merchant bankers would have a say in the selection of the registrars and underwriters. The merchant bankers resented this arrangement.[2] In order to encourage them to improve their services SEBI suggested that they could have their own body to lay down norms and follow uniform practices. This was formed as The Association of Merchant Bankers of India (AMBI).

Pricing of the Issues

A major issue in the primary market was about pricing of the issues. When the Controller of Capital Issues was in place (1946-1992) the issue price was determined by him. After liberalization the companies were given the freedom to price the issues. Their point was that underpricing led to a large number of applications and clogged up the system.

At SEBI we recommended to the Government that there should be a cap on the premium to be charged and such issues should be underwritten so that the investor would be

---

2. Merchant Bankers, Business Times, 6.6.1991 < Appended on page 176 >.

"Bankers find SEBI means business"

Faced with a no-win situation, merchant bankers are falling in step with SEBI guidelines and coming together to form a self-regulatory organisation,

reports Sucheta Dalal

Ramakrishna made it clear that SEBI doesn't want to watch over every bank, that it wants to regulate but not control

Money World, THE ECONOMIC TIMES, Sunday 30 June, 1991

assured that the risk of under subscription is shared by the issuer and the investor. However, underwriting itself was beset with a number of problems of collusive action between the underwriter and the issuer.

At that time there was great enthusiasm for liberalization in all fields. This was led by Montek Ahluwalia, the finance secretary and Ashok Desai, the chief economic adviser. The latter saw me as a bureaucratic hindrance in the mission to liberalise the capital markets. This feeling manifested in several matters and persisted even after he left the ministry due to differences with Ahluwalia. He wrote articles in which he was critical of SEBI, and me in particular. I did not reply to any of them, as his diatribe against me was well understood and derated by many readers of his articles. We however continued to be overtly polite to each other.

In the new found enthusiasm for deregulation, Government thought it best to leave it to market forces. Eventually it was left to the investor to judge whether the premium was reasonable. In my speeches, I had warned the investors that going into a free pricing regime was like jumping into a sea infested with sharks. Several promoters took advantage of free pricing and sold their shares at unjustified premia, and many of them just vanished after collecting the money. Later in 1994 and 1995, free pricing and misuse of funds had an adverse impact on investor confidence and the market as a whole, but few people knew that SEBI had tried to minimize the damage.

Investors lost their money in the primary market, and their faith in the free pricing system. The JPC (Joint Parliamentary Committee) report of 2002 on stock market scams, (in para 11.28 on p 259) dealing with vanishing companies, points out that SEBI had identified 229 listed companies which collected funds through public issue and are not available now at their registered offices. Subsequently, SEBI and the Department of Company Affairs (DCA) were able to trace 160 out of 229 companies and the balance of 69 companies still remain to be traced.

Another issue related to the use of the money raised by issue of shares. In the case of loans there is an arrangement of the lending institutions to monitor use of funds, but there is no such arrangement for the use of capital raised by the companies. Companies found it convenient to raise large sums as capital and use the money for speculation of various kinds and for rigging up the share prices of their companies. Several big companies would show 'other income' as a significant item in the profit and loss account. The practice of having investment in 'off balance sheet items' was also gaining ground. (This reached its limits in the US recently when Enron made it a fine art of deception). SEBI had suggested that, at least, for capital raised above certain limits, say Rs. 200 crores, the use of funds should be periodically verified. Ashok Desai, who saw this as one more manifestation of my pro control mindset, recommended that my proposal should be turned down. It was accordingly turned down.

Other intermediaries in the primary market were registrars who made the allotments and the underwriters. Regulations were framed for them also with minimum net worth fixed for underwriters at Rs. 20 lakhs.

Under the liberalized conditions, over 900 companies entered the market to raise Rs. 18,000 cores in 1992-93.

Postal Ballot

One of the important grievances of the small investors was the lack of corporate democracy, particularly in large companies. Major decisions like mergers and demergers, fresh issue of capital, pricing of rights issues, inter corporate lending etc, were all taken without considering the views of the small shareholder. SEBI went into the matter to ascertain the correct legal position.

The small shareholders were affected when FERA companies sold equity at low prices to the parent companies. I therefore, suggested that public financial institutions should voluntarily abstain from voting their large shareholding so that small shareholders could have a say in the matter. I did not suggest differential voting rights. Some news reports misunderstood my suggestion.

According to the Companies Act, there are about thirty sections under which Special Resolutions are required for approving certain decisions. Apart from this the Articles of Association of the company can stipulate additional items that would require a Special Resolution.

A Special Resolution requires a 75 per cent majority of those present (in terms of voting rights) for approval. While new shares were required to be sold all over India in order to enable the small investor to acquire shares, the meetings of the company can be held in only one place; sometimes this is fixed in a remote place. The small shareholder could not spend the money to travel for the AGM (Annual General Meeting) and vote in person. Therefore, the General Body meetings were attended only by a small number of investors. The SEBI study showed that in many cases the meetings were attended only by the promoters and the employees with a total voting power of about 10 per cent. A Special Resolution was carried with 75 per cent of those present and voting. Small shareholders had very little say in important decisions affecting their interests.

In order to rectify this situation, I had proposed in 1993 that there should be a system of ascertaining the wishes of the small shareholder through a postal ballot on special resolutions dealing with important matters.[3] Since notice of a meeting had to be sent to all the share holders, the company should, along with the notice, send a ballot paper stating the Resolution and providing space for the indication of approval or disapproval by the share holder. Interested shareholders can then return the ballot paper to an independent SEBI appointed auditor to classify the votes and report the results to the annual general meeting. This was received with dismay by the company managements. In any case an amendment of the Companies Act was required to make this compulsory.

Later, in 1996, when the Companies Act review committee was formed, I was in the Disinvestment Commission. I wrote to the chairman of the committee, T.S. Krishna Murthy and requested that my earlier proposal be taken into account. At first there was reluctance, and the pro corporate elements in the committee almost rejected the proposal. I pressed for fresh consideration. As a concession

3a. Postal vote... Financial Express, 27.9.1993 < Appended on page 177 >.

3b. Postal vote... Financial Express, 16.9.1993 < Appended on page 178 >.

3c. Postal vote... The Economic Times 19.9.1993 < Appended on page 179 >.

to me, they agreed to recommend an enabling provision in the Companies Act leaving it to the companies to have a postal ballot if they so chose. Naturally no company will take advantage, rather the disadvantage, of this provision. The Parliamentary Committee also did not look into this aspect. Perhaps, some one will take up this matter once again.

Several issues hinge on this provision even today. When companies are merged or demerged, it is important to protect the share value of the small investor in these companies. However the small shareholder has no say in this. With regard to delisting of companies by foreign and Indian managements, the interests of small shareholders are vitally involved. If the law and the authorities are indifferent to their interests they have no other recourse.

With regard to take over of companies also, the interests of the small shareholder would be better protected if they had a postal ballot. I requested my friend Rajendra Chitale[3d] of the well known auditor firm of M.P. Chitale & Co. to give me a note on the subject. This note is appended.

In order to protect the Government and in public interest, I had proposed that apart from keeping 26 per cent shares, as a veto against special resolutions, (as required under the law), the articles of association be amended to provide for a few more decisions requiring a special resolution and this may be made before a strategic sale. If this had been accepted, the VSNL situation could have been avoided even if the shareholders agreement was lax on this aspect.

3d. Postal Ballot as Takeover Defence < Appended on page 180 >.

In March 1993 there was the bomb blast in the stock exchange. I visited the exchange and found that extensive damage had been caused to the basement garage and a number of cars were damaged and a number of people were killed. The Maharashtra Government was fully supportive, and in agreement with SEBI, wanted trading to continue. The brokers cooperated and business did not stop.

The International Organisation of Securities Commissions (IOSCO) was formed in 1990. In 1991, SEBI was admitted as a member. Although it had no statutory status we took active interest in IOSCO. Pratip Kar was a popular representative from SEBI who accompanied me to the meetings. In 1992, SEBI was voted as chairman of the Asia Pacific group for two years. In IOSCO several issues of regulation of the capital markets were discussed. We found that many other countries had progressed more than India. The concept of the National Depository was discussed at the Taipeh meeting in 1993. They had a limited facility for demat shareholding. In India, under the able leadership of C.B. Bhave, the NSDL (National Securities Depository Limited) has come to acquire a central place as a national data depository.

Secondary Markets

The Stock Exchanges

Indian stock exchanges grew fast in 1990 and 1991. There were 23 exchanges, 5500 stockbrokers and lakhs of subbrokers.

Our stock exchanges were not functioning in a very efficient manner. Their systems, procedures and infrastructure were outmoded. Brokers were partnerships or proprietary concerns. There was practically no corporatisation among Indian brokers. The governing boards consisted wholly of brokers. Some of the office bearers were themselves violating the rules of the exchanges. They act as closed clubs, restricting the membership to a limited few. Arbitration proceedings were not implemented in many of the stock exchanges and many of rules and regulations were not enforced for the protection of investor interests. I had to remark in my speeches that the exchanges were of brokers, for brokers and by brokers. This was resented by the broker community, just as they resented a number of things that I did later.

It is not only fraud and dishonesty that can distort the proper functioning of the market. Differential access to information also can have the same effect. Rules regulating the availability of, and access to, information relevant to the exercise of sound commercial judgment on securities play an important role in the operation of orderly and efficient markets. The stock exchanges had a role to play in ensuring that there was adequate and timely disclosure by companies of the information needed to enable investment decisions to be made. They were lax in this respect also.

In the investor grievance cell of SEBI there were several complaints of delays in share transfers in the name of the purchasers. The Companies Act had provisions for these but there was no enforcement. SEBI took up these matters with the companies.

The secondary markets attracted my attention, as there were a number of complaints about the way in which brokers transacted their business against the interests of the investors particularly the small investor. After an inspection of the Bombay Stock Exchange, which typified other exchanges, I said, once again, that the stock exchanges were not run as institutions serving the market or the public interest but were run by the brokers, as private clubs of the brokers, for the benefit of brokers. I also said that self-regulation had not worked anywhere in the world and most of the market oriented countries had strong regulatory bodies for the capital market. This raised the hackles of the brokers, particularly of the Bombay Stock Exchange, which was the largest and oldest stock exchange in India. Even when I pointed out that they were not following their own Byelaws and regulations of the exchange prepared by Jeejeebhoy, a pioneer who built the exchange and office towers on Dalal Street, they were not impressed.

The Press was supportive and even pointed out the untenable position in which SEBI had been placed, without powers for regulating the capital market. Industry leaders also saw the point. SEBI was called the 'toothless tiger' in the media. We said that we had strong jaws from which teeth will soon grow!

In the meanwhile I worked on a simple way of getting statutory powers. Earlier when I joined SEBI, I found that a comprehensive new legislation was being prepared running into hundreds of pages. I knew that this would not be passed for several years by Parliament because of the complexities of legislative procedures.

I started on a short SEBI Bill which had the essentials and which gave the Government the right to frame regulations in a number of areas covering brokers, merchant bankers, mutual funds, registrars, underwriters and others engaged in the capital market. This was sent to the Government and followed up by regular visits to Delhi to explain the whole set up to the ministry of finance and also the law ministry. After several visits an Ordinance was passed in January 1992. Later, a SEBI Act was passed in April 1992, nearly two years after I joined SEBI. Section 11 of the Act gave wide-ranging powers to SEBI to regulate all the players in the capital market.

Mutual Funds

The mutual funds were major players in the secondary market. Starting with the oldest and the largest, UTI, there were the funds started by public sector institutions like the banks and the insurance companies and later by private parties, both Indian and foreign. By the end of 1993 there were 25 mutual funds of all categories.

My first public engagement came in October 1990 when I was invited to speak at a function organized by Assocham at the Oberoi Hotel in Bombay. The subject was Mutual Funds. It was well attended with several persons from the capital markets. The Chairman was Nimesh Kampani, the influential Chairman of J.M. Financial, one of the leading market intermediaries. S.A. Dave, Chairman of UTI was one of the main speakers. I had known Dave from my days in the Industry ministry when he was an executive director of IDBI. He was a soft-spoken professional who was also a good friend of mine. When SEBI was formed by an executive order in 1988, Dave was appointed Chairman. Later in 1990 he was appointed Chairman of UTI, and was placed in additional charge of SEBI. At that time Dave as chairman of SEBI was asking for UTI to be regulated by SEBI. He later changed his view when I began to plead for the same after SEBI came into existence as a statutory body![4a]

At the Assocham meeting Dave spoke of the need for change. He said that a 'surgical' change was necessary in the capital markets. I made the following points. Indian mutual funds were violating every norm that was followed internationally, They offered assured returns but did not inform the investors of the risks, they did not publish scheme-wise details of investment, NAV (Net Asset Value) etc. The mutual funds floated by public sector banks gave the impression to the public that they were in fact public sector and had the backing of the Government, when this was not the case. The audience was somewhat taken aback at what I said especially when I was so new to the job. Later events proved that assured returns promised by the mutual funds cost the government thousands of cores of rupees, as in the case of Canara Bank and UTI.[4b]

From the early days I was asking the Government to direct UTI to submit to SEBI inspection under the regulations, which applied to all the mutual funds. A number of meetings were held in the finance ministry and letters were exchanged. We pointed that SEBI had notified the Mutual Fund Regulations under which it had to inspect all mutual funds, and also that UTI was in violation of these rules. Dave himself, in his address to the unit holders of UTI, had referred to UTI as the 'largest mutual fund in the country'.

4a. Mutual Funds, Midday, 5.8.1991 < Appended on page 183 >.

4b. Assocham Information Post, 15.10.1990 < Appended on page 184 >.

And yet the specious argument was put forth that it was a statutory body and hence should not be brought under SEBI regulation. I pointed out that the manner of constitution should not alter its obligation to come under SEBI regulation, which was also statutory. I asked them whether UTI did not conform to the municipal laws when they made alterations in their building. I also pointed out, in one more letter to the Finance Secretary, that there were a number of transgressions that were happening in US-64 and other schemes.[5] SEBI was merely asked to discuss the matter once more with UTI. The Finance Ministry continued to support UTI and would not allow inspection by SEBI. In his latest book *Face Value* Debashish Basu has commented on this attitude of UTI and the finance ministry.[6] He has put it bluntly as follows:

> Until 1992, UTI was being used as an arm of the ministry of finance. If the market needed to be supported, the ministry would call UTI's boss. In 1992, this could have changed. SEBI, set up to regulate the market, got G.V. Ramakrishna as the chairman while the new team in the ministry of finance functioned in a less feudal manner. Ramakrishna framed guidelines for all the funds to follow.
>
> However UTI was a law unto itself. It fought to protect its bogus sense of autonomy (now we know what it was trying to hide) and so, under the affable chairman S.A. Dave, UTI mulishly refused to be regulated by SEBI, citing arcane laws and structures. It was a notorious campaign to dodge public accountability. Dr. Dave's argument to escape SEBI's supervision were that UTI is a homegrown institution that has stood the test of time, nobody should tamper with its unique structure of lending, underwriting and equity investment rolled into one. UTI claimed that it had a mixed portfolio of assets such as real estate, unlisted debt etc., which could not be valued on an ongoing basis. In fact Dr. Dave went on to

---

5. Letter to Montek and reply < Appended on page 185 >.
6. 'Face Value', D. Basu, p 42, 43, 45.

> claim that UTI disclosed much more than other funds and there was strong internal accountability.
>
> These preposterous arguments went virtually unchallenged in public. As has been proven time and again, arguments like 'don't touch, this is uniquely local' are just tricks to carry on with bad old ways and stay unaccountable. Unfortunately, the collective 'wisdom' of the then finance secretary (Montek Singh Ahluwalia), economic adviser (Ashok Desai) and the finance minister (Dr. Manmohan Singh) killed the first and last chance to get UTI to be transparent before it could inflict further damage. A victorious UTI bottled up the problem of poor returns and collected more money from the public – to lose more.
>
> The real issue was a corrupt nexus of politicians, brokers and UTI officials. No wonder, when the UTI was bailed out in 1998, it continued with its old tricks. Its equity portfolio became peppered with illiquid, unlisted, hollow and defaulting companies, while the debt portfolio worsened. This led to another crisis in July 2001, when it froze the sale and redemption of US-64 units forcing the government to sack and arrest UTI's chairman, P. S. Subramanyam.

At this stage it would be useful to refer to the Joint Parliamentary Committee (JPC) Report of 2002, which quotes, in para 13.47, from the earlier JPC report of 1992 as follows:

> The Committee recalls that the 1992 JPC had drawn attention to, in para 2.8 of its report on the 'very damaging approach (which) seems to pervade, that of transferring responsibility downwards. This distressing lack of fibre in the apparatus of governance can only debilitate the state.' Regrettably, notwithstanding the passage of nearly a decade since that Report, nothing seems to have changed.[7]

Because of my continued pressure, sometime in September 1993 they appointed the Vaghul Committee which went into the matter and essentially supported my

7. JPC Report, Dec. 2002, p 320 para 13.47.

THE ECONOMY

The Change of guard at SEBI

THE HINDU *Sunday, January 09, 1994*

More serious have been the obstacles placed before the SEBI while it attempted to fulfil its crucial task of regulation. These are too well known now and do not require repetition. After all, the broker's displeasure with the SEBI has been intermittent. What needs to be emphasised, however, is that none of the financial intermediaries, now being subject to the SEBI's control, has had to face even minimal regulation by an authority. Armed with considerable number of years these intermediaries have considered the role of the SEBI to be an intrusion and the regulatory body itself to be redundant.

Which is a pity because the cardinal principle behind any regulation is to bring about better market practices, which in turn would lead to an all-round development of the capital market. Fortunately for the SEBI its corporate message was to first convince the investor at large that it is so. Investor protection become the driving force behind the SEBI's functioning and it is here that most of its achievements lie.

C. R. L. Narasimhan
in Madras

views. I was soon out of SEBI in January 1994 and the matter was shelved. The JPC on the 1992 scam recommended that UTI should come under SEBI, but nothing was done. The scam of 1998 in UTI which cost the exchequer Rs. 3,300 crores proved my point, but at high cost to the exchequer, the small investor and illegitimate benefit to a number of individuals. The later, and bigger scam in 2001 cost the exchequer and the investors several times more. Above all, a large number of investors, who were led to believe that the UTI was like the *Titanic* and could not sink, saw their life savings vanish in the morass of corruption and mismanagement. It was only after the second scam that UTI 'voluntarily' agreed to submit to SEBI inspection all the schemes launched after July 1994 (which excluded the US-64 scheme which was launched earlier). If this is how the Government allows a market player to treat the regulator it does not augur well for regulation. UTI has since been split into two and is striving to get back on its feet. It is not clear how long this will take.

Under SEBI guidelines, based on international practice and regulation, inter scheme transfer is not generally allowed. In fact, each scheme should have a separate fund manager who would deal with other fund managers on an arms length basis. UTI had, in many cases indulged in inter scheme transfers because they were shielded from SEBI inspection. I had pointed out this violation, with facts and figures, in my letters to the Finance Secretary in July 1993.[8] The JPC drew attention to this in its report of December 2002 as follows:

---

8. *Ibid,* p 350 para 16.21.

> The Committee noted that the UTI management sanctioned inter scheme transfers to boost the income and liquidity of some schemes, that these decisions were not taken by individual fund managers, but by the Chairman and the Executive Directors, and that brokerage was paid on such transfers in violation of UTI's own guidelines.[9]

The Vaghul Committee report presented in September 1993, had recommended that:

> 'It would be in the interest of UTI and UTI's investors if the regulatory jurisdiction of SEBI was extended to UTI's mutual fund schemes.[10]

The Joint Parliamentary Committee in its report of December 2002 went on to point out the attitude of Government and UTI management as follows:

> The Committee concluded that between 1992 and 1996 the Ministry had identified the need to delink the UTI's mutual fund activities from its term lending activities, the need to bring UTI's mutual fund activities under SEBI regulations, the need to do away with IDBI's role in UTI, and the consequent need to amend the UTI Act. The Ministry's own view regarding the need to amend the UTI Act also had the mandate from Parliament as well as the backing of the Central Bank and the Capital Market Regulator. Only the top management of UTI was reluctant to amend the Act and restructure the institution, and the Ministry indirectly supported the status quo in UTI by implementing interim measures.

The interaction between the ministry of finance and UTI, and the statements of former finance ministers, Manmohan Singh, Chidambaram and Yashwant Sinha are given in detail from pages 418 to 426 of the report.

---

9. *Ibid,* p 412 para 20.3.
10. *Ibid,* p 418 para 20.5.

Though the government's responsibility for UTI was not written into the UTI Act, 1963, accountability for UTI's US-64 scheme to Parliament became obvious when the scheme was kept out of the purview of the market regulator. (Para 20.13)[11]

Regrettably, negligent management by UTI and inadequate monitoring on these fronts contributed in significant measure to the crisis in UTI generally and US-64 in particular. (p425 JPC).

UTI is a classic case of grave dereliction of duty, leading to thousands of crores of rupees loss to the investors and the taxpayers. No one has been held accountable under law so far. The earlier attitude of the finance ministry to keep UTI out of the purview of SEBI is difficult to pass off as the usual bureaucratic lethargy. Basu has brought it out well in his book *Face Value* quoted earlier.

The Scam

It is necessary at this stage of my story to deal with the infamous Scam of 1992. The best and most detailed account of the events leading to the Scam and the roles of the various parties has been presented in the excellent book by two of our outstanding economic investigators, Sucheta Dalal and Debashish Basu.

What came to light in April 1992 was not the beginning but the culmination of a series of actions and circumstances dating from 1986. It is not necessary, for the purpose of this book, to go into the arcane world of money markets, bond markets, ready forwards, bankers receipts and the like.

---

11. *Ibid* page 425 para 20.13.

The bond market is an esoteric and closed market in which only a few operate – out of the public view. This is because bonds are not publicly quoted, and the bond market is closed to the public; only the banks, insurance companies and certain other institutions buy and sell Government securities. There are a separate set of money market brokers who usually have links with stock brokers.

When banks buy and sell Government securities they rarely exchange paper. The selling bank issues the SGL notes to the buying bank which then deposits them in the Public Debt Office of the RBI which keeps the SGL account of the trading banks and institutions. If the selling bank does not have the bonds in its SGL account, the SGL bonuces. The RBI acts as the banker of the banks and the securities are like currency.

To simplify, and even oversimplify matters, the process started with the discovery that the money market involving Government loan securities, public sector bonds and short-term call money markets was several times bigger than the equity or stock markets.

The situation in 1992 was that bond trading was about Rs. 1,500 to 2,000 crores a day as compared to Rs. 100 to 200 crores of equity trading per day. The situation has changed now with equity trading around Rs. 8,000 to 10,000 crores a day and derivatives about Rs. 15,000 to Rs. 20,000 crores a day and bond trading about Rs. 3,000 to 4,000 crores a day.

It was, however, little known to our brokers and the public sector banks that while margins in bond trading were thin, the volumes were huge, and aggregate earnings could be rewarding. So it was necessary to use this source to generate money for multiplication by fair and foul means. The only people who were familiar with the rules and the tools of this game were the foreign banks. The calculation of how much a bond, carrying a coupon rate of interest, maturing some years later, would be worth today and how it would compare with the prevailing market rate of interest was important. It was complicated and little used in the Indian market, but well known in western markets and foreign banks in India who had ready-made tables to facilitate the calculations. The foreign banks outwitted the Indian banks in this matter in the early years from 1986 to 1988. They made huge profits at the expense of the Indian banks.

The second factor was the large Public Sector Undertakings (PSUs) raising money in the market through tax-exempt bonds and other bonds at high rates of interest. This was partly because they wanted to raise money to meet future needs for their projects and partly because of the encouragement given to them by the Government of tax benefits. They had huge surpluses, far in excess of their needs, and had to find a way of getting some interest on it. The banks entered the picture as they were also keen to show high deposits. Brokers offered to get the banks handsome returns provided the profits were shared with them. The brokers used this money to rig up prices of shares of all kinds of companies.

The third strand was the clutch of mutual funds of the public sector banks and insurance companies. They had collected a lot of money from the public and from large companies. They also had to earn a return.

With so many sources of money, a clever and unscrupulous man like Harshad Mehta found a number of accomplices in various places, to put the money to use in areas where it could be multiplied. Apart from the money markets the obvious place was the stock exchange. He set up a number of new companies, named after flowers, like Lotus, Jasmine etc., hence called 'flower companies' in current jargon. With so much money it was not difficult to rig up prices of particular shares by buying heavily. The usual tussle between the bulls and bears continued. The bulls bought long (without money in hand) in the hope of future price increases and the bears sold short (without having the shares in hand) in the hope of a price fall. Both groups operated without putting out the money or the shares in the first instance. Margin requirements were unequal between the bulls and the bears and were administered by the Stock exchange in a biased, self-serving manner.

The fourth contributory factor in raising money in an irregular manner was the archaic system of keeping the securities accounts of the banks with the Subsidiary General Ledger (SGL) of the RBI. Each bank had an account in the SGL in which its government securities were held. When they sold the security in the market their account was debited and the buyer's account was credited through SGL notes. Brokers took advantage of the time lag in adjustments, to sell the same security twice. The use of Bank Receipts (BRs) given by banks for transactions in bonds and units came in handy. These receipts, issued for securities received in a sale, were supposed to be non-negotiable and the securities were to be returned when the party returns the money. Later BRs became tradable, and they were sometimes forged and traded for raising further money.

In 1991, the Government raised the interest rates on Government bonds. When this was leaked out, the information was used by insiders to make huge profits.

The transactions between the National Housing Bank and the Grindlays Bank became a matter of dispute around Harshad Mehta who benefited by Grindlays transferring a huge sum of Rs. 622 crores directly to him. He used this money to save himself from the discovery of his fraud on the SBI, from whom he had taken money, without giving government securities. This transaction had not been discovered in the ledgers of the RBI.

I had an unexpected role in Delhi when the scam came up in Parliament in May 1993. There was a furore, especially after the F.M. said that he would not lose his sleep over stock prices. Government had decided that the Finance Minister should make a statement in Parliament. The Finance Secretary had gone abroad. When I met Finance Minister, Dr. Manmohan Singh, he asked me what should be done. I said that the matter was mainly related to the abuse of the banking system to raise money for deploying it to rig prices in the stock markets. It would therefore be better to have an investigation made by the RBI, and he should make a statement to this effect in the Parliament. He was initially reluctant but asked me to give him a draft statement. I sent him the draft the same evening. When I met him the next day in Parliament House, just before he was due to make his statement he was still reluctant. The Minister of State, Rameshwar Thakur was present and he agreed that it would be best to accept my suggestion. F.M. eventually agreed to make the statement. On the basis of the statement, RBI later constituted the Janakiraman committee, which went into the whole matter and estimated the loss to the banking system at about Rs. 4400 crores. Even this was incomplete, as the loss to the investors in the stock exchange was not taken into account.

The Joint Parliamentary Committee (JPC) was constituted and I was one of the witnesses to go before it. In my evidence, given over three hours, I explained how, in my view, the scam arose because of a variety of reasons involving the banks, the brokers, the stock exchanges and a host of dishonest individuals. I also explained that during the period the scam took place over a period of four or five years from 1986, SEBI was not in the picture. At SEBI, we had noticed the fast growth of the Stock Exchange index with share values in many cases going to unprecedented levels. SEBI was still without any statutory powers when the scam broke out. It had no powers to call for broker records or even to look at stock exchanges both of whom resented the very existence of SEBI. I also explained at length, the various steps that had been taken by SEBI to improve the functioning of the stock markets. The problems we had with the brokers were also well known by then.

The Janakiraman Committee met me and we discussed the link between bank finance and the stock market. They realized that stock brokers led by Harshad Mehta had drawn money from various sources like banks, mutual funds and public sector undertakings and deployed the ill gotten resources in a rigged market to defraud the investors. They also realized the Public Debt Office (PDO) and Subsidiary General Ledger (SGL) of the RBI needed to be modernized to provide online data on trading in securities.

JPC, in its report, fully supported the steps being taken by SEBI and went on to say that 'the brokers and the stock exchanges needed strong regulation'.[12]

The moral of these scams is that as long as accountability for negligence or wrongdoing is not established quickly and punished, there will be no end to such scams, which will continue to occur from time to time.

Broker Registration

I thought the first step towards disciplining the brokers was to ask for registration with SEBI under the Regulation. After the SEBI Act was notified on 4th April 1992, the brokers were asked to register themselves. On the 10th April 1992, broker fees were initially fixed at Rs. 5 lakhs for brokers in A category exchanges, Rs. 3 lakhs in B category and Rs. 1 lakh in the C category. The brokers reacted strongly. The chairman of the Calcutta Stock Exchange said that they were already members of the stock exchanges which were also 'regulatory bodies', and there should be no 'dual registration'. This was refuted and it was pointed out that for several decades brokers were registered with the Securities and Exchange Commission of USA (SEC).

There was also some confusion among the brokers about the fee for registration. At first the BSE chairman wanted the graded flat fee to be reduced, and I agreed on the 19th April to reduce it to fifty per cent, payable in five instalments. The next day he met me and said that he felt that a flat fee would be unfair to the smaller brokers he

---

12. JPC Report, p 176 para 8.49.

wanted a turnover based fee. I agreed to this also. The fee was fixed at one per cent of one percent that is for a turnover of Rs. one lakh the fee would be Rs. 10.

The brokers went on strike in late April 1992. Most of the Press was against the strike.[13] They made representations to the ministry. I told the finance minister that it would be best if they left it to SEBI to handle the matter and he was so good as to agree and also informed his officials to redirect the brokers to approach SEBI. The industry leader H.S. Singhania, who was then, Vice President of the International Chamber of Commerce, came out openly in the Press supporting the SEBI stand.[14] He said that whatever SEBI was trying to do was good as there should be some order in the market. After the strike ran for about seven days the brokers resumed work. The Press commented on this action of the brokers. The brokers then wanted to exclude certain types of trades in government securities from the fee. I appointed a committee on 4th December 1992, consisting of the respected R.S. Bhatt, former chairman of UTI; Mayya, the executive director of BSE; N.J. Jhaveri and a SEBI official to go into the matter. They called the BSE and others for discussion and recommended, on the 18th December 1992, that the fee for trading in government securities may be one tenth of the rate of fee for stock market transactions. I agreed and orders were issued accordingly. In the meanwhile several stock exchanges had gone to the High Courts from January 1993 onwards, to challenge the levy of fees. Some High Courts asked them to pay a minimum fee

---

13. Selected extracts from editorials and news reports on broker's strike, 7 extracts in all < Appended on page 190 >.
14. H.S. Singhania, Business Standard, 10.5.92 < Appended on page 195 >.

pending further hearing. After I left SEBI, matters were not pursued actively in the courts and the cases dragged on. Eventually the Supreme Court had to take on all the cases and the decision was in favour of SEBI. Even after court orders, the enforcement of the SEBI rules was tardy.

Having brought the brokers in line for registration, the next task was to revamp the boards of the exchanges which consisted only of brokers. When I suggested that they should have a majority of public representatives the exchanges again objected. We finally settled for a fifty-fifty arrangement and I carefully picked persons of integrity willing to spare time and placed them on the Boards. There was a distinct improvement in the functioning of the Boards in matters of investor complaints, margin collection, issue of contract slips, arbitration and disciplinary action against erring brokers. This fell into disuse later. Now there is a move towards demutualisation of the exchanges. Mutualisation, or the cosy arrangement between brokers for their own benefit is reduced by a process of demutualisation.

There were three other areas where SEBI wanted to improve broker services to the investors. Although the regulations provided for contract notes to be issued to the investors, showing the nature of shares to be sold or bought, the date of the transaction, the price of sale or purchase, the broker's commission and other details, this was mostly followed in the breach. The exchange managements were not interested in enforcing this rule as brokers' books were rarely audited. Very often the investors were given less than what was realized by sale or charged higher than the actual purchase price. They could not complain to the exchange authorities, who generally ignored them. The popular term for this common practice was 'gala'. SEBI directed the brokers to give contract notes with all the details.

The second problem was to ensure that investor funds were not mixed up with brokers' own funds and directions were issued for this also. The exchange authorities were reluctant to enforce this.

The third important issue was to prescribe capital adequacy norms in accordance with international practice. This was fixed at eight per cent, and was to be reached in 18 months by moving from three per cent to five per cent and finally to eight per cent. The brokers were unhappy with this also.

All this provoked M.G. Damani, who had formed a Brokers' Forum, to comment that 'SEBI has a biased outlook towards brokers' and 'the good old days of CCI were much better, do we really need a white elephant like SEBI?' In a constructive mood he said 'reforms should be by way of education not punishment'.

In May 1992, I recommended to the Finance Minister that the capital market could be broadened and deepened, (apart from getting foreign exchange in a non-debt creating manner), if we allow qualified Foreign Institutional Investors (FII) to invest in India. Dr. Manmohan Singh agreed and we drafted rules and an application form. At first the FIIs were somewhat supercilious and complained that the application form called for too much information and the clearance by SEBI was delayed. The form was somewhat simplified without giving up any of the essentials and clearance was given fast. We took care to exclude hot money flows, as they tend to destabilize markets. Later Non-Resident

Indian (NRIs) and OCBs (Overseas Commercial Bodies) were also allowed to invest. From 1993 up to May 2002, FII amounted to $ 14.8 billion and NRIs and OCBs brought in $ 1.97 billion. This figure has now risen several times.

In May 1992, I also recommended that a High Level Coordination Committee (HLCC) be set up with the Governor RBI, the Finance Secretary and the Chairman of SEBI for taking coordinated action to prevent and deal with aberrations in the financial and capital market. The finance minister agreed readily and set up the HLCC. The JPC report of 2002 in para 13.38 comments on the working of the HLCC.

The National Stock Exchange

Manohar Pherwani was Chairman UTI before Dave, and later was in charge of the Stockholding Corporation of India which acted as custodian for UTI and other public sector institutions. He was known as the original Big Bull before Harshad Mehta came on the scene. He had aggressively built up US-64 by accepting corporate money in a big way and it was generally believed that the money was used in the stock market to put up the prices of select shares. He used to meet me at intervals, just to find out what I was up to in SEBI. Around March 1993, the Pherwani committee, (which had been appointed by the Government to examine whether a new exchange could be opened for the bond market), gave a report recommending the starting of the National Stock Exchange for trading not only in bonds but also in the equity shares of small companies. When Pherwani met me to give me a copy of his report, I looked at the recommendations and asked him why he had made a half-hearted suggestion for the setting up of the NSE. He said that he still had a soft corner for BSE (the Bombay Stock Exchange), where he had traded big for a number of years, and did not want to cause harm to it, and wanted to give it a chance to improve. I wrote to the Government that I had been trying hard to improve the performance of BSE but was encountering resistance at every stage, with the result that the investors were seriously affected. I wrote that if the Bombay Stock Exchange authorities did not show any serious interest in reforming themselves within a period of six months I would recommend that the NSE should be a full fledged exchange competing with BSE. The NSE would be a modern exchange with electronic online trading. Even then the BSE did not wake up. Eventually the NSE was formed and steadily displaced the BSE and increasingly the business went to the modern transparent exchange. The BSE market share has come down from over 48 per cent in 1999 to 17.4 per cent in April 2003. The gainer has been the NSE. One recent Press comment says 'NSE leaves behind a battered BSE'. The stockbrokers and their leaders should realize at least now that they were themselves responsible for this state of affairs. If they had accepted the various measures proposed by SEBI in 1992 and 1993, without resisting them and fighting SEBI tooth and nail all the way, BSE would have been in a position to give a fight to the NSE in the market. Unlike the BSE and other older exchanges, the NSE was managed by a board, which did not have a single broker. It had been promoted by UTI and other institutions and their representatives sat on the Board. BSE and other exchanges had earlier rejected my suggestion to take outsiders on their boards. They were now pleading for some representation for themselves on the NSE Board.

'Badla'

The next big issue was the question of "badla trading" which was a peculiar feature of the Indian exchanges. In normal cash trading a person having shares, sells for cash. A person wanting to buy shares buys for cash. In *badla,* a person can buy without having the money and borrow the money when there are more buyers not having the money compared to sellers not having the shares. Such borrowing was called *vyaj badla.* Conversely, where they sell without having shares and postpone the deal, by paying some amount of money or by borrowing interest bearing money from money lenders to get the shares from some one else for a short period is called *undha badla.* The interest rates were fixed for different shares at the badla session following settlement. To put it simply, cash trading and badla trading going together and indistinguishably, was like playing football and rugby, (or tennis and badminton), which have quite different rules, in the same ground at the same time. The cash buyer or seller does not know what the fair market price is, and incurs a loss whether he is buying or selling.

When the exchanges refused to stop *badla* trading, I gave them plenty of time, writing to the exchanges and meeting them in August, September and November 1993. They were evasive and clearly unwilling to make the change. On 13th December 1993, I had to pass statutory orders to stop further *badla* trading and giving them time to unwind their existing positions over three months. This again raised a furore and the exchanges stopped work for sometime. The chairman of the first JPC called for drastic action against the stock exchanges. The fast moving events of those days are captured in the articles[15] of December 1993 and later. When they found that the Government was backing me they resumed trading normally, but without *badla*.[16] Damani was, as expected, critical of the SEBI action and called it 'spiteful and without basis'[17]. In an interview given as late as 5th February 1996, in the *Business Standard*, Mayya, the former Executive Director of the Bombay Stock Exchange stated that the 'carry forward is an excellent system'.[18]

A committee was appointed in 1995, after I had left SEBI, to go into the matter. The Committee while in principle agreeing with the stoppage of *badla* suggested some relaxations in *badla* trading, but stipulated audit trails of trades. This did not satisfy the brokers. They continued with informal *badla* trading while pressing for total revocation of the earlier orders banning badla. Eventually the Government had to intervene and put a stop to *badla* in 2001. News reports and headlines of May 15, 2001 give a sense of *deja vu*.

While opposing badla, I suggested that the stock markets should provide opportunity for hedging (or distributing risks) by opening the derivatives market. Other modern exchanges around the world have derivative trading in options and futures as a means of hedging for investors. I had encouraged brokers to look at the derivative option seriously but there was little interest. SEBI arranged seminars presented by experts, but this was not picked up by the

---

15. Ban on badla – news reports and editorials (13 cuttings) < Appended on page 195 >.
16. Business Standard, 21.12.93, The Times of India 23.12.1993 < Appended on page 206 >.
17. M.G. Damani, Indian Express, 16.12.1993 < Appended on page 207 >.
18. M.R. Mayya, Business Standard, 5.2.1996 < Appended on page 208 >.

brokers. After six or seven years, the brokers saw the merit of my proposal. Then the Act had to be amended to provide for derivatives trading. It has now been started since 2002. This process was facilitated by the growing strength of the National Stock Exchange with its clean, no nonsense administration.

In order to streamline cash trading, I wanted to bring them in line with world practices regarding settlement of trades within a time limit. The T+5 mechanism (settlement of transactions on the fifth day after the date of trade) was suggested as a first step. The brokers and the exchanges were lukewarm. And nothing much happened while I was in SEBI, but later they agreed mainly because of the coming into existence of the National Securities Depository, and the better practices of NSE.

At SEBI we prepared consultation papers on the take-over code and arranged for a discussion. There was little interest among the companies. Today it has come to occupy centre stage with big companies like Grasim, L&T, ACC and Gujarat Ambuja getting involved in SEBI adjudication of take overs.

Similarly, we prepared a paper on insider trading which evoked even less interest. Even today action in insider trading cases is not being pursued with vigour perhaps because of lack of interest, or adequate powers of search and seizure, or both.

Some Interesting Cases

There were a few interesting cases that were being investigated by SEBI in 1992 and 1993. In the case of the bearings company, Tata-Timken, there was a flaw in the allotment of shares. I had regard for the Tata house, and had known JRD since my days in Washington when I had to sign the government guarantee for the U.S. Exim Bank loans for the purchase of Boeing aircrafts. In 1992, he had invited me for a lunch with the Directors of Tata Sons where I spoke about the coming WTO regime. The Indian company was first called in and the irregularity was pointed out. The foreign collaborator was informed of the SEBI notice and within a few days the compliance officer of Timken flew in from the US and met me along with a senior vice president. They readily accepted the SEBI position and agreed to make amends by compensating those who did not get the allotment and also fired the officer of the company responsible for the wrongdoing.

There was another case of a large company, Raymond Synthetics, not allotting shares or refunding money to the investors. When asked, they said that the share certificates were burnt in a train accident and therefore the certificates were not sent or the money returned. It was pointed out to them that only the certificates were burnt but not the money, which was in their bank, earning interest. They saw the point and agreed to pay interest for the delay in issuing share certificates or in refunding the money.

Later in 1993, there was the case of Reliance, which came to SEBI in connection with their mega issue of about Rs. 3,000 crores through an innovative convertible debenture, which provided for two-tier conversion, at intervals, into equity, and the remaining amount a pure debenture. We had several rounds of discussion and changes were made in the terms to make them more investor friendly to which they agreed. Then it was noticed that share prices were going up sharply and it was found that share prices had been rigged by the process of circular trading. When the trading sheets of the brokers were summoned it was obvious that the same shares were traded among two or three brokers at higher and higher prices. I sent for the Ambani brothers to meet me. I had known Dhirubhai and his sons for some years and we had cordial relations. I drew their attention to the trading sheets showing circular trading to put up prices. They agreed that there was circular trading, about which they were not aware, and agreed to reverse the trend and not to do it again. We parted on good terms with no hard feelings. After a few days Dhirubhai sought an appointment to meet me and came to see me at my flat. He thanked me for clearing the mega issue. After a general discussion on the economy, the meeting ended on a cordial note. Since then I have met the Ambani brothers on several meetings, on friendly terms.

These three cases showed that a vigilant SEBI could make an impact on market discipline. The Press and the public began to regard SEBI as the guardian of the small investor.

With electronic trading it should not be difficult for the SEBI to get the summary of trades during the day, by the same evening. Thereafter, a team of SEBI officials should go through the trades and examine the top ten trades and see who the buyers and sellers are. Next morning the concerned brokers should be called in and asked for further details. This kind of real time surveillance is the solution to prevent the frequent aberrations and scams in the market.

Towards the beginning of May 1991, Rajiv Gandhi sent for me and I called on him when I visited Delhi for a meeting. He was cordial and invited me to his small private drawing room and library. He said that he was sorry they had pulled me out of Brussels where he had sent me for three years and asked me how I was doing in SEBI and whether he could help in getting through the SEBI Bill in Parliament. I said things were on track and I would ask for his assistance if necessary. The mid-term poll was on after the Chandra Shekhar Government had fallen a few months earlier. He said he was going on a tour of Orissa and the South, that after the elections he would need my assistance and hoped that I would be available. This was indeed a remarkable transformation since my days in Petroleum when he was angry with me for the way in which I handled the HBJ contract.

Then he called in Vincent George, his personal secretary, asked him to give me his direct personal phone number and said that whenever I wanted to meet him (Rajiv), I should be given priority. George went out and brought a slip of paper with his telephone number and gave it to me. Rajiv then shook hands warmly with his charming smile and I left. That was the last I saw of him before he was assassinated a few days later.

Exit

While the tussle with the brokers continued on the three issues of registration, fees and *badla* trading, there were rumors that I was likely to move out of SEBI. My enquiries through friends revealed that there was an attempt by some officials in the ministry of finance to show that my three year term was over. They started count from the time of my appointment in a purely administrative capacity in August

1990 and not from the date of statutory appointment in May 1992. The legal department had almost agreed, when the F.M. wanted the matter to be referred to the law officers in the Ministry of Home Affairs. They advised that my term of three years was fixed under SEBI regulations and I had taken over as the Chairman of the statutory body in May 1992, and therefore the three year term should be reckoned from that date, and not the date of my appointment to the administrative post. It is another matter that the same Finance Ministry later proposed a five year term for the Chairman.

The provocation for this detailed enquiry about my term was manifold. The brokers who were beginning to feel the pinch of my insistence on their registration, payment of fees and stopping of *badla* trading, began using their political influence to get me out of SEBI. A more important reason was my investigation of a matter concerning a close relation of a VIP in Delhi who was involved in violation of rules in dealing with the rights issue of a company in Hyderabad.

When the JPC was in session, there were news reports of wrong-doing in the share allotment by the company and the JPC wanted Central Bureau of Investigation (CBI) to look into the matter. When they got the report, I was giving evidence about the scam. The JPC then wrote to the Finance Minister that they were not satisfied with the CBI report and that they would like to have the matter investigated by SEBI. The Finance Ministry wrote to me to get the matter investigated. I then asked my officers to look into the matter.

SEBI officials had prepared a detailed report showing the misappropriation of some crores of rupees. In my report, sent to the JPC through the finance ministry, I stated that there was a *prima facie* case which warranted a detailed enquiry by an inter agency group of RBI, Income Tax, SEBI and the CBI. JPC accepted my recommendation. This set the cat among the pigeons and hastened the process of my departure. When it was found that legally they could not consider my term over, efforts were made to persuade me to take on a 'bigger' job as member of the Planning Commission with the rank of Minister of State. My friends advised me that this was the best option for me at this stage.

So, in January 1994, I left SEBI and took up the job in Delhi.

The Press commented on my work in, and departure from SEBI in several articles and editorials.[19]

The finance minister wrote a nice letter to me about my work in SEBI, which I cherish till today. [20]

Comments continued to be written long after I had left SEBI, and a few of them are interesting.[21]

---

19. News reports and editorials on leaving SEBI, (5 cuttings) < Appended on page 208 >.
20. Letter from Finance Minister < Appended on page 213 >.
21. Economic Times 6.11.95; Financial Express 2.4.2001 < Appended on page 214 and 215 respectively >.

APPENDED REFERENCES

< Merchant Bankers, Business Times, 6.6.1991 >

BUSINESS TIMES *Bombay, Thursday, June 6, 1991*

PUBLIC ISSUE PROSPECTUS

SEBI, Merchant bankers lock horns

By Debashis Basu

Bombay, June 5.

The Securities Exchange Board of India (SEBI) and some of the leading merchant bankers do not see eye to eye over what SEBI describes as "due diligence" the merchant bankers are supposed to exercise in scrutinising prospectuses relating to public issues.

Worse, merchant bankers have been giving evasive and unsatisfactory answers to SEBI's specific queries on lack of clear and adequate information in some recent prospectuses with which these merchant bankers have been associated.

SEBI wants merchant bankers to take much more responsibility and care while pushing public issues. Since the prospectus is the only document which allows investors to judge the quality of an issue, SEBI has been insisting that merchant bankers must scrutinise prospectuses thoroughly and be responsible for them. In other words, they should exercise "due diligence." ...

... SEBI has gone through an elaborate process of consulting and informing the merchant bankers of what it thinks is due diligence. The merchant bankers first ignored SEBI. Now they are answering only some of SEBI's queries on whether due diligence has been observed or not and that too in a manner that SEBI feels is unsatisfactory. ...

... Having received these certificates, over the past two months SEBI combed scores of prospectuses, drew up a list of points and wrote 24 letters to various merchant bankers asking them to clarify what diligence they have exercised as regards these.

Amazingly, out of these, just three replies have completely satisfied SEBI. Almost half of these 24 queries (13) have simply been ignored. The others are either partly satisfactory or not satisfactory at all. ...

... When asked about these queries and the SEBI's dissatisfaction over the response, a top executive of SBI Capital Markets, the biggest merchant bankers, said that "we are not in conflict with SEBI and we have exercised due diligence." ...

< Postal vote, Financial Express, 27.9.1993 >

FINANCIAL EXPRESS *New Delhi, Monday, September 27, 1993*

SEBI chief takes up cudgels for public shareholders

From Sanjeev Sharma

New Delhi, September 27.

The chairman, Securities and Exchange Board of India (SEBI), Mr G.V. Ramakrishna, has asked the Government to introduce changes in the Companies Act to give public shareholders the right to have a say in fixing the price and quantum of rights issues offered to foreign and Indian promoters. ...

... Mr Ramakrishna has proposed that these matters may include aspects like (a) proportion at which further shares may be offered to the shareholders; (b) price at which such shares are being offered; (c) issue of share to any section of the shareholders like institutional or foreign shareholders on terms which are more favourable than those offered to the Indian shareholders, should be subject to receiving positive consents from a specified percentage (say 25 per cent to 30 per cent) of the individual shareholders. ...

... Mr Ramakrishna has added that these proposals are relevant in the context of the recent proposals for allotment of rights shares to foreign partners in various Fera companies at prices much below the market prices and the objections of Indian shareholder to such unduly favourable terms being offered. "This has resulted in bitterness amongst the Indian shareholders." ...

... Also, many Indian shareholders have been feeling bitter about the offer by Fera companies to their parent outfits to raise their stake at prices much below the prevailing market rates. ...

< Modified postal vote, Financial Express, 16.9.1993 >

FINANCIAL EXPRESS *Thursday, September 16, 1993*

CHEAP EQUITY SALE BY FERA COs CAUSE CONCERN

SEBI for modified postal vote to protect small investors

By Manika Gupta

New Delhi, September 15

The Securities and Exchange Board of India has suggested marginalisation of financial institutions' votes and for weightage to be given to individual shareholders, who are losing heavily due to FERA companies selling equity at a cheap rate to parent companies.

This could be achieved through a modified postal ballot system.

SEBI feels institutional investors are more inclined towards multinationals, specially when the premium is fixed in their favour.

The board suggests a system be devised, whereby companies take a view of the house minus FIs. The weightage given to FIs during annual general body meetings should be reduced in the interest of the individual investor.

While this is SEBI's answer to the problem of multinationals picking up a stake in FERA companies cheaply, other government departments are still looking for the most effective way of curbing this practice without endangering the present round of liberalisation.

Since the decision to allow parent companies to increase the stake in FERA companies from 40 per cent to 50 per cent is in tune with liberalisation, the Government is finding it difficult to let the equity be sold at heavy discounts to multinationals.

It may be recalled that the Castrol issue had created a major controversy when the parent company was offered a Rs. 10 share at a premium of Rs. 100. Shareholders put their foot down and pointed out that Castrol share was being quoted at Rs. 1,000 on the market.

Close on the heels of this controversy, Colgate announced that it was offering its parent company, 11 per cent stake at Rs. 50 per share. By offering a 1:1 bonus and 1:10 bonus on the right issue, share holders were silenced.

According to an official spokesman involved in solving this vexed problem, the practice could be detrimental to the interest of small investors as well as the national exchequer which is losing due to this practice.

< Change in Sec 81 of Cos Act, The Economic Times 19.9.1993 >

THE ECONOMIC TIMES *Sunday, September 19, 1993*

SEBI wants change in Sec 81 of Cos Act

Our New Delhi Bureau

New Delhi, September 18

... This had been, however, interpreted by DCA as SEBI prescribing differential voting rights for individual and institutional shareholders. DCA feels that SEBI wants FIs to stay away from voting on issues like issuing of shares to foreign shareholders on terms more favourable to those offered to the Indian shareholders.

On the basis of this interpretation, DCA held discussions with ministries of law and finance. Both were of the opinion that FIs cannot be refrained from voting.

SEBI chairman, however, clarified to *The Economic Times* that he never suggested that FIs should abstain from voting on important issues. SEBI is only suggesting that in addition to voting by institutional shareholders and promoters, the consent of atleast 25 to 30 per cent of the individual shareholders should also be taken before the resolution is passed.

Mr. Ramakrishna said he is of the opinion that FIs should exercise their rights in larger public interest and the interest of the companies' public shareholders. SEBI chief has also written a letter to the finance secretary, Dr. Montek Singh Ahluwalia stating this.

In his letter to Dr. Ahluwalia, Mr. Ramakrishna has said that consent of atleast 20 to 30 per cent shareholders will avoid the need for any external controls on the pricing of rights issues.

< Postal Ballot as Takeover Defence >

Postal Ballot as Takeover Defence

By Rajendra P. Chitale

1. A wide cross-section of our private sector is controlled and managed by Industry Houses with relatively small shareholdings. Even some large credible Business Houses feel nervous, if not threatened, of becoming targets of hostile takeovers. The extent of nervousness is inversely related to their percentage of shareholdings. The smaller the shareholding, the greater the nervousness. The ongoing debate on corporate governance may ultimately result in redefinition of the role of Indian financial/investment institutions as significant shareholders in several frontline Indian companies. This could add further to their concerns.
2. The Indian private corporate sector has, till now, shown a rather distinct apathy to view postal ballot as a harbinger of true corporate democracy: A framework which facilitates convenient, yet meaningful, participation of the vast and growing public shareholding population geographically dispersed all over India.
3. Besides the shareholdings of Promoters Groups, FIs and other institutional investors, only a tiny fraction of the public shareholding makes it's presence felt at AGMs/EGMs. It will be presumptuous to say that public shareholders are anyway not interested in participating in the company's affairs or in exercising their rights.
4. A large majority of public shareholders may, in fact, like to endorse their support to a competent and credible sitting management/promoter group when the company becomes a takeover target by a predator. Postal ballot can bridge the geographical distance between such public shareholders and the AGMs/EGMs, without the sitting management/promoter group resorting to a proxy collection drive. In this manner, postal ballot can become an effective takeover defence to credible and competent sitting managements/promoters groups. This would be particularly true where public shareholding is rather large, say, over 30%. Faced with the prospect of such surging support of public shareholding to sitting management/promoter group, the predator may have no choice but to offer a higher price to lure the public shareholding into selling, or to retract from the acquisition. Increasing the offer price would step up the takeover cost. Besides, such activated public shareholders' support would necessitate acquisition of additional shareholding beyond the minimum 20% offer required under the takeover code. This would benefit the minority shareholders if the predator succeeds, and the sitting managements/promoter groups if the public shareholders do not exercise the offer of the predator.

Contd...

...Contd...

5. Of course, postal ballot will be a double edged weapon. If the sitting management/promoter groups loose credibility or are seen as less competent than the predator, postal ballot could act as a catalist for the predator with a surge of support from public shareholders. This could enable the predator to limit the mandatory offer under the takeover code to the minimum 20%. This too would only advance the interests of the target company by facilitating change of management to the one which is perceived by its shareholders as more credible and competent than the sitting management/promoter group.
6. Viewed in the above perspective, there is perhaps a case for the various Chambers of Commerce and Industry Association to not support but suggest introduction of postal ballot.
7. It should be possible to weave a set of legislative provisions in the new company law reportedly taking shape, to make the concept of postal ballot not only possible but practicable as well. Not all decisions need to be brought under the postal ballot concept. Postal Ballot could be confined to important matters which could be identified through wider consultations. These could include appointment and remuneration of directors, inter corporate investments beyond prescribed limits, subsidiarisation, desubsidiarisation, inter corporate lending beyond prescribed limits preferential/public issue of equity or convertibles, and corporate restructuring including spin offs, demergers and mergers.
8. The concept of "postal ballot" is not common in developed capital markets. But they are largely institutionalised markets with most of the investment in corporate equity flowing through collective investment pools such as mutual funds, social security funds, pension funds etc. These institutional investors have the where-withal to make their presence at shareholders meetings if they so wish. Therefore, this concept is of no relevance there. In any case, some legislative precedents of the concept do exist elsewhere. The "voting by correspondence" for all or specific agenda items, in place of passing resolutions at the meeting of capital participants in a limited liability company under the company law in Switzerland is an example (Swiss Code of Obligations, Vol. II).

Outline of Postal Ballot Procedure:

9. Briefly put, a share holder should be sent along with the notice of AGM/EGM (including shareholders meeting summoned under direction of Company Court's orders in demergers and spin offs), a form indicating in brief, each of the proposed resolutions and advice the shareholder to indicate there against his vote as "In favour" or "Against". The shareholder may complete the form indicating his vote on each resolution and mail it back in a 'business reply' cover (postage payable by addressee), which should accompany the notice of AGM/EGM sent by the company. Shareholders attending the AGM/EGM themselves or through proxies should also bring the voting form duly completed and leave it in the ballot box to be kept at the venue of the AGM/EGM. If resolutions are put to vote at the AGM/EGM by show of hands (if this system is

Contd...

...Contd...

continued even under the new concept) the result thereof as announced by the Chairman of the meeting should be made legislatively) subject to the ballot box and postal ballot.

10. Postal ballot, for it to be considered valid, should be received for counting not later than say, 15 days after the date of the AGM/EGM. Results of the ballot should be communicated to the shareholders either by correspondence or through newspaper advertisement. To ensure free and fair ballot, a new professional category of independent "scrutineers" should be given statutory recognition. Their task would be to receive the postal ballots directly from the shareholders, verify signatures for authenticity, count them and the ballots cast in the box at the AGM/EGM venue, and report their results to the Company for onward publication and announcement.

11. If Registrars and Transfer Agents of the Company itself are given this task of "scrutineers", it must be mandatory for the company to appoint an independent supervisory scrutineer, such as a qualified Company Secretary, a qualified Chartered Accountant or a firm of Chartered Accountants or Solicitors to supervise and monitor the fairness of the process. For any of these to qualify as "scrutineers" or "supervisory serutineers", registration with a regulatory body such as SEBI should be prescribed, which will monitor their respective conduct as "scrutineers". Severe penalties should be prescribed for wrongdoings of scrutineers and abetting company managements.

12. In addition, care must be taken to anticipate and identify avenues of possible abuse of the suggested system of postal ballot (such as impersonation, forgery, vote-banking, etc.). Adequate safeguards to pre-empt such abuses must be provided for in the provisions of Company Law.

Mumbai, February 7, 1997

< Mutual Funds, Midday, 5.8.1991 >

MID DAY *Monday, August 5, 1991*

EXTRACTS FROM INTERVIEW WITH CHAIRMAN OF SEBI, G.V. RAMAKRISHNA

"Mutual Funds flouting international norms"

By Krishna H. Rao

The functioning of mutual funds in India is not in accordance with international standards and practices. The deviations are in several major areas. Firstly, while floating new schemes, they do not clearly reveal what they will do with the funds. So there is not enough differentiation between schemes; whether a scheme is high-risk and high-reward or medium-risk and medium-reward, whether a scheme goes only into the call-money market or into equities is never clear.

...a few months ago were guaranteeing minimum returns, which is alien to practices in any developed capital-market country. Recently, at our insistence, they have stopped advertising in that manner. ...

... In other countries mutual fund managers are required to state in their promotional literature that past performance is no guarantee of future performance. Here, since we have asked them to have a similar warning, they carry it but in the smallest possible print which you cannot read without a lens. ...

... And fourthly, the funds collected under each scheme should be treated separately, and the investor should be continually kept informed of the status of his investment in a particular scheme. Our mutual funds give the net assets value of each scheme every year, whereas abroad, the investor is informed everyday. ...

... Yet another much-required change, that has already been initiated, is in accounting practices in calculating net assets values of various schemes. We have asked all of them to standardise their policies, so that the investor can make proper decisions by comparing net asset values of different schemes. ...

... Several changes will have to come about before our capital market becomes a safe place for investors.

< Assocham Information Post, 15.10.1990 >

October 15.

... Mr. G.V. Ramakrishna, Chairman, SEBI criticised the functioning of stock exchanges and mutual funds and called for structural changes in the composition and functioning of the governing board of stock exchanges and the opening up of their membership to various financial institutions, corporate bodies and individuals.

As regards investor protection, Mr. Ramakrishna felt that there was inadequate disclosure and transparency in operations and that the investors' interests were not looked after.

While welcoming the growth of mutual funds, Mr. Ramakrishna was critical about the way in which the mutual funds went about attracting investment. He stated that the Indian mutual funds never highlighted or even pointed out the risk associated with such investments. Further, they assured a minimum return to the investor, which, in general, is not promised by mutual funds in countries with well-developed capital markets.

Mr. Ramakrishna favoured the monitoring of mutual fund performance on the basis of quarterly, half yearly and annual reviews. He also emphasised the need to have a central agency for regulation, but stressed that SEBI did not foresee itself performing such a role, but rather, it would like to promote Self-Regulatory Organisations (SROs) in all segments of the securities industry. ...

< Letter to Montek and reply >

CHAIRMAN

भारतीय प्रतिभूति
तथा एक्सचेंज बोर्ड
Securities and Exchange Board of India

IIMARP/10682/93
July 05, 1993

My dear Montek,

I am enclosing an analysis of the Balance Sheet of UTI as of June 30, 1992. The analysis brings out certain interesting facts about the operations of UTI and makes interesting reading.

I will only sum up the analysis to say, that although UTI is a hybrid of a Mutual Fund and a Financial Institution, all resources deployed by UTI for its activities as a Financial Institution such as term lending, underwriting have come through the Schemes of the Mutual Fund. Even as a Mutual Fund, the accounts are not maintained in the same manner as other Mutual Funds are required to under our Regulations and the restrictions on the limits and types of investments applicable for other Mutual Funds under the regulations have been exceeded. Further, even as a Financial Institution, its disclosures are not in line with those of other Financial Institutions.

With regards,

Yours Sincerely,

G V Ramakrishna

encl: a/a

Shri Montek Singh Ahluwalia
Finance Secretary
Department of Economic Affairs
Ministry of Finance
North Block
New Delhi 110 001

मित्तल कोर्ट, "बी" वींग, 224, नरीमन पॉईंट, बम्बई–400 021, फोन: 2028221 फैक्स: 2021073 टेलेक्स: 0118–5765 SEBI IN

Contd...

...*Contd.* ...

UTI as a Mutual Fund and a Financial Institution

An analysis of the balance sheet of Unit Trust of India as of June 30, 1992 reveals the manner in which resources have been deployed between its activities as a Mutual Fund and a Financial Institution.

1) Total investible resources of UTI as of June 30, 1992 is Rs. 31805 crores.

2) These resources have been allocated into four broad categories of Funds defined in the balance sheet as General Fund, Mutual Fund, India Fund and India Growth Fund.

3) The General Fund includes all domestic schemes of UTI, 7 open ended schemes and 28 closed ended schemes and 3 venture capital schemes except Mastershare. The names of the schemes are given below ...

...

6) The deployment of resources in terms of investible funds are as follows:

	Rs. in crores (Figure as of 30.06.92)
General Fund	30,426
Mutual Fund	673
India Fund	582
India Growth Fund	125
Total investible funds	31,806

7) These resources have been deployed as follows:

(Fig. Rs. in crores)

	Equity	*Pref.*	*Deb*	*Money Market*	*Term Loan etc.*
General Fund (All schemes)	7795 (26)	22 (.1)	6082 (20)	10221 (32)	6305 (21.9)
Mutual Fund	521 (78)	0 (0)	40 (6)	112 (16)	0 (0)
India Fund	443 (76)	0 (0)	53 (9)	86 (15)	0 (0)
India Growth Fund	103 (82)	0 (0)	11 (9)	10 (9)	0 (0)

Contd...

...*Contd.* ...

8) All Funds put together, the break up of the investments are as follows:

	Rs. (Crores)	(%)
Equity	8862	28.0
Preference	22	0.1
Debentures	6185	19.0
Money Market	10431	33.0
Term Loans etc.	6306	19.9
Total	31806	100.0

(9) ... <u>Besides, the "notes to account" shows a contingent underwriting liability for Unit 64 scheme to the extent of Rs. 227 crores.</u>

Although, the resources for these schemes are mobilised in the same manner as any other mutual fund, UTI does not conform to the following norms applicable to other mutual funds as per the Securities and Exchange Board of India [Mutual Funds] Regulations, 1993.

a) Maximum permissible limit for investment in money market instruments is 15 per cent.

b) Mutual Funds are not allowed to deploy their resources in terms loans, deposits, bridge finance etc.

c) Mutual Funds are not allowed to underwrite.

d) Mutual Funds are not allowed to provide venture capital assistance.

...

11) ... As a Financial institution it does not make the disclosures of the portfolio for its term lending activities as is done by the financial institutions.

12) Unlike the financial institutions, UTI does not give figures for the recoveries and outstanding interest in arrears, or for that matter interest that has been funded. ...

13) In the Mutual Fund accounting as per SEBI Regulations it is required that the Mutual Funds should indicate separately the non-performing assets and also provisions made in this regard. UTI's balance sheet does not indicate this separately.

10) However, UTI does provide for schemewise account for all its schemes where deployment of the resources and interscheme transfers have been indicated.

***

सत्यमेव जयते

वित्त सचिव
FINANCE SECRETARY

DO. NO. F 2020/FS/93

Chaima
8061

भारत सरकार
वित्त मंत्रालय
आर्थिक कार्य विभाग
Government of India
Ministry of Finance
Department of Economic Affairs
नई दिल्ली/New Delhi

12 July 1993

Dear G.V.

Please recall our earlier correspondence and discussions on the issue of the need to subject UTI to the same SEBI regulations as are applicable to other Mutual Funds. This issue has since been discussed further by the Joint Secretary (Investment) with representatives of both SEBI and UTI.

2. The Government's consistent view has been that irrespective of the fact that UTI is governed by its own statute, the relationship between UTI and its unit holders is essentially similar to that between a mutual fund and the investors therein, and as such it is necessary and desirable from the point of view of investor protection that this aspect of UTI's activity be subjected to SEBI regulation as for other Mutual Funds. However, the Government also recognises that UTI has certain special characteristics whereby the regulations of its activities cannot be achieved simply on the basis of duplicating the provisions which exist for Mutual Funds. The Government also recognises that the special characteristics of UTI, its unique position as the dominant mobiliser of saving, and its historical evolution, all need to be kept in mind in determining the appropriate modalities for regulation by SEBI.

3. As you know, we had earlier circulated, vide my letter of 18 March 1993, a discussion paper prepared in the Economic Division suggesting a possible framework for regulation based on bifurcation of UTI. The reaction of the UTI has yet to be received. As I had mentioned in my letter the proposal was meant for discussion and we would be willing to consider alternative approaches to achieve the basic objective of subjecting UTI to suitable regulation to ensure investor protection.

4. I understand some discussions are planned between SEBI and UTI to pursue these issues further. I hope these can be expedited to permit an early resolution of all outstanding problems.

Contd...

...Contd. ...

5. I am writing to Chairman, UTI also conveying the above.

With regards,

Yours sincerely,

(Montek Singh Ahluwalia)

Shri GV Ramakrishna
Chairman, SEBI
Bombay.

< Selected Extracts from Editorials and News Reports on Broker's Strike >

(1 of 7)

BUSINESS STANDARD *Monday, April 20, 1992*

SEBI Versus Brokers

"........ animosity of the stock exchange........new and intruding presence called........was prompted by the high-handedness of SEBI........if the brokers over-reacted........thoughtful pilots of a new agency should........both sides are willing to climb down - SEBI on the stiff and arbitrary registration fee........

Obviously, the arguments.....compulsory registration with SEBI.....stiff price.....are not seriously made.....only because the stock exchanges whose registration credentials the brokers flaunt are not famous for their regulatory prowess. They are in effect so many brokers clubs where the broker-members call the shots and sideline non-broker members to get all their daily sins in the marketplace absolved. SEBI after all became necessary just to end this state of affairs. How will such a state of affairs get corrected if the most important players of the stock-brokers insist that they have nothing to do with SEBI directly? Nor are the arguments about financing the so-called huge budget of the SEBI quite honest........ It is not a big enough budget for an agency charged with quite a few tasks ..... Rs. 25 lakhs to Rs. 2 crores unreasonable have no business to protest about the unfairness of a one-time SEBI registration fee of Rs. 10 lakhs! It was plain and simple poor public relations strategy..... issue easily....."

(2 of 7)

TIMES OF INDIA *Wednesday, April 22, 1992*

Wilful Brokers

The broking community's decisions to continue the stock market strike, even after the Securities and Exchange Board of India decided to halve the registration fee for brokers, has exposed the hollowness of the claim that the agitation was against the high fee SEBI has set. As several brokers have admitted, even while their colleagues hold the ordinary investor to ransom by keeping the markets closed, the fee

Contd. ...

...Contd. ...

suggested initially was not really steep. The agitation is actually against the concept of regulation which is being implemented. The SEBI Chairman's plan to implement certain capital adequacy norms, whereby brokers' trading volumes will be restricted to a fixed multiple of their capital base, is one of the major sore points with many of the striking brokers. Not only will this keep errant brokers on a leash, the capital adequacy principle, accepted worldwide as a means to maintain market health, will require greater transparency in the accounts of broking firms which today are a closely guarded secret – concealing incomes from the tax authorities as well as information from the regulators. This is why brokers are asking, who is the SEBI to ask us questions?

..... The Government must take all necessary steps to fully empower SEBI to regulate the markets to ensure that a handful of brokers do not push the market to the brink of collapse. With the stock exchange boards having failed miserably in checking malpractices, there is no alternative to strengthening SEBI's hands. Some brokers have been trying desperately to lobby with members of Parliament to take up cudgels against SEBI – and have engineered a continuation of the strike despite SEBI's willingness to compromise on the issue so that it is kept alive to enable some MPs to raise it in Parliament. Their attempts to exert this kind of pressure must be defeated."

(3 of 7)

FINANCIAL EXPRESS *Friday, April 24, 1992*

A Demand for Friendliness!

While on Monday we had warned against pressure being brought on the SEBI to retreat, this is just what is being done........ This is no way to treat an agency that, by statute, should discipline the fraternity of brokers, not bow before them. When we see all the mayhem, one might regret the fact that North Block has done nothing to defend the SEBI and warn the brokers to return to the trading floor........ It is, indeed, the responsibility of the Union Finance Ministry to not just safeguard but even enhance the authority of the Board and to tell the brokers and the exchanges where they get off........ As we pointed out earlier in these columns, one can object neither to the Board's requirement that the brokers should register themselves with it nor the fee structure it had worked out.

........We carried a Calcutta-based report in this newspaper on Wednesday, which quoted the President of the local stock exchange, Mr. Ajit Dey, as saying that the Securities Exchange Commission of the United States did not have any provision for the registration of

Contd. ...

...*Contd.* ...

brokers. Mr. Dey told the Financial Express, over the telephone, from New York that the US Commission, on which the SEBI was modelled, did not have the brokers registered with it and charged no registration fee. And mark his words, "it provides guidance to the brokers and is quite friendly." If friendliness is what the exchanges and brokers expect of SEBI, then, obviously the latter should not be there. It must be wound up! The 1991 World Development Report of the World Bank said something about a market-friendly development strategy. Now, we have a responsible member of one of India's leading stock exchanges demand that SEBI should be broker-friendly, when the brokers everywhere are anything but friendly. If the idea is that the Board should smile at whatever the brokers do and do nothing even when they are bent on setting records in disorderliness, there is no case for the SEBI being there. Mr. Dey was, of course, exaggerating the way the Securities Exchange Commission behaved and was putting things in his own perspective. The truth is that the Commission comes down hard on errant behaviour and Mr. Dey should know that it will not be broker-friendly in the face of what goes on day in and day out in his own territory, the Lyons Range.

(4 of 7)

THE WEEKEND OBSERVER *Saturday, April 25, 1992*

Shackling SEBI

The boycott of trading........after the Securities and Exchange Board of India made it clear that while the fee issue could be held in abeyance, it was sticking to its stipulation regarding registration, is likely to strengthen the impression that brokers are unwilling to submit themselves to any kind of regulation........not only against SEBI........ Unfortunately, monitoring by stock exchange governing bodies, controlled by the broking community, have been ineffective in preventing malpractices. Nor can it be argued that brokers did not get sufficient time to familiarise themselve with the functions of SEBI and its application to their business since the Securities and Regulations Act came into being in end-January. The Act contains a clear provision that SEBI would register and regulate the working of stock market intermediaries.

While the reluctance of brokers to submit themselves to regulation is understandable, what is not is the encouragement they seem to have received from a section within the finance ministry........ This has contributed in no small measure to the obduracy with which brokers have refused to fall in line........ Now it appears that unless the finance minister intervenes to restrain his power-hungry bureaucrats and back SEBI to the hilt, stock markets will continue to function in the same unregulated manner as before hurting millions of investors in whose name the SEBI was set up.

(5 of 7)

THE ECONOMIC TIMES *Saturday, April 25, 1992*

On A Weak Wicket

The stance taken by the country's broking community over the issue of registration with the Securities and Exchange Board of India (SEBI) is unjustified and untenable. The finance ministry should not be cowed down by the brokers' refusal to trade and threats of legal action. The continued boycott of trading shows the extreme irresponsibility of the brokers towards investors and the country at large. There can be no objection to registration *per se*. Dual registration with the stock exchange and a body like SEBI is a worldwide practice.........What SEBI should immediately do is to make it clear that registration will be automatic and all existing brokers will be registered by it even if all the information it has sought cannot be supplied immediately.........If the brokers still try to buck registration, the finance ministry could intervene by making it clear that registration with SEBI is a non-negotiable issue and it will not be cowed down by brokers refusing to trade. If such a firm stand is taken by Government after making it absolutely clear that brokers need not fear disqualification by SEBI on application for registration, the brokers are bound to see reason and return to the trading ring........In the final analysis, there can be no getting away from the fact that all markets need to be regulated. Self regulation is fine, except that it does not always work. That is why exception, and the sooner they realise this, the better it will be.

(6 of 7)

INDIAN EXPRESS *Saturday, April 25, 1992*

Brokers Strike SEBI

The impunity with which share brokers have got away with the protest strike which forced the prolonged closure of the country's leading stock exchanges is truly amazing........The striking brokers have been treated with astonishing indulgence even though it was obvious that the breather provided by the stock exchange closure would enable the bulls to push up share prices in an overheated and narrow market........It was made out as if the strike was all about the stiff registration fees announced by the Securities and Exchange Board of India (SEBI) although it was obvious that the real purpose was to blunt SEBI's powers to call brokers and other financial intermediaries to account........Share brokers are now up against registration with SEBI: why duplicate registration when, as members registered with stock exchanges, they are governed by regulations, of the parent associations?

Contd. ...

...*Contd.* ...

Such libertarian anguish does not wash though. It is the share brokers who dominate the governing bodies of the stock exchanges which wink in concert at violations of the very regulations by which they now swear. What is important in the current context is that powerful corporate interests use share brokers to groom the market, that is, jack up the premium at which share issues, including rights offers, are made and manipulate the prices at what debentures are converted in shares........Though share brokers are the most visible, defenders of the *status quo*, the companies and the institutional investors prodding them have a vested interest in manoeuvring the markets. Powerful forces are thus at work in the stop-go strike to scuttle the bid to open up the investments markets to fair trading. It will be a pity if the Government yields to the siege within and maims SEBI.

(7 of 7)

THE OBSERVER OF BUSINESS AND POLITICS *Monday, April 27, 1992*

Trading Must Resume

"........it appears that the brokers of the Bombay Stock Exchange will not trade in the ring today as part of their continuing agitation against the recent move of the Securities and Exchange Board of India to enforce registration of brokers with it........The brokers are in a defiant mood and intend to stubbornly refuse to trade unless their demand, that the registration move be dropped, is accepted. This hardheaded attitude deserves to be severely condemned.... there is no justification for completely suspending trading unilaterally........Not only does it amount to blackmail, it strikes at the very root of a stock market which is after all supposed to provide a channel for free and fair exchange of securities........they seem to be confused about exactly why they want to do that........but SEBI has indicated its willingness to pare the charges to more reasonable levels and also claim it only when the registration is actually done........ the brokers are up in arms against the very idea of having another body, especially a government one with sweeping powers, to oversee their functioning and conduct........there was ample room for dialogue and debate to clarify any misgivings, but the brokers have chosen to take an agitationist line........SEBI has been established to ensure that the investor is protected and registration of brokers would be one step in that direction. Keeping the markets closed forcibly harms investors' interests.

The authorities must ensure that this blackmail does not succeed........it is the duty of the Government and the various agencies which oversee the stock markets to ensure that trading is resumed as early as possible.

< H.S. Singhania, Business Standard, 10.5.1992 >

BUSINESS STANDARD *New Delhi, Sunday, May 10, 1992*

Singhania backs SEBI's market regulatory role

From Our Special Correspondent

New Delhi, May 9.

Noted industrialist and vice-president of the International Chamber of Commerce Hari Shankar Singhania has supported the recent SEBI guidelines making registration mandatory for stockbrokers. He said that whatever the SEBI was trying to do was good as there should be some order in the market.

Singhania, the first industrialist to come out in open support of SEBI, following the countrywide agitation by stockbrokers, said that while big brokers should be allowed to operate in the primary market, small brokers should be left to deal in the secondary market. ...

< Ban on Badla – News Reports and Editorials >

(1 of 13)

THE PIONEER *Bombay, Thursday, December 16, 1993*

Ban to prevent another scam, claims SEBI

PTI

The Securities and Exchange Board of India (SEBI) on Wednesday strongly defended its ban on forward trading, saying it was to prevent the recurrence of "the 1992 situation", an obvious reference to the stock scandal, and to protect investors.

"There is no substance in the allegation that the ban is sudden and that the conditions for liquidation of outstanding positions are harsh", SEBI said, justifying the move which has come under fire from brokers, leading to their boycott of trading for the last two days.

Contd. ...

...*Contd.* ...

SEBI said in a statement that it intervened only after adequate discussion on three occasions with the stock exchange authorities and their inability to restrict excessive speculation. ...

... Not only had sufficient advance notice and warning been given to the exchanges, but also the time for liquidation of outstanding positions had been extended to nearly two months, it said. ...

(2 of 13)

FINANCIAL EXPRESS *New Delhi, Saturday, December 18, 1993*

The brokers are wrong

For the first time in several months, Indian stockbrokers have managed to win the sympathy of the masses. Many investors agree with stockbrokers that the Securities and Exchange Board of India (SEBI) was wrong in imposing a ban on forward trading on December 13. Consequently, when these stockbrokers decided to suspend trading on the Bombay Stock Exchange, to protest against the stand taken by SEBI, they found that this time they had not aroused the investors' ire.

But the stockbrokers are wrong. And they compounded their wrongs by boycotting trading. If they have the sympathy of investors, it is possibly because SEBI's stand has not been understood.

First the brokers are wrong in saying that SEBI's action was too sudden, and that it came without warning. On the contrary, there was enough warning, including the one issued on August 26 this year, and which was widely reported by all newspapers. The SEBI's Chairman had then clearly stated that it might be compelled to impose a ban on forward trading if the stock exchange authorities did not take measures to curb speculative trading. A second warning was issued on November 24 this year. Then came the ultimatum from the Executive Director of the Bombay Stock Exchange (BSE) directing all members to square up and reduce their outstandings by at least 25 per cent before the next settlement which is due in the first week of December. However, an analysis of the settlement showed that outstanding had been reduced only by 10 per cent. Obviously, the stockbrokers were in no mood to listen to orders. They were not willing to bridle their speculative urges. Consequently, the ban on forward trading became inevitable. They were literally asking for it.

Second, it is surprising that the brokers should now suspend trading when they had already accepted an earlier directive from the BSE authorities banning forward trading in 10 major scrips which account for 80 per cent of the weightage of the BSE Sensitive Index. No stockbroker protested at that time that the ban was imposed too

Contd. ...

...Contd. ...

suddenly. It was possibly because, by then, the stockbrokers themselves had shifted their attention to other scirps.

Third, there is no denying that the markets were getting highly speculative. The rise of the stockmarket indices was not on account of actual trading, but on account of forward deals. Actual delivery of shares comprised not more than 13 per cent (though some counts put this figure even lower at 9 per cent) of the total volumes traded. There was, obviously, the danger that the runaway boom would cause other funds from manufacturing to get diverted towards speculative activities, like it happened during 1991-92. ...

... Fourth, there were few other options left for SEBI, but to impose a ban. For instance, even when controls had been imposed by the stock exchange authorities in the past, they were applied so discriminatingly and selectively, that they did not really amount to much. For instance, audit after audit conducted by SEBI on the books of all the country's major stock exchanges have shown how margins were evaded by most members who had close ties with the members of the governing council. A notable example is a leading stockbroker who has continued to evade margins with impunity each time they have been imposed. Since neither the brokers nor the stock exchange authorities were interested in restraining themselves, such controls had to be imposed from outside.

Fifth, even when it come to other measures aimed at streamlining the markets, it is sad to see well-entrenched (and prosperous) stockbrokers displaying the maximum recalcitrance. For instance, even in the force of SEBI's directive that stockbrokers must achieve capital adequacy norms, older and prosperous members are allowed greater latitude than new members. ...

... Lastly, it is extremely ironical to see stockbrokers' amazing ability to assemble and to decide on suspension of trading in a matter of just a few minutes, given the claim that they could not decide on how to curb speculative fires over three-and-a-half-months! Each time they have boycotted trading, such decisions have been taken swiftly and almost unanimously. But when it comes to self-regulation, they have dragged their feet on one pretext or the other.

Till recently, Indian stockbrokers have broken laws with impunity. ...

... Obviously, the brokers are wrong. And it is ridiculous to watch them trying to act pious instead.

(3 of 13)

THE TIMES OF INDIA *Bombay, Saturday, December 18, 1993*

Ban On Forward Deals

The decision by brokers of the four major stock exchanges to boycott trading in protest against the ban on forward trading by the Securities and Exchange Board of India (SEBI) is plainly unjustified. The brokers have effectively held over 18 million investors, 128 foreign institutional investors and 15 mutual funds to ransom by refusing to trade. The SEBI is, quite rightly, attempting to prevent a recurrence of the 1992 speculative bubble which led to the securities scam. But the brokers have learnt no lessons and have chosen to paint the SEBI's action as hasty, arbitrary and one that curbs the operation of free markets. These charges, which are being given wide credence, are misleading. The SEBI first warned stock exchange authorities in early August that it would consider banning forward trading if speculation was not controlled. The warnings have been repeated several times but the exchange authorities have been unable to exercise effective control. The fact that excessive speculation is responsible for the soaring index is clear from the fact that only 93 out of over 2,500 companies listed on the Bombay Stock Exchange are in the forward section. Even here speculation is concentrated around the 30 shares which form the BSE sensitive index, with seven shares responsible for 60 per cent of the capitalisation of index scrips.

Moreover, the SEBI ban does not prevent trading. It only requires buyers and seller to make their payment and delivery within a fortnight and stops speculators from selling shares they do not possess and postponing payment for shares they cannot afford. Investors and brokers only complain when brakes are applied under bullish conditions. There are no protests when restrictions are imposed and revised every other day to arrest a fall in prices. It should also be remembered that such decisions always draw protests from vested interests, and the broking community has yet to accept a single regulatory measure proposed by the SEBI. The wide support to the campaign against the SEBI is also explained by simple human psychology; nobody wants his increasing paper profits to be curbed by sensible regulation. The SEBI not only needs to be supported in its battle with the brokers, but it should be allowed to find a way to prevent brokers from boycotting trading in future if the Indian stock exchanges hope to find a respectable place on international capital markets.

(4 of 13)

INDIAN EXPRESS *Bombay, Thursday, December 16, 1993*

$250m ADB loan led to *badla* ban

By V. Shankar Aiyar & Raghu Nandan Dhar

Has the century-old *badla* system which oiled the stock markets across the country been sacrificed at the altar of conditionalities imposed by the Asian Development Bank (ADB) for a $ 250 million loan sought by the Government of India for the development of the capital markets? ...

... However, Securities and Exchange Board of India (SEBI) chief G.V. Ramakrishna -- now at the centre of a major imbroglio -- clarified that the step to ban *badla* and the directive calling for compulsory squaring up of positions is "a decision of the board and is not influenced by the Government. What I can say is that the Ministry has been kept informed of the moves." ...

... Incidentally, the ADB loan for capital market development has specified among its conditions:

- Setting up and operationalising the National Stock Exchange (which incidentally is happening by the beginning of 1994); ...
- ... Strengthening the regulatory mechanism in the Indian capital market by giving more teeth to SEBI (... the watch dog agency).

Although the conditionalities do not directly specify the banning of *badla* as one of the points, the clause on modernisation of the stock exchanges is being interpreted by members of the financial sector as being a clear indication of change required. It is an accepted fact that the *badla* system is inherently flawed and vulnerable to misuse as also being capable to misrepresenting real market trends.

What is perplexing even the proponents of the "decision based on conditionality theory" is why there has been no move to initiate and introduce the futures and options market before embarking on the drastic course of action. It is their belief that the introduction of futures and options market is a foregone conclusion now and could happen any time in 1994... sooner than later. ...

(5 of 13)

DATELINE BUSINESS CORPORATE WATCH *December 16-22, 1993*

RAMAKRISHNA DEFIANT ON TRADING BAN

Brokers say their positions were not large enough to justify the step

Dheer Kothari

... The SEBI Chairman, Mr. G.V. Ramakrishna, told Dateline Business, the ban was justified as brokers had built up excessive speculative positions and this was precisely the reason why they have called off trading. ...

... In fact, the authorities had struck a note of caution by moving ten volatile scrips in Bombay to the cash section. Besides, compulsory reduction of outstanding positions to the extent of 25 per cent had forced bulls to lighten their commitments. ...

... Denying that the ban was imposed without adequate notice, Mr. Ramakrishna remarked that he had discussed the ban with the stock exchange authorities twice since November as the market was getting overheated. ...

... Mr. A.N. Kolhatkar, executive director, Bombay Stock Exchange, replying to Mr. Ramakrishna's observation, said that the BSE had taken precautionary steps and had immediately shifted ten highly volatile scrips to the cash section and had also directed members to reduce their outstanding commitments by 25 per cent in the first week of December. But SEBI probably felt that these measures were not enough. ...

(6 of 13)

THE ECONOMIC TIMES *Bombay, Thursday, December 23, 1993*

No talks till erring brokers are punished, says SEBI chief

Sanjeev Sharma

New Delhi, 22 December.

The SEBI chairman, Mr. G.V. Ramakrishna has categorically said that SEBI will consider the brokers' point of view only after they return to the trading ring and action is taken against those who did not reduce their outstanding positions as directed by the stock exchanges.

Contd. ...

...*Contd*...

Mr. G.V. Ramakrishna said that the respective stock exchange governing boards will strictly monitor the action taken against errant brokers in this regard. He added that though DSE has issued show cause notices to errant brokers, BSE and CSE are yet to take any action against them. He said that CSE does not even have information on these brokers.

Mr. Ramakrishna, while outlying his main priorities said that establishing the depository system, increasing the transparency of the stock exchanges and introduction of futures and options trading were the main items.

(7 of 13)

THE TIMES OF INDIA *New Delhi, Thursday, December 23, 1993*

43 BSE brokers account for outstandings

By Sucheta Dalal

Bombay, December 22.

The figures presented by the Bombay Stock Exchange (BSE) to the Governing board today indicate that 43 brokers account for almost all the outstanding positions by 25 per cent with impunity but in fact except for seven brokers the rest have increased their positions.

The figures confirm the SEBI charge that stock exchanges have consistently failed to monitor and ensure compliance with their own restriction and regulations. ...

... The figures confirm the position of Mr. Manu Manek as the king pin of the market, who operating through the firm of M/s. M.M. Patel, has a whopping outstanding position of Rs. 39.58 crore. The broker has also doubled his position between the 18 and 19 settlement instead of reducing it even by a fraction. ...

... According to brokers, this only indicates that the broker was completely confident of being left untouched. As against this, the next highest defaulter has been the broker U.M. Kamdar who has nearly trebled position from Rs. 2.74 crore to Rs. 6.37 crore with a default figure of Rs. 4.32 crore.

Another example is of the broker Chandu Chunilal who had virtually quadrupled his position between the two settlements from just Rs. 29.02 lakhs to Rs. 106.11 lakhs. ...

... It is now felt that if proper penal action had been taken after the last settlement, SEBI would not have resorted to drastic measures across the board action like banning forward trading.

Contd...

...*Contd.* ...

When asked about the strident anti-SEBI stand taken by the Brokers Forum, some brokers cynically charge that the Forum itself is controlled by the biggest rule breakers.

Interestingly, even as several brokers have begun to demand that those who have violated the BSE's rules should be strictly penalised immediately, the BSE executive director has taken the stand that he is not in favour of punishment but would rather give them a chance to comply with its rules.

The figures also raise questions about how little the general body of brokers knows about the big operators' business, say market sources. They feel that had the true positions been known when SEBI made its announcement, brokers would have demanded that the speculators be punished rather that boycotting trading.

While the trading boycott continues, at least four top brokers operating on behalf of foreign financial institutions have struck spot deals between FIIs and financial institutions. There include S.S. Kanti Ishwar, Enam Financial Services, Dalal and Borcha and Ajit De of Calcutta.

(8 of 13)

FINANCIAL EXPRESS *Bombay, Friday, January 07, 1994*

TONE OF SE CHIEF'S LETTER DEPLORED

SEBI warns brokers of penal action

From Our Delhi Bureau

January 6.

... The Board took serious note of the letter written by the presidents of the stock exchanges and 'disapproved of the tone of the letter'. It has stated that the points made in the earlier board letter 'were absolutely crucial and will have to be discussed before any resumption of forward trading is considered'. ...

... The Board pointed out that the bye-law of the stock exchanges required that no trades are carried forward beyond the period of 90 days and that this was a precondition set by the Government in 1983 when the stock exchanges were allowed the facility of carrying forward trades from one settlement to another.

SEBI, it may be pointed out, in its letter dated January 4, 1993 to presidents of the stock exchanges, stated that before SEBI can consider the resumption of *badla* trading and any representations that may be received from the stock exchanges, it would like to discuss with the

...*Contd.* ...

...Contd. ...

four stock exchanges, the matters which include that *badla* trading and cash trading in specified shares should be separated from the beginning with separate slips for cash and carry forward trades.

Cash and *badla* trades should be on seven day settlements and audit trail of all *badla* trades to be kept so that they are terminated within a maximum period of 90 days as required under bye-laws (Bye law 48 and 52A of BSE). Jobbers should be separately registered and they should keep separate *sauda* sheets and accounts for jobbing business and broking business.

Client transaction and clients' money should be segregated from brokers' money and transactions and reported as required under bye-laws and SEBI directives. ...

(9 of 13)

ECONOMIC TIMES *Bombay, Thursday, January 06, 1994*

SE chiefs decline to meet SEBI deadline to prune outstandings

Our Bombay Bureau

Bombay, 5 January.

... In a strongly worded letter to SEBI today, the stock exchange chiefs of Bombay, Calcutta, Delhi and Ahmedabad have tried to wriggle out by claiming that they need a clear mandate of their broker members before they can negotiate on the issue which is of vital importance to the functioning of the markets. ...

... The SE chiefs claimed that SEBI's January 4 letter had threatened this process of dialogue. What is more, discussion of the present crisis has been made conditional upon prior discussion of more fundamental issues like separation of *badla* and delivery transactions *ab-initio,* shortening of trade cycle and permanent separation of jobbers and brokers, the letter noted. ...

(10 of 13)

INDIAN EXPRESS *New Delhi, Thursday, December 23, 1993*

Mirdha calls for drastic action against SEs

ENS Economic Bureau

New Delhi.

Ram Niwas Mirdha, who chaired the Joint Parliamentary Committee (JPC) on the securities scam, said here on Wednesday that drastic action must be taken to reform the stock exchanges of the country.

The exchanges continue to operate in an unhealthy manner "in spite of what we (JPC) have written (in the final report)", he said at the release of CPI MP and JPC member Gurudas Dasgupta's book on the securities scam.

"There is no desire in the stock exchange authorities to change. There is so much resistance to change that something drastic has to be done." he said. He said the supervisory system at all levels and in all systems had collapsed whether it was Ministry of Finance, the Reserve Bank, stock exchanges, public sector undertakings, nationalised banks or foreign banks.

"The most surprising feature is that all these institutions did not follow their own guidelines and rules. This was the cause of the entire scam," Mirdha said.

(11 of 13)

ECONOMIC TIMES *Bombay, Thursday, January 06, 1994*

SE chiefs decline to meet SEBI deadline to prune outstandings

Our Bombay Bureau

Bombay, 5 January.

Presidents of four major stock exchanges have sought to stall the decision of the Chief, Securities and Exchange Board of India (SEBI), Mr. G.V. Ramakrishna, on the ban on forward trading by politely declining to meet SEBI's January 10 deadline. ...

(12 of 13)

THE ECONOMIC TIMES *Monday, April 30, 2001*

Liquidating *Badla*

... The proposed ban on carry forward products from July 2, the day rolling settlement is to be introduced in all specified stocks, will achieve the much needed separation between cash and futures-type of transactions. Almost a decade ago, the first Chairman of SEBI, G.V. Ramakrishna, had realised that the basic malaise in Indian markets and had banned *badla*. Unfortunately, the powerful broking lobby not only saw to it that Ramakrishna was shifted out of SEBI but also ensured that the system was re-introduced in a revised form later. Since then, there has been much debate over the *badla* system and its recent *avatars* ALBM and BLESS. But invariably, the 'liquidity' argument would be used to stymie any forward looking proposal. It is time to call this bluff.

The much talked about volume in our bourses derives from excessive speculation. A good measure of the level of speculative trading is the volume-to-market capitalisation ratio; in our case this is three times the US ratio. It's not going to hurt much if we trade a bit of that speculative volume for an orderly market. ...

... For years, the carry forward mechanism has been used for excessive speculation and manipulation to the detriment of genuine investors. It is time to make bold and take steps to develop cash and futures markets separately. It's a new world – with automated systems and alternatives like futures markets for those who wish to take positions – and there is no need to hang on to relics like *badla*. ...

(13 of 13)

THE ECONOMIC TIMES *Tuesday, May 15, 2001*

SEBI bans *badla*

... According to Mr. Mehta, while the cash market will be relatively easier through the T+5 rolling settlement system, those who want to play the speculative market can go to the derivatives segment for which the index futures and stock-specific options will be made available. ...

... The finance minister Yashwant Sinha had announced the need for reforms in the capital market and the J.R. Varma committee too had recommended the introduction of the derivatives products. Accordingly, the SEBI took its decision to replace the *badla* system with rolling settlements." ...

< Business Standard, 21.12.1993 >

(1 of 2)

BUSINESS STANDARD *New Delhi, Tuesday, December 21, 1993*

Finance Ministry backs SEBI

By Anil Padmanabhan & Jayanthi Iyengar

The finance ministry is backing the decision of the Securities and Exchange Board of India (SEBI) to temporarily suspend forward trading on the stock markets. Top finance ministry officials ruled out intervention, independent of SEBI, to solve the imbroglio which has sparked off a trading boycott by brokers on the major stock exchanges.

"We are working in tandem with SEBI. The ministry had made it clear to all the parties involved that it is necessary to go through SEBI", says a finance ministry official. ...

... The BSE executive director was told in no uncertain terms that the finance ministry would intervene, if at all, through the offices of SEBI. ...

... SEBI is now insisting that the exchanges should take action against errant brokers and resume trading. It will initiate talks with brokers only after these conditions have been met. ...

... It is reliably understood that the Unit Trust of India has threatened to cancel its orders if the brokers continue to stay away from the trading floors. ...

(2 of 2)

THE TIMES OF INDIA *New Delhi, Thursday, December 23, 1993*

Govt not to intervene in SEBI-brokers row

New Delhi, December 22 (UNI).

Trading in major stock exchange remained suspended for the seventh successive session today in protest against the ban on forward trading order issued by the Securities and Exchange Board of India (SEBI).

... SEBI took this decision in a bid to check the unabated rise in share prices since the beginning of December this year. ...

... Meanwhile, member brokers in different stock exchanges, who were planning to move the court against the SEBI's order, did not do so following popular view that SEBI was empowered to take the "harsh" decision under section 16 of the SEBI Act.

Meanwhile, a spokesman of the finance ministry made it clear that the ministry will not intervence in the SEBI-brokers tussle. ...

< M.G. Damani, Indian Express, 16.12.1993 >

INDIAN EXPRESS *Bombay, Thursday, December 16, 1993*

BAN ON FORWARD TRADING AND 'BADLA'

"Spiteful and without basis"

By M.G. Damani

The most tragic aspect of the current controversy is that SEBI which was formed for investor protection, development of the market and then regulation has left investor open to the wolves, strangulated the market and made regulation its prime motive. It is one of most unreasonable and uncompliable orders ever seen... and legal luminaries will bear me out that an uncompliable order is a bad order in itself.

Lastly, SEBI must realise that regulation should be in doses like poison. A little poison is good and curative. In excess it can only kill the system.

(The author is the chairman of the BSE Brokers Forum and an elected director of BSE's governing board.)

< M.R. Mayya, Business Standard, 05.02.1996 >

BUSINESS STANDARD *Monday, February 05, 1996*

'Carry Forward is an excellent system' (Extracts from an interview with MR Mayya)

You could call 'carry forward' a replacement of the earlier system, with checks and balances. It is an excellent system. It provides a hedging facility, it acts as a market stabiliser, it improves liquidity, it also provides for a stream of finance.

... With options, the payment of a market-determined premium reduces the effectiveness of hedging. With carry forward, you buy at the same price whether it is for delivery, jobbing or for carry forward, which makes it a better hedging medium. ...

(MR Mayya is the former executive director of the Bombay Stock Exchange and a member of the G.S. Patel Committee. The only ED to have served two terms on the BSE, he initiated the computerisation of the exchange. Mayya spoke to Urmik Chhaya on a wide range of market-related subjects.)

< News reports and editorials on leaving SEBI, Jan. 1994 >

(1 of 5)

TIMES OF INDIA *Friday, January 07, 1994*

Wrong Signal

The union government's decision to remove Mr. G.V. Ramakrishna from the chairmanship of the Securities and Exchange Board of India (SEBI) when it is engaged in a crucial battle with a recalcitrant community of brokers, sends a wrong signal to the financial markets. While the brokers understandably have been jubilant about the move it is the silent majority of investors who must feel let down, for SEBI, under Mr. Ramakrishna's leadership, had become a guardian of their interests. Apart from being an affront to the Joint Parliamentary Committee (JPC), which conferred a singular honour on Mr. Ramakrishna and the SEBI by supporting all their actions, the decision comes as a rebuff to a man who has become the symbol of a rule-based reform of the financial markets. If the Government has taken this decision for

Contd. ...

...*Contd.* ...

reasons which had nothing to do with SEBI's confrontation with the brokers, then it must clarify that while Mr. Ramakrishna has been given another position, the policies he had come to represent will stay. The JPC's endorsement of the SEBI's stand covered practically all regulatory moves, whether it was the ban on forward trading, inspection of brokers and stock exchanges, regulation of Unit Trust of India or the check on excessive speculation. These regulatory powers had been wrested by it from the finance ministry in tiny doses through close inspection and exposure of malpractices. In this respect, the scam helped the watchdog body to silence its critics for over a year and hastened the transfer of regulatory powers from Delhi to Bombay.

It needs no reiteration that the SEBI's tough moves to regulate every segment of the capital market met with fierce resistance. But this is true of every country which has sought to discipline its markets. The difference is that most of these countries have managed to overcome such opposition instead of giving in to vested interests. The latter include companies forced to make humiliating disclosures of price rigging and manipulation to investors; banks and promoters deprived of ill-gotten interest by blocking almost Rs. 1,600 crores of investors' funds collected through over-subscription and delayed allotments; merchant banks which were awarded penalty points for failing to display due diligence; and bankers, bureaucrats, politicians and government officials who were caught helping themselves to huge chunks of shares from the promoters' or employees' quotas. It is important that the Government emphasises the fact that a free market does not mean a free for all market.

(2 of 5)

DECCAN HERALD *Monday, January 03, 1994*

Wrong signals

The transfer of Mr. G.V. Ramakrishna, Chairman of the Securities and Exchange Board of India (SEBI) as member, Planning Commission, has come at an inappropriate time. Though the official view is that the decision is of a routine nature, and that the matter has been pending before the Government for over a month, there are grounds to believe that Mr. Ramakrishna has been "kicked upstairs" because his continuation as the SEBI chief could be embarrassing for the Government. It was only last August that the Government had extended his tenure by six months, which was to end in February. There has been no explanation as to why the Government decided to terminate his stay with SEBI just two months before he was due to lay down

Contd. ...

...*Contd.* ...

office. The timing of the Government's decision has given rise to speculation on two different counts. The first is Mr. Ramakrishna's role in the investigation by the Joint Parliamentary Committee (JPC) into the banking scam. The other is the strong stand he took in banning forward trading in the Bombay Stock Exchange last month as a measure to curb excessive speculation.

Mr. Ramakrishna is one of the very few economic administrators whose work has been appreciated by the JPC. It was, in fact, his letter to the Finance Ministry warning the stock exchanges months before the banking scam surfaced which proved to be an important piece of evidence in the JPC's indictment of the Ministry. The news of his transfer, within days of the JPC report being made public, is thus seen by some as an indication of the Government's displeasure of his role in the investigation. Moreover, the brazen manner in which some Bombay brokers have expressed their delight at the SEBI chief's impending departure makes it difficult not to believe that his role in trying to bring some order in the exchange has not been fully appreciated by the powers that be. Even if it is true, as the Government spokesmen have maintained, that this episode has had nothing to do with his transfer, one can be sure that the decision has emboldened those who believe that the stock exchange is a place where wealth is made by rigging the market.

(3 of 5)

BUSINESS STANDARD *Calcutta, January 06-12, 1994*

A pyrrhic victory

This could turn out to be a pyrrhic victory for the big time stock brokers who refused to see merit in the reforms being initiated by Mr. G.V. Ramakrishna, Chairman of the Securities & Exchange Board of India (SEBI). What, however, cannot be denied is that the stock exchanges as they are run now leave investors of all kinds at a disadvantage *vis-à-vis* the brokers. Since level playing field is the catchword of the present times, then what is wrong in asking the brokers to suitably amend the trading practices in phases so that the system becomes evenly balanced among all the participants in stock trading. May be, because the Indians in general are not at ease when old rules of the game are dispensed with fast. The brokers were never comfortable with Mr. Ramakrishna who was made the chief of the regulatory body on the specific understanding that the archaic rules and regulations would be dispensed with within a given time frame and the

Contd. ...

...Contd. ...

brokers used to taking too much liberty would be reined in. The brokers would not accept the fact that whatever Mr. Ramakrishna was doing had the unreserved support of the union finance ministry. After all, the reforms of the stock exchange form a part of the overall liberalisation of the Indian economy. The mistaken perception that many of the SEBI chief's actions did not have the sanction of the finance ministry led the brokers to seek relief in the corridors of power in Delhi. While they did draw a blank in that, they again and again restored to closing down the market, much to the discomfiture of investors. The Foreign Institutional Investors (FIIs) on whose buying the recent improvement in the sensex is to be largely attributed have in no uncertain terms expressed their unhappiness over the frequent closure of the market in India. Last month, the market went into comatose once again when the exchange authorities failed to ensure that all outstanding speculative positions were cut by 25 per cent and the SEBI imposed a temporary ban on *badla*. To put the record straight, Mr. Ramakrishna had forewarned the exchange authorities about the rapid build up of speculative positions and impressed on them the need for squaring up of portions of them. That the brokers did not heed his advice was perfectly in tune with their mindset. The brokers no doubt are happy that the Government is withdrawing Mr. Ramakrishna from SEBI a few months before his five-year term ends and putting him in a largely sinecure Planning Commission job. For whatever reasons, the relationship between the SEBI chief and the brokers has become so strained that the Government is right in bringing about a change at the top of the regulatory body. Perhaps it will be easier for the brokers to deal with the new incumbent. They will be, however, entirely wrong in believing that Mr. Ramakrishna alone authored the SEBI decisions. He himself has said that "the SEBI decisions are not Ramakrishna's decisions. They have been approved by the SEBI board. They also have the backing of the finance ministry. There will be continuity in policy and actions by SEBI". Whoever replaces him at SEBI will be given the same mandate to cleanse the stock exchange. Mr. S.S. Nadkarni who is tipped to become the next SEBI chairman wears a veil of suavity, but the brokers will come to grief if they think the can take liberties with him. He will be required to do the same things as Mr. Ramakrishna, but he will certainly go about the job in a different way. Everyone has his own style. Mr. Ramakrishna has done well to draw attention to how the Bombay Stock Exchange Board has allowed the bye-law to the effect that "no transactions shall be allowed to be carried forward for more than 90 days" to be violated with impunity. The observance of it would have spared the present impasse in the market. He also wonders how many brokers, as required by another BSE bye-law, "indicate in each transaction whether they are entering into it on their own account or on behalf of their clients." It will be interesting to watch how the new SEBI chief phases out *badla* system and introduces options and futures trading, as prevalent in the more developed stock markets.

(4 of 5)

THE ECONOMIC TIMES *Bombay, Thursday, December 23, 1993*

Well done SEBI

By A.K. Maheshwari

Pune, December 16.

Sirs: The steps taken by SEBI to stop the rampant speculation of the Bombay Stock Exchange are more prudent though not exactly in tune with market oriented processes.

While such a move would be condemnable in a mature market in the current context, SEBI has rightly argued that if the boom is really due to FII buying then there is no reason why the market will crush since there is no restriction on buying for delivery. ...

Obviously even mature markets don't mind using the rod once a while to discipline spoilt grown up children. Rightly, so, since otherwise the stockmarkets will really be considered a gambling den for rich people which is the last thing it really is.

(5 of 5)

BUSINESS WORLD *November 27-December 10, 1996*

The Real Story

The real story can now be told. Former Securities & Exchange Board of India (SEBI) chairman G.V. Ramakrishna is widely believed to have been shifted from his post by the Narasimha Rao Government because of his confrontation with powerful brokers in Mumbai over the *badla* issue. Actually, Ramakrishna was not moved out for this at all. He was shifted for his report to the Joint Parliamentary Committee (JPC) on the scam.

The JPC has asked Ramakrishna to file a report on the scam after hearing him depose before it in the capital. Ramakrishna flew back to Mumbai and instructed SEBI staff to work on the report. It would also mention Goldstar Steel & Alloys, of which Rao's son, P.V. Prabhakar Rao was Director.

Soon, pressure was mounted on Ramakrishna to dilute his report. Ramakrishna declined to do so and went ahead – and got his marching orders after the report was submitted. He might have been unceremoniously dumped, had it not been for Manmohan Singh. Singh interceded and Ramakrishna was moved to the Planning Commission as a member.

< Letter from Finance Minister >

सत्यमेव जयते

वित्त मंत्री
भारत
नई दिल्ली

FINANCE MINISTER
INDIA
NEW DELHI
January 7, 1993

Dear G.V.

I have received your letter of 7th January submitting your resignation as Chairman SEBI, consequent on your appointment as Member of the Planning Commission. I would like to take this opportunity to express to you my sincere appreciation for the tremendous work you have done in SEBI.

Under your stewardship, SEBI has grown in stature and has established itself as an institution with high credibility. Both the professionals in the field and also the general public view it as an effective body working for healthy development of the capital markets and serving the interests of investors. The regulatory framework that has been put in place in this short period is impressive by any standards. I have no doubt that as this framework is effectively implemented it will bring our capital markets rapidly up to the standards of transparency, fairness and efficient functioning. I would like to congratulate you, and through you all other members of SEBI, for the excellent work that has been done in this period.

I would also like to extend to you my warmest congratulations on your well deserved elevation as Member Planning Commission. I have no doubt that with your experience and wisdom you will make a vital contribution in the work of the commission which is especially challenging as we steer the economy through this difficult period. I look forward to continuing interaction with you in your new capacity.

With regards,

Yours Sincerely,

Manmohan Singh

(Manmohan Singh)

Shri G V Ramakrishna
Chairman
SEBI
Bombay

< The Economic Times 6.11.1995 >

THE ECONOMIC TIMES *Monday, November 06, 1995*

Time to recount Ramakrishna's legacy

Second Opinion Debashis Basu

... At this point it is worth recounting Ramakrishna's contribution to the stockmarket in just two years he had been the SEBI chairman. I am picking up only the issues that are relevant to the current imbroglio.

> Mr. Ramakrishna's successors in SEBI never displayed the initiatives and understanding to keep the exchanges and companies in line.

- Insisting on greater disclosure that led to Reliance twins (REPL and RPPL) admitting on the covers of their prospectuses that the quoted price was rigged up. This was far more damaging than a three-day suspension that BSE handed out. Ramakrishna handled it deftly — Ambanis privately made some noise but then quietly accepted the disclosure requirement. He did not need newspaper editorials exhorting him to stand up to the Ambanis.
- Exposed the BSE for the mess it is. His moves to register brokers brought the best out of M G Damani, known more for his lung power than any constructive or progressive ideas. Ramakrishna, labelled by the brokers as arbitrary and autocratic, caught BSE red-handed not implementing its own bye laws, not collecting margins on time and not being able to control price rigging. In short, Ramakrishna showed that BSE was generally a failure as a self-regulatory body. In the Reliance case, ironically, it is the BSE which comes across as capricious and vindictive. (One of the BSE board members wanted to suspend Reliance scrip for six months!)
- Pushing for the creation of National Stock Exchange, Reliance's key weapon in the slanging match and the nemesis of BSE. Teaming up with the late S S Nadkarni, Ramakrishna ensured that the NSE got off the ground quickly. This was after both the ministry of finance and SEBI were quite fed up with the stubborn resistance of BSE brokers to change. BSE refused to increase the number of brokers, bumbled along with computerisation and continued to jeer any of the progressive ideas coming from Ramakrishna, including the modified system of forward trading.

The BSE brokers are generally so clueless that they did not realise that in NSE, Ramakrishna has opened a new front which would soon be impossible to guard if they do not shape up quickly. BSE brokers should

Contd. ...

...Contd. ...

ask themselves what would Reliance have done if there was no NSE to migrate to? The Ambanis would have been burning with impotent rage and of course the sensible lot of BSE brokers would not have got an opportunity to see how vulnerable their exchange is. By digging in their heels, BSE brokers have allowed a better competition, NSE, to emerge.

Ramakrishna also fought hard to make the BSE administration more sensible. He pushed for a change in the composition of the Board and made sure there are more public representatives. Clearly, in virtually every area, touching the current fight between BSE and the Ambanis, Ramakrishna's legacy is obvious.

Unfortunately, he was removed when he was only half-done, especially with the stock exchanges. Despite the threat of NSE and maladministration of BSE, the message just never went in. Worse, Ramakrishna's successor never displayed the initiative and understanding to keep the exchanges and companies in line. After Ramakrishna's departure, total inaction from SEBI and BSE allowed prominent brokers like Bharat Seth to continue to dodge serious investor complaints. Right now, when the market is down, price rigging in BSE is rampant which the exchange and SEBI are watching almost helplessly.

The BSE brokers were gleeful when Ramakrishna was removed. Will they (excluding M.G. Damani) now think back coolly and recount what he would have done for them to save for them from themselves?

< Financial Express, 2.4.2001 >

THE FINANCIAL EXPRESS *Monday, April 02, 2001*

IT'S ALSO A POLITICALLY UNDESIRABLE ENTITY
SO DON'T HOLD YOUR BREATH

A no-nonsense regulator is a good regulator

Sucheta Dalal

... It is important to recall that SEBI itself was modelled after the powerful Securities and Exchange Commission (SEC) of the US. Yet, within a couple of years its most powerful chairman G.V. Ramakrishna, was moved out because he was tough; being "market friendly" became an important qualification for SEBI's subsequent chairmen. It is also important to recall that Mr. Ramakrishna struck terror among market intermediaries without half the powers that SEBI enjoys today. SEBI is a good example of how automation and development alone cannot substitute supervision and punishment. ...

Contd. ...

...Contd. ...

... Supervision has to be swift, even handed and ruthless in order to send a deterrent message to market intermediaries and speculators. This was the quality which made SEBI so powerful under Ramakrishna; the market knew that he meant business and would find a way to punish wrong-doers irrespective of their financial muscle or financial clout. ...

... The message is clear. A regulatory or supervisory authority needs a person with the right attitude to head it. Today SEBI has a strange combination of a Chairman who is reluctant to regulate; and a deputy (J.R. Varma) who is openly against excessive regulation and supervision. In fact, Varma was the lone dissenter in SEBI's action against former BSE President Anand Rathi. ...

GLOSSARY OF STOCK MARKET TERMS

Backwardation/ ***Ulta Badla/ Undha Badla*** **:** The payment of money charges made by a seller of shares which he borrows to deliver against his sale. These charges become payable only when there are more sellers who are not in a position to deliver against their sale. These charges become payable to the buyer, when the seller is not in a position to deliver the documents to the buyers who demand delivery.

Badla **:** Carrying forward of transactions from one settlement period to another without effecting delivery. This is permitted only in specified securities and is done at the making-up prices which is, usually, the closing price of the last day of settlement.

Badla **Charges/Contango :** Consideration or interest paid to the seller by buyer for carrying over a transaction from one settlement period to another.

Broker : A member of a Stock Exchange who acts as an agent for clients and buys and sells shares on their behalf in the market. Though strictly, a stock broker is an agent, yet for the performance of his part of the contract both in the market and with the client, he is deemed as a principal, a peculiar position of dual responsibility.

Brokerage : Brokerage is the commission charged by the broker for purchase/sale transaction through him. The maximum brokerage chargeable, as stipulated by SEBI, is at present 2.5 per cent of the trade value.

Carry Forward Trading : Carry forward trading has evolved in response to local needs in India and it refers to the trading in which the settlement is postponed to the next account period on payment of contango charges (known as *vyaj badla*) in which the buyer pays interest on borrowed funds or the backwardation charges (known as *undha badla*) in which the short seller pays a charge for borrowing securities.

Closing Out : Where a party to a contract does not make delivery against sale or payment against delivery of documents, the other party can close out the transaction against the defaulting party, the gain or loss arising from the closing out being borne by the defaulter.

Delivery : Presentation of securities with transfer deeds in fulfilment of a transaction.

Depository : A system of organization which keeps records of securities deposited by its depositors. The records may be physical or simple electronic records.

Derivative Markets : Markets such as futures and option markets that are developed to satisfy specific needs arising in traditional markets. These markets provide the same basic functions as forward markets, but trading usually takes place on standardized contracts.

Escrow : A separate account set aside to be used to pay for the shares allotted to the account holder.

Forward : A commitment to buy (sell) an asset at a future date for a price determined at the time of commitment. May be applied to currencies, equities, commodities or other assets.

Forward Trading : Forward trading refers to trading where contracts traded today are settled at some future date at prices decided today.

Future Contract : An exchange-traded contract generally calling for delivery for a specified amount of a particular grade of commodity or financial instrument at a fixed date in the future.

Hedge : To reduce risk by taking a position which offsets existing or anticipated exposure to a change in market rates or prices.

Hot Money : Short term international capital movements, motivated by interest rate differential or revaluation hopes/devaluation fears.

Insider Trading : Trading in a company's shares by a connected person having non-public, price sensitive information, such as expansion plans, financial results, takeover bids, etc., by virtue of his association with that Company, is called insider trading.

Lead Managers : The member of an underwriting syndicate charged with the primary responsibility of managing the affairs of the syndicate and the proposed issue of the security.

Margin : In this report, margin refers to a good-faith deposit (of money, securities or financial instruments) required by a futures or commodity exchange to assure performance. Futures and options exchanges often require traders to post initial margin when they enter into new contracts. Margin accounts are debited or credited to reflect changes in the current market prices on the position held. Members must replenish the margin account if margin falls below a minimum. The system of margin payment for stock exchange transactions in large company shares has been announced by SEBI recently.

Market Price : The last reported sale price for an exchange traded security. For over the counter securities, (OTC) represents the consensus among market makers.

Odd Lot : A number of shares that are less than the market lot are know as odd lots. These shares are illiquid in nature, as they cannot be transacted on the Exchange.

Off-balance-sheet Activities : Banks' business that does not generally involve booking assets or liabilities. Examples include trading in swaps, options, futures and foreign exchange forwards and the granting of standby commitments and letter of credit.

Option : The contractual right but not the obligation to buy or sell a specified amount of given financial instrument at a fixed price before or at a designated future date. A call option confers on the option buyer the right to buy the security. A put option involves the right to sell the security.

Price Rigging : When persons acting in concert with each other collude to artificially increase or decrease the prices of a security, the process is called price rigging.

Prospectus : Document containing an invitation to invest. The document explains the workings of the company, provides financial details of the project and also contains the application form for investment.

Rights Issue/Rights Shares : The issue of new securities to existing shareholders, in a fixed ratio to those already held at a price which is generally below the market price of the old shares.

Selling Short : Manoeuver in which an investor sells securities he does not posses in the hope of buying them later at a lower price for delivery.

Settlement : The completion of a transaction, wherein the seller transfers securities or financial instruments to the buyer and the buyer transfers money to the seller.

Speculation : Employment of funds by a person to assume a relatively larger risk in hope of a gain.

Spot Delivery : Delivery and payment on the same day of the contract or the day following the day of the contract.

Stock Holding Corporation of India : Set up in October 1988, it provides post trade services including safe custody in respect of securities dealt with on the Stock Exchange for client organizations.

Trust Deed : Detailed legal document which sets out in precise legal terms the rules under which a trust works, for operating Mutual Funds. It explains its aim, the fees and charges that are created, plus the responsibilities of the Manager and the Trustee.

Trustee : A person who holds the property of the Mutual Fund in trust for the benefit of the investors.

Underwriting : An individual or institution guaranteeing subscription in part, or in full, of a security issue made to the public to make up the shortfall in subscription for a fee known as Underwriting Commission.

Unit : When someone invests in a mutual fund scheme, he is issued units. Units can be held in close-ended or open-ended schemes. Close-ended schemes have a specific closing date when the investor get back the value of his investment at the prevailing price (net assets value). In an open-ended scheme, the investor can sell his units at any time at the prevailing price. In both schemes, the unit holder will get periodic dividends out of the surpluses of the scheme.

(In India Units refers to Units issued by the Unit Trust of India.)

Unit Trust : Fund where money subscribed by many people is pooled and then used to purchase a variety of investments. All investments are held in the name of the trustee, but investment decisions are made by the fund manager. All the various rights and duties of the trust holders are set out in the trust deed.

Writer : The party that sells an option. The writer is required to carry out the terms of the option at the choice of the holder.

Dr. C. Subramanian presenting the Investor Mitra Award to the author, Chennai, 1993

With Montek Ahluwalia, New Delhi, 1993

With members of Bangalore Stock Exchange, Bangalore, 1993

With George Soros,
Purnendu Chatterjee,
and Shanker,
New York, 1992

With Shri Dharam Vira
and Prof. Y.K. Alagh,
New Delhi, 1995

Dr. Manmohan Singh
at the opening of the
Southern Regional O
of SEBI, Chennai, 19

12

The Planning Commission

IN the Planning Commission, I was given the subjects of energy (power, coal, petroleum), and transport (railways, roads, air, sea ports and shipping). This was the core of the infrastructure. I was already familiar with the energy sector, having been Secretary Coal and Secretary Petroleum.

It did not take me long to get into controversy once again. As the country was going through acute power scarcity, the Government decided to frame a new policy for attracting foreign interest in power generation. The new power policy had been enunciated in 1992 and was under implementation in the Centre and the States. Under the new policy, the main aim was to get Indian and foreign parties to invest in power projects by offering several incentives. The Government sent out a team of senior officers to the US in 1992 to explore the possibility of inducing private power producers to come to India. The policy consisted of giving the investor an actual 30 per cent return on the investment not heard of anywhere in the world. The fuel would be that of the investor's choice. Most of them chose petroleum, natural gas and coal.

The policy stated that the 16 per cent return would be for 68.5 per cent Plant Load Factor (PLF) and would go up by 0.7 per cent for every 1 per cent increase in PLF. The normal Plant Load Factor for a gas-based generator was normally 90 per cent. Plant Load Factor means the actual number of hours of generation out of the total available time. So, for a power plant operating on gas with 90 per cent PLF, the rate of return would be over 30 per cent on investment. Since the power had to be sold to the State Electricity Boards for distribution and as the State Electricity Boards (SEBs) were in dire financial straits the foreign investors asked for a State Government guarantee backed by a Central Government counter guarantee. An association of Independent Power Producers of India (IPPI) was formed. At one of their meetings, inaugurated by the Power Minister and the Prime Minister, statements were made by Government representatives that any power was better than no power and we wanted power at any cost! This was an open invitation for gold plating the costs and getting very high returns unheard of elsewhere in the world. A number of foreign and Indian, Independent Power Producers (IPP) came to India hoping to make a quick buck.

The States were encouraged to enter into MoUs (Memoranda of Understanding) with the foreign power producers on the above terms. As the Central Government had laid down a deadline of 28th February 1995, state governments worked overtime with all kinds of private parties till late at night to register half-baked MoUs before the deadline. Within a year or so, from 1994 to 1995, 245 Independent Power Producers (IPPs) had entered into MoUs, hoping to get the benefits that Enron had got. None of them resulted in any power. In 1995 there was a change in policy and competitive bidding route was mandated. 51 projects were registered, but none of them were taken up seriously. Only four of the earlier projects in the private sector materialized, namely, BSES (500 MW) Hazira (515 MW), Trombay (180 MW) and Jegurupadu in A.P. (158 MW).

On the whole the private sector power policy was a failure. The public sector, NTPC and BHEL, saved the situation to some extent, by stepping in where the private sector did not come forward owing to the failure of the policy. The Eighth Plan target for additional power generation capacity was achieved to the extent of only 52 per cent.

I pointed out in several notes and in speeches that the policy was deeply flawed, one sided and would result in high cost power and was not sustainable.[1] A few years before the Indian officials visited the US in 1992, the energy department of the US had brought out a paper prepared by the Livermore Laboratory which pointed out that the utilities in the US were buying power on the basis of competitive bids as this was the most economical way of pricing power. The Indian authorities ignored this. The World Bank, which had agreed in principle to provide $ 2 billion for the power sector, said that the policy of non-transparent and non competitive pricing of the Government of India was not acceptable and refused to have anything to do with financing the power sector. I drew attention to all the global evidence and practices and suggested a review of

1. Criticism of Power Policy – Extracts/cuttings from four news reports < Appended on page 236 >.

the policy. I said that power should be purchased on the basis of competitive bids for power rates and not on the basis of guaranteed rates of return on inflated investment costs.[2] There should be arrangements by which the power producers could sell power directly to the main consumers on the basis of their bank guarantees, This raised hackles all round, particularly in the Power Ministry. When one of my speeches[3] appeared in a major newspaper the matter was brought to the notice of the P.M. that a member of the Planning Commission was openly criticising Government policy and he should be spoken to. I met the Deputy Chairman of the Planning Commission and explained that my numerous notes on the subject (sent through the deputy chairman) had not reached the P.M. and hence I thought the P.M. would know my views at least through the Press!

Enron started in 1985 as a natural gas transport company located in Houston, Texas. Enron officials in India led by Rebecca Mark, developed close connections with high level personalities which was to prove helpful in developing their business in India. Enron US made generous contributions to Presidential campaigns of both Sr. and Jr. Bush. When the three-member Indian official team landed in Houston in 1992 the first persons to meet them were the Enron representatives. They knew that India was keen to add a new power capacity as quickly as possible and offered full cooperation and arrived in India a few days after the Indian team returned. They established close connections with the

---

2. Competitive bidding for power purchase – three news reports < Appended on page 240 >.
3. Government Guarantees, Economic Times 25.8.94 < Appended on page 241 >.

political big wigs in Delhi and Bombay. It is believed that they even had a hand in framing a power policy advantageous to themselves.

Enron had a record of false starts in setting up power projects in Egypt and the Philippines, with their political connections in the US ensuring that they got aggressive diplomatic support. When they came to India, Enron had set up a total worldwide generation capacity of 3,000 Mega Watts. They teamed up with large equipment manufacturers like G.E. They had the strong support of Frank G. Wisner the US Ambassador who had earlier tried to help them in Egypt and the Philippines. After Enron left India, he joined their Board in the US.

The terms they were able to negotiate with the Indian authorities were not heard of anywhere. In fact, at the same time, Price Waterhouse had prepared a professional bidding document for the Electricity Generation Authority of Thailand (EGAT) which was based on competitive bidding for power rates. I procured a copy and sent it to the Ministry of Power. The Asian Development Bank had also assisted the Bangladesh Government with a loan for power generation based on international competitive bidding. All this was not recognized in India even after the World Bank refused to lend $ 2 billion because of the opaque procurement procedures. The Maharashtra State Electricity Board (MSEB) was one of the better Boards in the country. Enron entered into an agreement with them for setting up a power generating capacity of about 2100 MW in two phases. They got a State Government guarantee and also sought a Central Government guarantee. Most of the financing of rupee costs would come from Indian sources. The equipment would be procured by Enron at prices of their choice. Other contracts would also be given to parties of Enron's choice at prices determined by them.

After the Power Purchase Agreement (PPA) was signed, there was a change in the Governments, both in Maharashtra and in Delhi. The new coalition Maharashtra Government in 1995, disowned the PPA and threatened to 'dump the agreement in the Arabian Sea'. There was a hue and cry in the Media, the US embassy and the Industry associations that this would discourage further foreign investments in India. They said that India would become a 'pariah' in the world of Investments. Indian business misread that situation totally and succumbed to the pressures of foreign companies and the Media, India and foreign. The Maharashtra Government did a *volte-face*. First they appointed a committee under Kirit Parekh to have a second look at the Agreement. This committee suggested that the damage could be minimized if the second stage of the project was also approved for a further capacity of 1400 MW in addition to the first phase of about 740 MW. The Maharashtra Government forgot all about 'the Arabian Sea' and approved the full project and sought the guarantee of the Centre. There was a change of Government at the Centre in 1996, with a coalition broadly in line with that at the State. The coalition Government at the Centre agreed to give a partial counter guarantee for $1 billion to get the project going, a few days before it fell. The Dabhol Power Company (DPC) raised exhorbitant power bills on the State Electricity Board, between Rs. 5 and Rs. 7 per unit which the Electricity Board could not afford to pay. The matter then went to the State Electricity Regulatory Commission, which stayed the collection. The Indian financial institutions who had lent large amounts to DPC, got into the act to protect their interests. A flurry of cases and counter cases in the High Court, and arbitration proceedings in London further complicated the matter.

Several committees were set up to examine the contract and its impact on MSEB and the country. The latest was the Energy Review Committee headed by Godbole, set up by the Government of Maharashtra in 2001. This committee had other experts like E.A.S. Sarma, and Deepak Parikh. It went into the Enron power purchase agreement in detail and came out with some startling facts to show how one sided the whole arrangement was. It pointed out that the excessive payment terms would enable Enron to claim unjustly from MSEB, additional amounts under various heads amounting to Rs. 930 crores per year. The committee commented as follows:

> With respect to DPC (Dabhol Power company). The committee is concerned with numerous infirmities in the process of approvals granted in the project, which bring into question the propriety of the decisions. Arguments advanced to support these decisions appear unconvincing, and *prima facie* against public interest. The committee is troubled with the failure of governance that seems to have characterized almost every step of the decision.[4]

This confirmed the points, I had made, and brought out independently by the 'The Hindu Business Line' on March 21, 1995 about 'the extortionate Enron deal'.[5]

---

4. Energy Review Committee Govt. of Maharashtra, p 82 of Report.
5. Hindu Business Line, 21.3.95 < Appended on page 242 >.

When the Enron project came up for Government guarantee, I said that it should not be given. The F.M. agreed with me but later had to yield to political pressures.[6]

At a meeting of the deputy chairman with the minister of power, I was called in. I had to tell the minister that the power policy had a number of flaws and would not produce any power during the entire plan period. The minister was furious and said if the gas price was fixed he would guarantee investment of Rs. 50,000 crores! Subsequent events led by the Enron debacle, proved that the whole policy was misconceived and counter productive. The only additions to power during the Plan came from the public sector undertaking National Thermal Power Corporation (NTPC).

Persons in charge of negotiating the Enron contract did not take note of the history of the influential company, with its headquarters in Houston and high-level political connections. They did not realize that the company had earlier managed to use US diplomatic influence in the Philippines and in Egypt, and now in India, to get large contracts that were heavily loaded in its favour. Those contracts, as in India, failed and the company had to leave those countries. The recent exposures in the US about the company's wrong doings, leading to its bankruptcy and prosecution of its senior executives, only substantiate what was suspected for some years in the power circles.

The first phase of the project has been completed but disputes abound between the DPC and MSEB. This is the consequence of an *ab initio* questionable deal entered into

---

6. Counter Guarantee, The Times of India, 1.6.95 < Appended on page 244 >.

by the State and Central Governments against advice from several quarters. No one has been held accountable. No wonder, scams of various types continue to occur.

Coal for Power

India has over 90 billion tonnes of coal reserves, the world's second largest reserves, next to China. I had been taking the view for sometime, that in the long-term interest of the country we should exploit our large resources of coal for generation of power.[7] In many developed countries like UK and Australia, new technologies had been developed for coal mining, coal washing and power generation by using clean coal technologies, which protected the environment. This would reduce the dependence on imported fuels, petroleum and natural gas. The Coalmine Nationalization Act needed amendments and there was little enthusiasm for doing this. Later a partial amendment was made to enable power generation companies to undertake coal mining for captive use. Nothing much happened about this proposal, as power-generating companies were not interested in investing in coal mining.

An important development was the setting up of a High level Committee under Shri Chari, an eminent expert on coal, who had been Secretary in the Ministry of Coal. This committee made comprehensive recommendations for liberalizing the coal mining and pricing policy by throwing it open to the private sector. In 1995 an attempt was made to amend the Coal Mines Act to allow private sector, but

7. Coal News Reports – The Economic Times, Business Standard, Indian Express < Appended on page 245 >.

at the drafting stage, changes were made to provide for private mining only to those companies that were setting up power stations.

The Oman Gas Pipeline

The proposal to import gas from Iran through a land pipeline had fallen through, because Pakistan did not permit the German consultant Pipe Line Engineering (PLE) to survey the route in its offshore area, for the Iran - India pipeline route. The pipeline was to go through Sir Creek, a disputed part of the Pakistani offshore area. India was also unwilling to take the risk of taking the pipeline on land through Pakistan. An alternate proposal was mooted to transport Iranian gas offshore to Qatar and from there to India through a deep-water pipeline. At this stage, Oman stepped in and said that it could also supply gas to India by means of a sub-sea pipeline.

In January 1994, a proposal was mooted by the Ministry of Petroleum to import natural gas from Oman by means of a high pressure 1400 km pipeline, 3-4 km under the sea carrying 59 million cubic metres of gas per day for 25 years. The proposal envisaged two pipelines, each carrying 28 million cubic meters of gas, one of them to feed the Southern Gas Grid, as there was a demand from the Southern states that they should have a share of the HBJ gas which was not feasible.

Many people believed that the real reason for the interest in the project was the impending elections in 1996 and the effect of such a big investment on the electorate in the Southern States. Capt. Satish Sharma, the Petroleum Minister, with the support of the Prime Minister, evinced interest in the proposal, which was pushed through with some diligence. In an unusual arrangement, John Deuss, an enterprising but controversial oil expert headed the Oman Gas Company. The project feasibility was in doubt. I raised several objections [8] before the Planning Commission about its technical and financial feasibility. Although the Ministry of Petroleum could not give satisfactory replies to my objections, they obtained the approval of Pranab Mukherjee, the Deputy Chairman. Officials hastened to give technical approval. In July 1994, a technical team led by Uddesh Kohli, Energy Adviser in the Planning Commission, went to Oman to work out the pricing formula. The Prime Minister, P.V. Narasimha Rao later went to Oman to witness the signing of the MoU. The stakes were huge with the contract providing for the import of gas worth $ 59 billion for supply over 25 years. The new Petroleum Secretary, Vijay Kelkar, who had earlier worked with me in the Ministry, had misgivings about the financial implications. The Petroleum Secretary questioned the pricing formula. Some international experts also questioned the technical feasibility of the project. International oil companies, like Shell, with gas interests in the region, raised questions about the availability of gas reserves in Oman. Huge investments of over $ 50 billion were proposed for this project, which involved a long-term commitment to buy the gas from Oman. The project was the first of its kind in the world. The users of the gas had not been tied up. Huge investments of over Rs. 50,000 crores would be required for power projects that could use the gas and this was nowhere

8. Oman Gas – Telegraph 16.3.96; Indian Express, 25.7.94; Telegraph 25.8.95 < Appended on page 246 >.

in sight. If domestic buyers got other options at lower prices they would not take the gas. The project also meant that we should produce less from our own Bassein gas field. I raised all these questions about the technical and financial viability of the project. In August 1995, a high level team consisting of the Petroleum Secretary, the former Chairman of the Atomic Energy Commission, Dr. P.K.S. Iyengar and senior officials of the GAIL (Gas Authority of India Ltd) was sent to the US to discuss the matter with the Oman Gas Company, and the project was put on hold. The experts expressed doubts about the feasibility of moving gas in a pipeline at a depth of 3.5 kilometers under the sea over 1400 kilometers distance. The matter came up in Parliament and the Petroleum Minister strongly defended the proposal. Eventually, after the elections, the project was given up in March 1996. A major mistake, as in the case of Enron, which could have caused the loss of several thousand crores to the Government had been averted.

According to recent reports, the Indo-Iran off shore pipeline project has come up again. Iran seems to be keen on selling Liquefied Natural Gas (LNG), but the Government is pursuing the idea of the offshore pipeline. While the investment in the LNG supplies would be that of the Iranians, the offshore pipeline will mean large contracts financed by India, at least in part. The questions raised in 1994, by the technical committee for the Indo-Oman pipeline, would be relevant even now.

Developed Oil Fields

The Ministry of Petroleum had decided to hand over some oil fields of ONGC to private parties without proper recovery of the costs of exploration and development which had already been incurred by the public sector company. I raised this point and the Planning Commission wrote to the Ministry but no satisfactory reply was given. The matter later figured in a Report of the Comptroller and Auditor General (CAG) but nothing much came of it.

When I looked into the Railways plan for 1995-96, I found that there were a number of projects that were uneconomical but were pushed through for political reasons such as the Bolangir line in Orissa. There were a number of unfinished projects, which, because of delays, faced escalation in costs. Even the Railway officials were not happy with the proposals they sent for the approval of the Planning Commission. The result was that not enough money was available for safety and revenue earning projects.

Sugar Enquiry

An interesting episode occurred in 1995. I was sitting in the Planning Commission when there was a phone call from the Cabinet Secretary to say that I would be called soon by the Deputy Chairman to discuss an important matter. Soon enough, I got the call when the Deputy Chairman was sitting in the Commerce Ministry, as he was in additional charge of the post of Commerce Minister. He spoke to me directly and asked me if I could meet him urgently.

I went to the Commerce Ministry and was warmly received. He ordered tea and broached the subject. For sometime the Press had carried stories about the 'sugar scandal' and there was a discussion in Parliament. The import of sugar had been regulated for sometime. When there was shortage, imports were being considered. At first, private parties were permitted and they placed orders at the prevailing price in the international market. The State Trading Corporation (STC) had also sought the permission of the Commerce Ministry to buy in the market. The Ministry delayed permission and in the meanwhile prices went up. When, after about 10 days, orders were given to STC, it entered the market and had to pay prices that were higher than those contracted for by the private parties. STC had to buy from the private parties who had contracted earlier at lower prices. Later when STC had to sell in the domestic market, prices had to be subsided. After the Opposition parties raised this matter and alleged wrongdoing leading to loss to Government, it was agreed to institute an enquiry.

The Deputy Chairman said that after discussion with Opposition parties it had been suggested that I should conduct the enquiry. He asked me if I could take it up. I asked whether the Government would accept a fair and impartial enquiry. He looked up at the ceiling and started laughing, but gave no reply. He quickly wound up the meeting and said I would be told later. I heard nothing more about the matter. A few days later, I had the occasion to mention the matter to the finance minister, Manmohan Singh and he confirmed that at the political level a decision had in fact been taken to entrust the enquiry to me. In the event, a retired Comptroller and Auditor General, held the enquiry and the report was placed before Parliament. I was actually quite relieved that I had eventually, not been asked to conduct the enquiry. When they had asked me to conduct the enquiry, the Government had perhaps overlooked my earlier investigations in SEBI conducted at the instance of JPC!

My tenure in the Planning Commission was marked by the formation of the Construction Industry Development Council (CIDC). I have further elaborated upon this in Chapter 14.

When the Government changed in 1996, the members of the Planning Commission resigned in accordance with convention.

APPENDED REFERENCES

< Criticism of Power Policy - Extracts/cuttings from four news reports >

(1 of 4)

THE ECONOMIC TIMES *Thursday, December 28, 1995*

PPAs that could mean a fortune

Following are the main features of the power purchase agreements (PPAs) signed by the Government of Madhya Pradesh:

Incentives

• For achieving a PLF above 68.49 per cent private companies setting up power projects have been allowed a maximum incentive of 0.7 per cent on equity.

Forex protection

• If the generating company brings equity in the form of foreign currency, it has an option of getting a maximum return at the rate of 16 per cent in the foreign currency itself.

Insurance

• The PPA with Essar provides that in case of breakdown at the plant after it has completed 12 years of commercial production, the insurance amount would be divided equally between the company and the MPEB after payment to debtors.

Accidents and calamities

• In case of an accident due to any natural calamity, MPEB will not pay any amount to the company.

Capacity and capital costs

• In the Essar pact, company had to demonstrate its installed capacity through a dependable capacity test for each unit after the commencement of commercial production. If the actual capacity is less than estimated, the capital cost would be slashed proportionately.

In the agreement with Daewoo, it has been decided that if the dependable capacity is lower than the installed capacity, then the payments would also be reduced.

Tariff depreciation

• Whatever interest accrues on the depreciation amount, would be deducted from the rate of electricity. Such a condition has not been mentioned in any other PPA.

Rate of electricity

• No PPA has been signed on the basis of the project cost, or the rate of electricity.

Contd. ...

...Contd. ...

Penalty for delays

• In the agreement with Daewoo, if the commercial operation does not start within the agreed period, the company will pay penalty at the rate of US$ 15,000 per day. However, this amount cannot be more than $3 million.

(2 of 4)

THE HINDU BUSINESS LINE *Thursday, November 17, 1994*

Powerful sell out

The Detailed Guidelines announced by the Centre to its counter guarantees for the half a dozen fast track private power projects confirms – if confirmation was needed – the apprehensions of the opponents of the Government's private power development policy. The guidelines are nothing short of a complete give-away to the foreign power majors despite the Centre's protests and assurances to the contrary. In its public posturings earlier, the Government, stung by criticisms that it was going overboard with incentives to lure foreign investor into the power sector, had tried to give the impression that counter guarantees would be temporary, and that adequate safeguards would be tucked in to prevent a rip off. A few months ago the Government had even initiated an exercise apparently to tighten norms. But the guidelines now announced by the Centre make nonsense of the assurances.

That should come as no surprise. The Centre, and particularly the Power Minister, Mr. N.K.P. Salve, had always maintained that the Government had no choice but to accept the terms of the international power majors to bridge the growing demand-supply gap in electricity. 'No power is costlier than no power', the minister is often fond of reminding his critics. But the fear is private power generation may be too costly for the country in the long run. No less a body than the World Bank had cautioned developing countries against providing counter guarantees in the power sector. Internationally acclaimed management experts and the Planning Commission had warned the Government that counter guarantees and absence of competitive bidding would stifle competition. But the Centre had no use for such unsolicited advice. ...

... If the electricity boards are in the red – many of them are chronically sick – political parties must take much of the blame. Political patronage, overstaffing and tariffs dictated by competitive politics have told on the health of the electricity boards. Unless state governments give up their 'divine right' over the working of the electricity boards, the problem will remain.

(3 of 4)

PIONEER *New Delhi, Wednesday, October 5, 1994*

GVR blasts policy on power sector

Special Correspondent

Planning Commission member G.V. Ramakrishna on Tuesday strongly advocated the cause of a "level playing field" for the Indian capital goods industry and said Government policy, particularly in the power sector, had effectively kept Indian firms from competing.

In an apparent reference to Finance Minister Manmohan Singh's comment at the Euromoney Conference last year that nowhere in the world is there anything like a level playing field, Mr. Ramakrishna said he totally agreed with this, but would like to add a footnote.

"All over the world, the tilt is in favour of domestic industry", he said and contrasted it to the situation at home where "we have been reduced to a situation where Indians are asking for equal treatment with foreigners." ...

.. .Mr. Ramakrishna said the Government could have laid down a simple policy for competitive bidding procedures. Observing that the Government argued that this was not possible because there were few takers initially and it had to take what was no offer, the Planning Commission Member added, "In the next sentence they say there are 75 people waiting in queue to set up power projects. If that is not a competitive situation. I would like to know what is"?

Competitive bidding, he said, would have provided equal opportunities to the Indian private and capital goods sector. Further, while the reforms initiated in 1991 were ostensibly aimed at greater transparency, market-orientation, efficiency and competition, was the power policy in consonance with these aims, he asked rhetorically. ...

... If Indian firms cannot compete in India, how can they do so abroad and conversely if they are competitive globally, how can they not be competitive domestically, Mr. Ramakrishna asked. ...

... Yet, he said, in India there was the reserve of "national treatment" with foreigners being treated better than domestic firms. "What Indian industry is demanding today is not protection but level playing field," he asserted.

(4 of 4)

FINANCIAL EXPRESS *Monday, November 13, 2000*

THE FOCUS SHOULD BE ON TAPPING DOMESTIC RESOURCES RATHER THAN IMPORTS

Formulating a viable energy policy

Policy makers in India have, over the years shown consistency in one particular aspect of policy making and implementation. They wake up only at the time of a crisis and hold seminars, make statements and everyone chips in with their advice. This happens when we have floods, during droughts and also during increase in oil prices. ...

... A viable energy policy should take note of some basic facts of the Indian situation. Some of these are: our own resource endowments of energy; the pattern of consumption; demand growth; elasticity of demand for different types of energy; domestic production; import dependence and the trends in the depreciation of the rupee. ...

... What should be the main features of such a policy?

First, there should be a clear statement that henceforth coal will be the main fuel for power generation. With about twice our reserves of coal, China produces three times or about a billion tonnes of coal per year. The usual arguments against the use of coal due to its impact on environment can be mitigated by carrying out mining in an environmentally friendly manner as has been demonstrated in countries which are more concerned than us for environmental protection.

Coal washeries can take care of ash content to a large extent. As large power stations based on pithead washed coal can save on transportation and transmission losses we could adopt commercially viable clean coal technologies available for power generation. Issues of global warming should be dealt with imaginatively and firmly. ...

... Second, infrastructure by way of water for washeries and HVDC transmission lines for evacuating power from the pit head power stations should also be thrown open to the private sector.

Third, Indian financing institution should give priority for lending to coal mining, washeries, coal based stations and for transmission lines. ...

... Another area which can help in making us self-reliant is nuclear power with thorium as the fuel. ...

... Less than 20 per cent of the hydro potential is being utilised but the problems of hydro power generation are quite daunting, going by past experience. The resettlement of displaced persons has not received the attention that it should have. ...

... Petroleum and natural gas will continue to be important and efforts for deep water exploration should be made by giving priority to those companies that have experience in successful exploration in deep waters. Incentives by way of marketing rights can be offered to such companies who make a serious commitment to explore in the deep waters of the Indian off-shore areas and economic zone. ...

< Competitive bidding for power purchase – three news reports >

(1 of 3)

FINANCIAL EXPRESS *New Delhi, Thursday, September 07, 1995*

FM favours competitive bidding

FE News Service

New Delhi, September 6

Finance Minister Manmohan Singh has advocated the need for competitive bidding to make the process of awarding contracts transparent and also to ward off allegations of corruption often levied on politicians and bureaucrats.

Addressing the annual economic editors conference here on Tuesday, Singh said that "the Ministry had been pursuing the Central Government departments as well as the state government to adopt competitive bidding process as was being done by the World Bank."

The Finance Minister's statement assumes importance in the wake of the Enron controversy, which was a negotiated project and several other offers awaiting approval in the power and other infrastructure sectors. ...

(2 of 3)

FINANCIAL EXPRESS *New Delhi, Thursday, September 07, 1995*

GUARANTEE ON RETURNS FOR POWER SECTOR INVESTORS

Harvard expert questions decision

ENS Economic Bureau

New Delhi

A leading management expert of the Harvard Business School, Prof. Michael E. Porter, has questioned the decision of the Indian Government to provide guarantees on returns to foreign companies investing in the power sector. He said that it amounts to a return to old system of controls and regulations.

Addressing a national seminar on "Developing Competitive Advantage in India," organised by the Confederation of Indian Industry (CII) here on Thursday, the Harvard don pointed out that international contracts make no reference to guarantees or returns whatsoever. ...

TELEGRAPH *New Delhi, Friday, February 17, 1995*

PLAN PANEL AGAINST COUNTER GUARANTEE

Competitive bidding in power favoured

From G. Srinivasan

New Delhi, February 16

Even as the shindy kicked up by the counter guarantee proposal in the power sector remains to be settled, the Planning Commission has firmly expressed itself against any such guarantee to lure private sector participation in power.

In a mid-term review of the power sector prepared recently, the commission said in no uncertain terms that for further power projects in the private sector, competitive bidding should be resorted to and "no guarantees need to be given but finances of state electricity boards (SEBs) should be improved." ...

< Government Guarantee – Economic Times 25.8.94 >

ECONOMIC TIMES *Thursday, August 25, 1994*

Ramakrishna flays govt on guarantees to private investors

United News of India

Bangalore, 24 August.

The Planning Commission member, Mr. G.V. Ramakrishna, on Wednesday came down heavily on the government scheme of providing guarantees and counter-guarantees to private investors in infrastructure development saying this would not bring any sustainable returns to the investors. ...

... Mr. Ramakrishna said, entry of private sector in infrastructure development in developing countries and democratic countries would be difficult.

In countries such as India, government agencies had been handling the sector resulting in most substandard and highly subsidised utilities and the private sector was brought after liberalisation.

Contd. ...

...Contd. ...

These utilities had over the years resource constraints in view of the subsidisation. This did not give them adequate returns that had led to inefficiency due to maintainance problems, resulting in the state electricity boards becoming financially weak, he said.

He said, it would be extremely difficult to blend these historical utilities with private sector entry unless the nation addressed the basic infirmities in them with bold policy decisions such as making the users of the infrastructure utilities pay for the services instead of burdening the taxpayer.

< Hindu Business Line, 21.3.95 >

THE HINDU BUSINESS LINE *Tuesday, March 21, 1995*

ONE-SIDED POWER PURCHASE AGREEMENT

The extortionate Enron deal

Rs. 547.26-crore pre-operative expenses	Massive cost padding up	IDBI objections brushed aside

N. Ram and V. Sridhar in Madras
Perez Chandra in Bombay

The Power Purchase Agreement (PPA) and a mass of associated documents on Enron's Rs. 3,029-crore ($ 946.55 million), 695 MW Dabhol Power Project reveal the framework, the methodologies and the devices through which huge project cost padding, an inflated dual component tariff structure (with indexation on several counts built in) and officially guaranteed extortionate returns have been negotiated and allowed by the Indian side. ...

... The Project

The 695 mega watt (MW) combined cycle gas-based power plant in Dabhol, Maharashtra, is being set up by Enron Corporation, a Texas-headquartered multinational giant having worldwide interests in gas and power. It will operate as a base load station for the State. The original proposal was to instal a 2,015 MW plant at Dabhol as a base load station but that was modified following techno-economic and public criticism. Now, the 695 MW plant, which is scheduled to

Contd. ...

...Contd. ...

become operational in 1997 (using imported distillates first and then liquefied natural gas), is Phase I of the project, in Phase II, the capacity will be expanded to 2,015 MW provided the Maharashtra State Electricity Board (MSEB) opts for it.

Dabhol Power Company - promoted as a 100 per cent foreign-owned private unlimited liability company incorporated in India by Enron, Bechtel (construction contractor) and GE (General Electric: equipment supplier), using the Mauritius tax-dodging route - is to launch the 695 MW project in 1997. The equity and loan components of the project are Rs. 909 crores ($ 284 million) and Rs. 2,120 crores ($ 662 million) respectively, which means a debt-equity ratio of 2.33.

Enron Corp. holds 80 per cent of DPC's equity - through a private unlimited liability company, Enron Mauritius Company, which is owned by Enron through a chain of holding companies. Bechtel Group Inc. and General Electric hold 10 per cent each of DPC's equity, using identical tax saving routes (see diagram showing ownership structure of DPC: Page 7). Enron is to shed 30 per cent of its holdings in DPC before commercial operations begin; given the attractive terms offered to the project, it is expected to make a tidy sum in the disinvestment process.

Following a visit to the United States by an official delegation (including the then Cabinet Secretary, Mr. Naresh Chandra, the then Finance Secretary, Mr. K.P. Geethakrishnan, and the then Power Secretary, Mr. S. Rajgopal) in 1992, Enron was nominated to develop the Dabhol project – without any pretense of open competitive tendering. The confidential documents make it clear that Enron, in turn, failed to follow any competitive bidding procedure for obtaining plant and equipment for the project. ...

... The PPA – cost rigging

The PPA and the accompanying Schedules and Annexures take us into the structure of the deal. They provide vital internal details on how capital cost padding and built-in tariff inflation have taken place. Mr. Kirit S. Parikh, an expert in energy economics, who has been sharply critical of the deal (while supporting the Government of India's decision to invite private investment in the power sector), has estimated that the Enron plant cost has been inflated by some 20 per cent, that the real equity to be brought in by the promoters will be only a fraction of what is claimed, and that the internal rate of return on the real equity will be extraordinarily high, perhaps over 90 per cent. The documents obtained by *Business Line* throw much light on these questions. ...

< Counter Guarantee, The Times of India 1.6.95 >

TIMES OF INDIA *New Delhi, Thursday, June 01, 1995*

Counter-guarantees to Pvt power units uncalled for: Panel

New Delhi, May 31.

The Parliamentary Standing Committee on Energy has observed that the grant of counter-guarantees for power projects in private sector was uncalled for, since several international private power producers were ready to implement projects without it.

"The controversial counter-guarantee instrument is a product of investor misgiving about reliability of state electricity boards", (SEBs) Mr. Jaswant Singh, chairman of the committee, told newsmen while releasing a copy of the 170-page report submitted to Parliament today.

... Mr. Singh said the Dabhol Power Energy (subsidiary of Enron) had neither insisted nor expected any guarantee on payment obligation except may be from the Maharashtra Government.

However, following the announcement of the policy of counter-guarantee by the Government, the company took advantage of it, he said. ...

... The committee felt there was no justification for giving counter-guarantees only to selective fast track projects. ...

... The current power policy provides for 16 per cent return on equity at 68.5 per cent PLF with additional incentive upto 0.7 per cent of return of each percentage of additional PLF.

Since a reasonably well maintained power plant would operate at 80 per cent in the first ten years and 75 per cent at the end of the 20th year, the committee observed that most of the private power projects cleared so far have been guaranteed off take of power well above 80 per cent PLF or allowed third party sales. ...

... The committee felt that private investors had a tendency to inflate costs which would finally translate into higher tariff, and emphasised the Government examine the desirability of adopting a standard practice of specifying a single rate at which private investors are asked to sell power.

(PTI)

< Coal News Reports; Extracts from three cutting:
The Economic Times, Business Standard and Indian Express respectively >

(1 of 3)

THE ECONOMIC TIMES *Thursday, December 21, 1995*

Coal Must be king

The report of Kleinwort Benson Securities on the Indian hydrocarbon sector says, quite rightly, that coal must not be treated as a poor cousin to oil and gas. The opening up of the coal industry is more urgent and important than the liberalisation of oil and gas. The report underlines the need for an integrated energy policy to intensify coal use in the economy (especially by setting up large pit-head power plants). Coal is the country's primary energy source. The oil sector's share of 31.8 per cent of total domestic fuel consumption is among the lowest in the world (China is the only major country with a lower share of 20 per cent). ...

(2 of 3)

BUSINESS STANDARD *October 20*

Need for coal-based power plants stressed

Our Special Correspondent

New Delhi

... Ramakrishna told *Business Standard* on his return from Tokyo that the power demand can be met to a great extent if the emphasis is shifted to coal-based power plants. He was also in favour of setting up pit-head generating stations for transferring power through long distance transmission lines. As far as the environmental aspects were concerned, he said, even if the effect of green house gases on global warming was taken into account, the solution did not lie in restricting the use of coal. ...

(3 of 3)

INDIAN EXPRESS *Thursday, December 19, 1996*

Ramakrishna for private participation in mining

Prees Trust of India
New Delhi, Dec. 18

Disinvestment Commission chairman G.V. Ramakrishna today said the private sector should be involved in commercial mining of coal as captive mining by private power producers had failed to yield any results. ...

... Expressing unhappiness over procedural delays in getting government approval of various projects, Ramakrishna said even the single window concept was not enough to speedily clear applications as no powers have been delegated to it.

He said due to the lack of an effective, adequate and impartial coal policy, the sector had not been able to attract enough investment. ...

< Oman Gas, Telegraph 16.3.96; Indian Express 25.7.94; Telegraph 25.8.95 >

(1 of 3)

TELEGRAPH *New Delhi, Saturday, March 16, 1996*

Govt pulls out all the stops to salvage Oman-India pipline

From R. Sasankan

New Delhi, March 15.

The Government is desperately trying to salvage the Oman-India off-shore gas pipeline project following reports that Oman is planning to back out. ...

... Energy experts feel that as the Iran-India pipeline is not going to materialise in the forseeable future, gas from Iran can be transported to Oman through pipeline and from there to the west coast of India through the proposed deep water pipeline.

Oman does not have enough proven reserves to sustain supplies for 40 years. India has also been negotiating with Qatar which claims to have huge gas reserves. Thus, supplies from Iran and Qatar can feed the pipeline even if Oman takes time to establish its reserves.

Contd. ...

...Contd. ...

At one stage Oman was keen to go ahead with the pipeline after experts confirmed the technical feasibility of the project which would have to go through 3.5 km depth of water. However, the sudden replacement of John Duees as the president of Oman Oil Company sent out signals that the Oman Government was no longer keen on the project.

Oman has been under tremendous pressure from the LNG (liquefied natural gas) lobby which wants to scuttle the pipeline project. According to unconfirmed reports, Shell, which is putting up an LNG plant in Oman, is leading the anti-pipeline lobby.

Prime Minister, Narasimha Rao had evinced great interest in the project from the very beginning. In fact, he went all the way to Oman to witness the signing of the MoU. The proposed southern gas grid will not take off without Oman-India gas pipeline. The ruling party has been planning to make political capital out of the project in the next election. ...

... The MoU with Oman envisages two pipelines each supplying 28 cubic meters of gas per day. The original plan was to restrict the life of the pipeline to 20 years. But downstream industries, to be set up in India, will have to be assured of supplies at least for 40 years. ...

(2 of 3)

INDIAN EXPRESS *New Delhi, Monday, July 25, 1994*

G. V. RAMAKRISHNA ISOLATED

Govt hurries to finalise Oman gas contract

by R. Sasankan

New Delhi

The Prime Minister's Office (PMO) and the Petroleum and Natural Gas Ministry are moving with uncharacteristic haste to finalise the $ 50 billion dollar contract for supply of Oman gas to India through a 1400 Km offshore pipeline.

Planning Commission member G.V. Ramakrishna who questioned the wisdom of rushing with the pipeline project has been isolated by obtaining the full backing of Planning Commission Deputy Chairman Pranab Mukherjee. Bureaucrats who earlier agreed with Ramakrishna have now fallen in line. However, the Petroleum and Natural Gas Ministry could not provide convincing answers to G.V. Ramakrishna's queries. ...

... The project aims at bringing in 56 million cubic meters of gas a day for 25 years. ...

(3 of 3)

TELEGRAPH *New Delhi, Friday, August 25, 1995*

Bid to hasten Oman-India gas pipeline project

From R. Sasankan

New Delhi, August 24.

A high-level team led by petroleum and natural gas secretary Vijay L. Kelkar is leaving for Houston tomorrow to listen to Oman Oil Company on the technical feasibility of the proposed 1,400 kilometer long Oman-India gas pipeline.. ..

... The high-level team comprises experts such as the former chairman of Atomic Energy Commission, Mr. P.K. Iyengar, and directors of Gas Authority of India, I.L. Budhiraja and C.R. Prasad.

Experts are still worried about the technical feasibility of this massive project. Even Mr. Iyengar who has been looking at the issue from India's side has found that various components of the project, in isolation, seemed feasible but has not yet been convinced about the feasibility of the pipeline at a depth of 3,500 km.

Even before this team is back from Houston, petroleum and natural gas minister Satish Sharma proposes to visit Oman to review the progress of the project.

Construction companies such as Snam Progetti, Bechtel and Mcdermott have been asserting that gas pipeline at such a water-depth is feasible although no such pipeline is in operation in the world. The most difficult problem is to ensure the required pressure and temperature to transport it in the gaseous form. ...

... India's risk is that many downstream companies will come up on the basis of an assurred gas supply. These units should not later feel that the gas supplied through the pipeline is uneconomical. ...

... Oman Oil Company, is headed by a non-Omani, John Duess, a dynamic but controversial oil man. His aggressive marketing strategy led to the signing of an MoU and later an agreement on broad principles without establishing the project feasibility.

With Shri K.C. Pant, New Delhi, 2002

Releasing the Second Report of the Disinvestment Commission, New Delhi, April 1996

FAMOUS as the crusty custodian of the capital markets, the redoubtable G.V. Ramakrishna, 66, received one more acknowledgement of his business sense last fortnight, in the form of the post of the Chairman of the Disinvestment Commission. Handed the mandate of determining the Government's strategy for lowering its equity holding in its crown jewels, the public sector units, Ramakrishna – who has been Chairman of the Securities & Exchange Board of India and Member-Secretary of the Planning Commission – will get the chance to test the political palatability of his celebrated no-nonsense approach.

— *Business World,* "Well Said", August 22 - September 6, 1996

13

The Disinvestment Commission

ONE day in August 1996, when I was packing up to go to Bangalore or Chennai for my retirement, I got a telephone call from P. Chidambaram, Finance Minister in the Deve Gowda Government. He said that I had been selected for the post of chairman of the new Disinvestment Commission (DC) and wanted me to accept the post. A little while later, Muralsoli Maran, the Industries Minister, spoke to me and said that he wanted me to take up the post as suggested by Chidambaram. After thinking about the matter for a day or two, I accepted. I learnt that the DC had been kept within the administrative purview of the Industry Ministry. This was strange as the subject was allotted to the finance ministry under the Allocation of Business Rules of the Government. The Finance Ministry had constituted the Rangarajan Committee, which had recommended the setting up of DC in 1993.

When I got the order of my appointment along with the terms of reference issued by the industry ministry, I called on Maran and said that I would like to start work and needed some logistical support from his Ministry. He said that I knew everyone in the bureaucracy and I could find accommodation and other facilities on my own. I told Jairam Ramesh, the dynamic Special Assistant to the F.M., that if accommodation was not found for me in the next few days, I could not function and would like to resign. He got to work and with the F.M.'s support he got me a good room in the Finance Ministry. Some thirty years ago, I was familiar with this room which was occupied by economic secretaries like Bhoothalingam and Jagannathan when I worked in the Department of Economic Affairs as Deputy Secretary and Director.

I drew the attention of the cabinet secretary to the fact that the DC had been placed in the industry ministry, which was inconsistent with the allocation of business. There was no reply.

When I saw the terms of reference, I noticed a number of restrictions and ambiguities. The DC could look into only those Public Sector Undertakings (PSUs) that were referred to it by the Government. As if to confirm what I had written to the cabinet secretary, the first batch of PSUs were referred to the DC by the economic secretary, Ahluwalia and not by the industry ministry. Even later the Commission had no correspondence with the Ministry of Industry but only with the Finance Ministry. The Core Group on disinvestment was serviced by the finance ministry.

The composition of the DC was good. The members were D. Basu, the highly regarded former Chairman of the State Bank; Suresh Tendulkar, an eminent economist who was a member of the Fifth Pay Commission; Dr. Nanjundappa, another eminent economist who was vice chairman of the Karnataka Planning Commission; and M.R.R. Nair the Chairman of SAIL.

The full commission called on the finance minister soon after the first meeting. At this meeting the F.M. said that the DC could look at all the Central PSUs and not only those that were referred to it and assured the members that the terms would be amended in a day or two. Nothing really happened. The Commission got down to business straight away to deal with the 24 PSUs that were referred to it.

It was necessary to assemble a nucleus staff for the Commission. As the right kind of staff was not available in Government it was decided to get staff on deputation from institutions like CRISIL and IDBI. We were fortunate to get the services of a capable officer P. Shanker, who was additional secretary (finance) in the Ministry of External Affairs. As the secretary of the Commission, he was of great help in organizing the work of the consultants, in preparing notes for the Commission and in drafting the reports. He had to leave on promotion after a year. DC got the services of another hardworking and efficient officer G. Ganesh, who studied the subject in depth and wrote two very good books on privatisation.

As a first step, two large seminars were arranged, in Delhi and in Bombay. The financial community and a number of foreign advisers and financial institutions attended. The finance minister inaugurated the seminar in Delhi and the Governor of the RBI in Bombay. All aspects of the process of disinvestment were discussed on the basis of a number of papers submitted by the participants. The experience of other countries was also discussed in some of the papers.

Thereafter, the Commission met a number of representative bodies of the industry like Confederation Indian Industries (CII) and all the Trade Unions. Economists having an interest in the subject were also invited to meet the Commission.

A background paper on the state of the PSUs, and the issues that arose in disinvestment, was prepared to help in the work of analyzing the PSUs. It was decided to engage Indian consultants who would study each one of the companies and make a detailed report of the industry in which the company functioned, its commercial, financial and staff strengths. Different consultants were engaged for each company. They made a detailed presentation to the members and several questions were answered. Any further information required by the members was provided and a final report was given. The DC took up each company for further discussion.

At this stage, the Commission met the chief executives of the PSUs, and the secretary of the ministry concerned, separately, to ascertain their views on the need for disinvestment and the modalities for the process. In some cases, the members available and the chairman visited the PSUs for discussion with the officers and the staff.

The Commission decided that each report of the DC would contain two sections, the first one on general recommendations and the second on specific recommendations on each of the companies. It decided to be transparent and provide the media with copies of the reports in a Press interview after it was submitted to the Government.

The First Report of the Commission was given in February 1997, four months after the first batch of companies was referred to it by the Finance Ministry.

In this report several important general recommendations were made. These dealt with the criteria for classifying the companies into strategic and non-strategic, core and non-core. It was recommended that the proceeds of disinvestment should be placed in a Disinvestment Fund and not taken into the general revenues of the Government, and that the Fund should be used for creating social infrastructure like houses, schools and medical facilities in the villages, for restructuring the PSUs before disinvestment, for providing VRS (Voluntary Retirement Schemes) and for retiring public debt. These recommendations were not implemented by the Government for several years. Although the budget speech of 1998, held out the promise, no action was taken. Only now in 2003, there is talk of creating a Disinvestment Fund but there is no implementation as yet.

The Commission recommended that, 'wherever appropriate, PSUs should be restructured before disinvestment in order to enhance enterprise value and intrinsic share value'[1]

One other recommendation was to encourage decision making by giving autonomy and to protect PSU officers from hasty criminal investigation. DC suggested the creation of a Pre-Investigation Board to examine the impugned decisions and to identify those which were just poor

1. Two news reports on restructuring Business India, Sept., 1996; Indian Express 19.9.96 < Appended on page 270 >.

commercial decisions, those which were rash, and those that were motivated by corrupt intentions or actions. Only the last were to be referred for criminal investigation. After several years the Central Vigilance Commission accepted this. The CVC, who was then Secretary of the Disinvestment Commission, wrote to the Prime Minister on the subject.

The DC recommended that the Boards be given greater autonomy and freed from the tight control of the Ministries. This led, in 1992 to the creation of a class of the larger PSUs as 'Navaratnas' which were given somewhat greater powers in some areas. In fact, the control of the Ministries has not diminished. For instance, in the case of bidding for the oil company HPCL, (Hindustan Petroleum Corp. Ltd.) the Petroleum Ministry directed the major oil company, ONGC (Oil & Natural Gas Corp.) not to participate in the bidding.

The DC recommended that PSU salary structures should be delinked from those of civil servants, and they should have incentives and disincentives similar to the private sector. A Committee under Justice Mohan, a retired Supreme Court judge, was appointed, but nearly after five years no action appears to have been taken.

After some time, DC reports mentioned the tardiness in Government decision-making on the various recommendations and commented on this in its subsequent reports.[2] When the Media picked up these comments and wrote about them, the Government did not like it.[3]

2. DC Report IV on Tardiness < Appended on page 272 >.
3. 'Many reports little action', Business Standard 13.11.97 < Appended on page 274 >.

In January 1998, a few months before the elections, an order was issued without any prior intimation to the DC drastically amending the Terms of Reference (ToR) of the Commission.[4] It is noteworthy that these orders were issued by the same Finance Minister, Chidambaram, who had earlier assured the members that the ToR would be widened to provide greater latitude for the DC. The new ToR stated that the DC would examine only those PSUs referred to it. The earlier terms, which provided for the DC to have a role in the implementation, were deleted. Chidambaram maintained that there was no such curtailment.[5]

In the new Government, the Ministers were Sikandar Bakht in industry and Yashwant Sinha in finance. The members of the Commission met these two ministers and protested that the drastic changes in the ToR were unwarranted and would hamper its working. They were promised that the matter would be examined and the action of the previous Government would be reviewed. Nothing came of it for some months. Later, the sentiment in the DC was for all the members and the chairman to resign and I met the Finance Minister and conveyed this to him. He said that very soon decisions would be taken after the budget in 1999. Nothing came of this also.

As the Government was regularly sending more companies for examination by the DC, we continued with our work and produced more reports. It was therefore decided to complete the work on hand and not to accept any more companies. When the three-year term of DC was

---

4. Copies of original ToR, and new ToR < Appended on page 275 >.
5. Chidambaram's statement, The Telegraph 4.2.1998; Business India Feb. 98 < Appended on page 278 >.

over by August, it was extended till the end of November. By the end of our term we had examined a total of 58 companies and twelve reports had been issued.[6] The Government withdrew six cases. Five cases were before the Bureau for Industrial and Financial Reconstruction (BIFR), and DC could not examine them. In several of these reports, DC reiterated the need for a Disinvestment Fund.

The DC said, in more than one report after the very first report, that disinvestment should be delinked from the budget and should not be used to reduce the fiscal deficit. This was ignored.[7] It continues to be ignored even today.

The anxiety to meet the budgetary shortfalls and to reduce the fiscal deficit for the year 2003-04 led to the Government's offer to sell its shareholding in as many as six companies with a total target of about Rs. 14,000 crores in a short period of three weeks in February-March 2004. This resulted in a sharp fall in the share prices of those PSUs. This provoked a strong reaction from Government sources concerned with disinvestment who felt that there was some market manipulation and price rigging. While this may be only partially true, many commented in Press that offering such a large volume of shares in such a short period will naturally result in a fall in prices. The capital market like any other market is also price sensitive to the basic law of supply and demand. Spacing of the sales over a period of about two or three months would have produced better results but that would not have met the objective of the Government to raise large amounts by the end of March

6. List of 58 PSUs, DC < Appended on page 281 >.
7. The Pioneer 22.11.97; Business Line 11.11.97; Financial Express 9.12.97 < Appended on page 284 >.

2004. Government had to direct the public sector financial institutions to buy, against their own commercial judgement, the shares of the PSUs and prop up prices. These officially sponsored purchases could arguably be considered as market manipulation which will not be conducive to the health of the capital market.

Budgetary support for PSUs over the last ten years has been given in the presentation of the Department of Disinvestment (DoD) of November 2000. It shows a total support of Rs. 61,211 crores from 1990-91 to 1998-99.[8]

During the first ten years of disinvestment, Government had got about Rs. 19,000 crores by the sale of shares. If this money had been placed in a Fund, it could have been used to build 40 lakh houses, 1 lakh schools and 5000 clinics in rural areas, apart from providing for payments under the Voluntary Retirement Scheme (VRS). Instead, this money which went into the general revenues reduced the fiscal deficit by only 0.02 per cent (from 5.72 per cent to 5.70 per cent) on an average for these ten years.

The opportunity was lost to prove to the people that the disinvestment process was development-oriented and not deficit-reduction oriented. Several groups, including political parties, employees and the public, were disappointed. They were not convinced about the purpose and advantages of disinvestment.

This also confirmed the saying, first heard in the U.K., that privatization should not be seen as 'selling the family silver to pay the butler'.[9]

8. Presentation of DoD, 21.11.2000 p 30 < Appended on page 286 >.
9. 'The view from No 11,' Nigel Lawson, p 238 < Appended on page 287 >.

The following interesting quote from the book *Privatisation, Principles and Practice* of the International Finance Corporation, Washington, gives some idea of how they looked at the problems of privatisation:

> 'To privatise', said an agency official, 'is to drive a two horse cart. The cart is the enterprise in question. One horse is called Political Goals and is flighty and fickle; the other is called Economics, and is slow and steady. They have to pull the cart along the Road to Privatisation which is a rough, boulder strewn track. The cart is full of cases of vintage wine, which is unfortunate because the horses, as often as not, are pulling in different directions. The bottles of wine which can be enjoyed only when the cart reaches its goal are labeled, improved efficiency, high sales price, effective corporate governance, economic investment and so on.
>
> Only the most skilful driver can negotiate this track; up the hill of Vested Interests (cases may have to be jettisoned here, and some horses are not strong enough to make it) across of Xenophobia (another case or two bumps off the back). Some carts are too weak and fall apart before they get to Privatisation. Sometimes it makes sense to give the flighty horse its head and fly the trail headlong, abandoning case after case in the way, sometimes it is possible to whip him into shape to follow its steadier partner. And many drivers simply give up, cut the horses loose and climb down and start back down the trail, hoping to find solace in the odd bottle that hasn't smashed.

Does this have any relevance to our own privatization?

The first country to start the process of privatization was U.K. Perhaps the best account of how the policy was conceived and implemented is given by one of the key participants Nigel Lawson, who was initially Energy Minister, and later Chancellor of the Exchequer in the Thatcher Government, in his book *The View from No.11.*

The importance of sale of shares to the public was realized first in the U.K., which started the whole process of privatisation in the world in the eighties under the Thatcher Government. In fact, their definition of privatization was different from what is now understood in India. For them, the exit of Government and the owning of shares by the people was privatization.[10] For the first ten years, they did not make any strategic sale and did not hand over the management to private parties. The Government at first wanted to call it peoples' capitalism but later Thatcher wanted it to be called 'popular capitalism'.[11]

The European experience of sale of PSU shares to the people has been brought out in the presentation of the DoD of 2000.[12]

However, to enhance share values of PSUs it is necessary to remove Government control which depresses prices.[13]

In November 1998, DC made a proposal that in regard to blue chip companies, like the oil companies and BHEL, NTPC and others, there should be no strategic sale to private parties, but the shares should be sold to the people and the residual shares should be kept with a National Shareholding Trust (NST) consisting of eminent persons with experience of business and industry.[14]

In the context of the present enthusiasm to offer, on strategic sale, the oil companies for bidding to Indian and

10. Nigel Lawson 'The view from No. 11', p 205, 207 < Appended on page 288 >.

11. *Ibid* 224 < Appended on page 289 >.

12. DoD presentation p 37-40 < Appended on page 289 >.

13. 'Get the Govt. out' Indian Express 23.10.2002 < Appended on page 290 >.

14. NST, Seven Press Reports < Appended on page 291 >.

foreign companies it is interesting to note the sentiment in the UK during their privatization process. In fact they showed a surprising degree of sensitivity to foreign holding in their privatized companies. For instance in the case of British Petroleum (BP), the Kuwait Investment Office (KIO) owned by the Kuwait Investment Agency, had acquired 10 per cent of the shares. KIO declared, on 18th November 1987, that it had acquired 10 per cent of the shares of BP and intended to buy more. This sent alarm signals in the company which approached the Government for intervention, as it saw Kuwait as a competitor in the global oil business. Meanwhile, KIO increased its share holding to 18 per cent. The UK Government took up the matter with the Kuwaiti Government at high diplomatic levels. When the Kuwaitis did not agree to withdraw, but instead, increased their holding to 20 per cent the British Government referred the matter to the Monopolies and Mergers Commission (MMC) of the UK. After a full hearing the Commission passed an order with the force of law that the Kuwaitis should reduce their shareholding to 10 per cent and not seek a place on the Board of BP. The following reasoning of MMC makes interesting reading in the present controversy about the strategic sale of HPCL.

> While it is not possible to predict the future of the oil markets or of the Middle East, we believe that there is high degree of probability that sooner or later situations will arise in which Kuwait's national and international interest will come sharply into conflict with BP's and HMG's interest. Such conflicts of interest would be even more likely to occur if a future Government in Kuwait was less well disposed to the West and the UK. We consider that if and when these conflicts occur Kuwait would seek, and be able to use its shareholding to influence BP in the ways we have set out... and that this may

be expected to be detrimental to, and will operate against the UK public interest'.[15]

Nigel Lawson in his book *The View from No.11* brings this out clearly.

It is important to note in the present context of the privatization of the oil companies HPCL and BPCL that at no time did the DC recommend privatization of the major oil companies or other major companies like IOC, NTPC, BHEL or financial institutions like SBI.

In 1997, I was appointed a member of the Prime Minister's economic advisory council. In the two meetings I attended, I stressed the need for a sound policy on disinvestment and explained the recommendations of the various reports of the Commission up to that time.

Since the Ministry of Disinvestment (MoD) was formed, there has been some acceleration of the process. However, it has been criticized, in several quarters, for a number of inconsistencies and contradictions in the disinvestment process.

A successful disinvestment process should have the support, in growing concentric circles, – within the Government, the party, the coalition, the Parliament and then the public. No effort has been made in this direction. On the other hand, recent discussions in Parliament in May 2003, brought out the lack of support for the process, from not only all the main opposition parties but also from some of the coalition partners. The Parliamentary Standing Committee on Disinvestment has, in its recent report of May 2003, pointed out, that the process is 'shrouded in mystery

15. Nigel Lawson p 778-779 < Appended on page 297 >.

and goes on a case by case basis'. It recommended that a comprehensive policy statement should be prepared.

The policy paper should deal with the policies – which should be people oriented, principles – which should be clear cut, and processes – which should be transparent.

As Minister of State for Energy, Nigel Lawson sent a note to Nicholas Ridley, the Financial Secretary, in connection with water privatization, in which he gave the justification as follows:

1. Experience shows that all businesses are more efficient and successful in the private than in the public sector.
2. The water and sewerage industry is a business like any other.
3. A quarter of industry is already in the private sector.
4. Of course it will need regulation.
5. Privatisation not only widens share ownership (desirable in itself), but increases employee share ownership which, previous privatisations show, leads to further improved performance.[16]

Valuation

Valuation can be used in two types of disinvestments – strategic sale and sale in the market to the public. In the case of strategic sale there is a premium attached to the management that the new buyer will have.

16. *Ibid* p 206, 237 < Appended on page 298 >.

For the purpose of determining a fair value for the strategic sale, by which the successful bidder gets the majority shares and the control of the company, there are several methods. Each company has to be valued separately on different bases. If the company is a running concern, the conventional valuation is based on the Discounted Cash Flow (DCF) method. I had pointed out, in one of my articles, the danger in applying this method to a public sector company with its lack of autonomy and other disabilities, like ministerial interference, demotivation, lack of incentives and the fear of criminal action for commercial decisions. The DCF in such a company will give different results from a private sector company with all the incentives for performance. The public sector has some very good managers, but they perform well below their counterparts in private sector companies. In fact, in the oil sector, the private oil companies hire public sector managers on three to five times the salary. So, the DCF method used to value a public sector company will generally understate its true value that will be realized by a private sector owner.[17]

Another aspect of valuation are the core assets and non-core assets of the company. Core assets are those that are used for the current business of their operations. Non-core assets are those that are not being used for current business or required in the near future for the regular business of the company. Private sector companies periodically resort to shedding non-core assets for realizing market value for the benefit of shareholders. Some years ago Philips did it.

---

17. 'Statics and Dynamics of DCF', Financial Express, August 2002 < Appended on page 299 >.

Recently, Hindustan Lever announced that they are shedding their non-core assets in Bangalore to realize market value.

In the early days, State Governments were anxious to get Central Government investment in their states and offered free land and other facilities for PSUs. When the PSU needed about 50 acres, they gave 100 or 200 acres of land. Because of this, today several PSUs have a lot of surplus land. These assets do not figure in the DCF method of calculation, and yet they have a market value and they should also be taken into account in fixing the reserve price. One of the criticisms of the Balco sale was that the surplus land and the employees' housing was not taken into account.

HPCL and BPCL

In particular, disinvestment in the oil companies Hindustan Petroleum Corporation (HPCL) and Bharat Petroleum Corporation (BPCL) had serious legal and constitutional problems. I pointed out that these two companies were acquired from the foreign oil companies Esso, Caltex and Burmah Shell, in the seventies by Parliamentary legislation which stipulated that the assets should be vested in the Government or a Government company, which by definition, had to have not less than 51 per cent of the shares. And, therefore, if there has to be disinvestment by which Government share holding would come down below 51 per cent , it would be necessary to get an amendment or repeal of these Acts. Government obtained the opinion of the Attorney General and I wrote a rebuttal of this opinion. Three retired judges of the Supreme Court, Justices

Krishna Iyer, Chinnappa Reddy and Sawant and a retired Chief Justice of the Delhi High Court, Justice Bhimsen Sachar and Shanti Bhushan (former Law Minister and Senior advocate) issued a public statement to the effect that Parliamentary approval had to be obtained before disinvestment in the two oil companies. The matter has now gone to the Supreme Court in a public interest litigation.[18]

The enthusiasm and energy shown by MoD (Ministry of Disinvestment) for disinvestment appears to be heavily weighted in favour of privatization of blue chip companies like HPCL, BPCL, and NALCO (National Aluminium Co.) and has created considerable controversy. Many political parties, and indeed large sections of the public, who have no objection to Disinvestment *per se*, have disagreed with the approach of MoD. They feel that a number of questions have to be answered and, if the process has to go forward with broad support, MoD should bring a note or White Paper before Parliament, after getting Cabinet approval, dealing, *inter alia*, with the following issues:

1. Should DoD not take a comprehensive view of all the Central PSUs including the 102 loss making units? The total losses of the loss making units has gone up from Rs. 5900 crores in 1997-98 to Rs. 13,000 crores in 2000- 2001. The aggregate losses in the five year period amount to Rs. 45,000 crores. The cash losses alone will amount cumulatively in this period to over Rs. 15,000 crores. This is the taxpayer's money going through budgetary support to meet these losses. What

---

18. HPCL, BPCL four news reports < Appended on page 301 >.

are the views of MoD on the resolution of this major problem? Have they classified these units into those that can be revived with restructuring before disinvestment and those that cannot.

2. Have the reports of the Disinvestment Commission been examined and taken to the Cabinet for decision on both the general and specific recommendations of the Commission. If so, what are the decisions on them.
3. What is the basis on which valuation is being done? How are foreign advisers appointed? DC had recommended that a domestic adviser should also be appointed in addition to the foreign adviser? Is this being done? Is the valuation discussed with the Finance Ministry?
4. How is the Shareholders agreement prepared? The case of VSNL raised considerable controversy about the shareholders agreement. When 25 per cent shares in the company were sold to Tatas along with management control for about Rs. 1,450 crores, VSNL had cash reserves of Rs. 1,200 crores which it had earmarked for meeting certain liabilities. VSNL also had large real estate properties in major cities but these were apparently not valued. There was no stipulation regarding the use of these funds and the new management promptly decided to use the cash reserves for supporting a sister company Tata Teleservices. In the case of the Airport Centaur hotel, the private party which bought the shares in a strategic sale for about Rs. 83 crores and sold them to another

party for Rs. 115 crores within three months. Why was no lock-in period and right of first refusal of Government provided in the shareholders agreement? Many sections of the public feel that no satisfactory answers have been given to these questions.

The CAG has now reportedly given a report critical of the sale process and quantifying the national loss to Government at Rs. 145 crores on account of the reduction in the lease rental rate.

Such a lock-in period was included in the shareholder's agreement for the sale of BALCO. The Supreme Court judgment in the BALCO case is interpreted as approval of the procedure whereas it merely upheld the right of Government to sell BALCO without Parliamentary approval. Even if it is taken as approval of procedure followed in that case, the lock-in period included in that case should have been followed. The explanation given is that in the BALCO case the clause was inserted to prevent 'asset stripping'. Assets are a part of the company that is sold. If this was prevented it would appear to be reasonable to assume that by the same logic the sale of the entire company with all its assets, would also be prevented by putting a lock in period. Too much reliance on that case may show that the procedure approved by the Court was not followed in this case.

5. Why was a monopoly created by the disinvestment of IPCL against the recommendations of the DC? It is not sufficient to say that legal advice was taken. Since when have political and public interest decisions been taken only on legal permissibility?

6. Legal opinion at the highest level was taken by DC before making the proposal for a National Share Holding Trust but why has this not been implemented? What are the objections to the proposal? Sale of shares to the public have been resorted to in many countries. Singapore has an arrangement similar to the NST. Why cannot this be tried out in the case of a few blue chip companies to enable a broad based public shareholding with residuary holding in the hands of the NST? With the removal of Government control, and widely acceptable persons appointed to NST, share values will go up for the benefit of the Government. The recent success of the sale of Government shares in Maruti to the public goes to confirm that the exit of Government from management promotes investor interest. Sales of Government shares in PSUs under Government management will not get the same response. The NST proposal offers a way out. The present discussions about an Asset Management Company (AMC) are vague. The idea is quite different from the proposal for the NST and may not enhance share values.

7. IOC was allowed to bid for IBP. Government got a good bid from IOC for IBP. Now ONGC is not allowed to bid for HPCL on the ground that a public sector company should not participate in disinvestment. Participation of PSUs will act as a reserve price and enhance the bidding levels. Stopping PSUs from bidding will lower Government receipt and help in handing over the PSU at a low price to private parties. This is against public interest.

8. How far does MoD want to go while privatizing blue chip companies? Will NTPC, BHEL, IOC, ONGC, NALCO and SBI also be privatized through the strategic sale route? Where will the line be drawn and on what criteria? The views of the Government may be explained in the white paper.
9. Why is the impression being given that strategic sale of the oil companies is the only way of going ahead with disinvestment or indeed of the reform process itself.

It is important to address these public concerns if the process has to go forward smoothly.

APPENDED REFERENCES

< Two news reports on restructuring
Business India Sept. 1996, Indian Express 19.9.1996 >

(1 of 2)

BUSINESS INDIA *September 9-22, 1996* **286**

INTERVIEW

Restructure first

G. V. Ramakrishna, former bureaucrat and the first chairman of the Securities and Exchange Board of India (SEBI), is one of the most agile economic administrators in the country. After leaving his mark on the evolution of SEBI as a capital market regulatory body, he has now been given another role as chairman of the disinvestment commission. As conceived by Ramakrishna, the commission is slated to break new ground in, not only how best to sell PSU shares but how best to restructure them to get a good price. GVR, as he is commonly known in government circles, spoke to Anjan Roy of Business India *on various issues relating to his new work. ...*

... Disinvestment has some pre-conditions. These have to be looked into and set right before the PSUs could be offered for sale. How good is the management of the units? What is the underlying value of the shares being offered for sale? A proper assessment of the capital market before the issues are offered. And, lastly, the timing of the issues. These will have to be examined before the disinvestment process can even be started.

All these factor will influence the prices received on sale of shares. The realisation on disinvestment will depend on the management of the PSUs since that will influence its performance. Excessive bureaucratic control on PSUs can dampen their share value. A measure of autonomy and accountability of management will have to be achieved before even profit making PSUs could be disinvested. In brief there has to be some restructuring. ...

... The public sector will very much continue to exist. These PSUs will remain active in critical areas. They will continue to play a crucial role in core sectors of the economy. And in the end their performance and fate will, to a large extent influence the entire Indian economy. ...

(2 of 2)

THE INDIAN EXPRESS *Thursday, September 19, 1996*

PSUs should be prepared before disinvestment: Ramakrishna

ENS Economic Bureau

New Delhi, September 18

Chairman of the Disinvestment Commission G.V. Ramakrishna said today that public sector units should be prepared before disinvestment in them. He said that in India there was inadequate preparation for disinvestment. He asked that the management be revamped, and that "elaborate preparation" should be done to ready them for disinvestment.

He said the PSUs were ill-equipped to deal with the competitive corporate world. For instance, they did not have experience in handling shareholders and many of them did not understand company law. ...

... He said that the aim of disinvestment should be the improvement of efficiency, broad-basing of share-holding, apart from resource generation. "We have to ask the question whether disinvestment is an end in itself or is it leading to something useful?" he said. ...

... Mere disinvestment would not help as the real question was of autonomy, he said. "I don't think any serious measures have been taken to provide autonomy to the profit making units," he said. PSUs were facing competition from joint ventures, domestic private sector and imports, but were not in a position to fight them.

Disinvestment will succeed only if the market felt that the PSU had a profitable future ahead of it. For this it is necessary that the PSUs consider their core competencies, market share and diversification plans and announce its future strategy before its shares are sold. ...

< DC Report IV on Tardiness >

1. General Issues and Recommendations on Disinvestment

Review of Progress in Disinvestment

... According to item 3(IX) of the terms of reference of the Commission (Annex B), it is required to monitor the progress of the disinvestment process. The Commission has taken due note of the progress of the disinvestment process over the past six months. Although there has been no formal communication from Government, based on the information available with the Commission, the action so far taken by Government on the recommendations of the Commission is reflected in the following tables:

TABLE 1

General Recommendations

Recommendations	*Government Action*
Establishment of Disinvestment Fund (I:3.1)	Decision awaited
Formation of Standing Empowered Group (I:4.1)	Core Group Empowered
Guidelines on-Offer of Sale-Book building for domestic and GDR issues (I:4.2)	Book building for GDR only
Guidelines on selection of Intermediaries (I:4.3)	Decision awaited
Retailing PSU shares to small investors & employees (I:4.4)	Decision awaited
Recommendation on joining NSDL (II:1)	Decision awaited

Contd. ...

...Contd. ...

TABLE 2

Corporate Governance: All PSUs

Recommendations for all PSUs	*Government Action*
• Professionalising the Board by induction of non-executive directors to be chosen by PESB (I:3.4)	Decision awaited
Provision for Elected Director(I:3.4)	Decision awaited
• Selection of Top Management (I:3.4)	
• Salaries and Incentives for Top Management (I:3.4)	
• Autonomy in Price Fixation (I:3.4)	Decision awaited
• Accountability (I:3.4)	Decision awaited
• Setting up of Pre-Investigation Board (I:3.4)	Decision awaited
• Strengthening the Investor Interface (I:3.4)	Decision awaited
Moderate Performers	
• Power to dispose off Assets (I:3.4)	Decision awaited
• Freedom of Investment within certain limits (I:3.4)	Investment Powers of the Board of Directors have been doubled from earlier limits for all PSUs.
Strong Performers	
• Powers to form Joint Ventures (I:3.4)	Decision awaited
• Full freedom with regard to Investment (I:3.4)	

< 'Many reports little action' Business Standard 13.11.1997 >

BUSINESS STANDARD *Thursday, November 13, 1997*

Many reports, little action

... The Government should find it even easier to refer all the enterprises in view of what it has been doing with the Commission's recommendations. Now it has become routine for parent ministries to "disagree" with the Commission's recommendations and to say that they want to do disinvestment their own way — or not do it at all. If this is permitted, then the Disinvestment Commission will become a typical Government committee — that is, it will become an instrument to put off decisions. ...

... In particular, the Government has completely stonewalled the Commission's recommendations regarding the setting up of objectively competent managements, and raising managerial salaries so that they are comparable with the private sector. These measures are not unsocialist; they are necessary to strengthen the public enterprises and to increase their value. In these circumstances, a reasonable doubt can now be entertained whether the Government is really on the same wave-length as the Disinvestment Commission. It will be a pity if the members of the Commission come to invest three years of their time, only to find that the Government had appointed the Commission simply to divest itself of the bother of doing something about public enterprises.

< Copies of original ToR, and new ToR >

APPENDIX I

Terms of Reference of the Commission

MINISTRY OF INDUSTRY
(Department of Public Enterprises)
RESOLUTION
New Delhi, the 23rd August, 1996

No. 11013/3/96- Admn. - In pursuance of the Common Minimum Programme of the United Front, Government hereby constitutes a Public Sector Disinvestment Commission, initially for a period of three years.

2. The composition of the Commission will be as follows:-

1. Shri G.V. Ramakrishna, Full-time Chairman
2. Shri Dipankar Basu, Part-time Member
3. Shri M.R.R. Nair, Part-time Member*
4. Dr. Suresh Tendulkar, Part-time Member
5. Dr. D. M. Nanjundappa, Part-time Member

The Commission will have a full-time Secretary who will be appointed separately. Shri G. Ganesh appointed Member Secretary vide Govt. of India Notification No. 13/18/97-EO (SMI) dated 11.12.97 vice Shri P. Shankar.

3. The broad terms of reference of the Commission are as follows:-

I. To draw a comprehensive overall long term disinvestment programme within 5-10 years for the PSUs referred to it by the Core Group.

II. To determine the extent of disinvestment (total/partial indicating percentage) in each of the PSUs.

III. To prioritise the PSUs referred to it by the Core Group in terms of the overall disinvestment programme.

IV. To recommend the preferred mode(s) of disinvestment (domestic capital market/international capital market/auction/private sale to identified investors/any other) for each of the identified PSUs. Also to suggest an appropriate mix of the various alternatives taking into account the market conditions.

* Shri Rajendra Singh, CMD, NTPC has been appointed part-time Member in place of Shri M.R.R Nair, vide Deptt. of Public Enterprises Resolution No. A-112023/2/97-Admn, dt. 14-10-1997

Contd...

...*Contd.* ...

V. To recommend a mix between primary and secondary disinvestment taking into account Government's objective, the relevant PSU's funding requirement and the market condition.

VI. To supervise the overall sale process and take decisions on instrument, pricing, timing, etc. as appropriate.

VII. To select the financial advisers for the specified PSUs to facilitate the disinvestment process.

VIII. To ensure that appropriate measures are taken during the disinvestment process to protect the interests of the affected employees including encouraging employees' participation in the sale process.

IX. To monitor the progress of disinvestment process and take necessary measures and report periodically to the Government on such progress.

X. To assist the Government to create public awareness of the Government's disinvestment policies and programmes with a view to developing a commitment by the people.

XI. To give wide publicity to the disinvestment proposals so as to ensure larger public participation in the shareholding of the enterprises.

XII. To advise the Government on possible capital restructuring of the enterprises by marginal investment, if required, so as to ensure enhanced realisation through disinvestment.

4. The Disinvestment Commission will be an advisory body and the Government will take a final decision on the companies to be disinvested and mode of disinvestment on the basis of advice given by the Disinvestment Commission. The PSUs would implement the decision of the Government under the overall supervision of the Disinvestment Commission.

5. The Commission, while advising the Government on the above matters, will also take into consideration the interests of stakeholders, workers, consumers and others having a stake in the relevant public sector undertakings.

S. TALWAR

Joint Secretary

APPENDIX V

MINISTRY OF INDUSTRY
(Department of Public Enterprise)
RESOLUTION
New Delhi, the 12th January, 1998

No. 11013/3/96-Admn. - In partial modification of this Ministry's Resolution No. 11013/3/96-Admn. dated 23-8-96 constituting the Public Sector Disinvestment Commission, Paras 3, 4 and 5 thereof are deleted and substituted by the following:-

3(i) The Disinvestment Commission shall be an advisory body and its role and function would be to advise the Government on Disinvestment in those public sector units that are referred to it by the Government.

3(ii) The Commission shall also advise the Government on any other matter relating to disinvestment as may be specifically referred to it by the Government, and also carry out any other activities relating to disinvestment as may be assigned to it by the Government.

3(iii) In making its recommendations, the Commission will also take into consideration the interests of workers, employees and others stake holders, in the public sector unit(s).

3 (iv) The final decision on the recommendations of the Disinvestment Commission will vest with the Government.

S. TALWAR
Joint Secretary

< Chidambaram's Statement, The Telegraph 4.2.1998;
Business India February 1998 >

THE TELEGRAPH *Chennai, February 4, 1998*

Selloff panel's powers not curbed: FM

PTI

Chennai, Feb 3

Union finance minister, P. Chidambaram today denied that the powers of the Disinvestment Commission had been clipped. He told a Press meet that the commission was only an advisory body to suggest disinvestment from public sector undertakings. It has no power to monitor the actual process. ...

... Decision flayed

Disinvestment Commission member and chairman of the National Council for Social Science Research D.M. Nanjundappa today termed as anti-national the order of the United Front Government to remove statutory powers of the Commission. ...

... He said the Commission has been set up to restore the health of the public sector enterprises in the country by taking various measures.

BUSINESS INDIA *February 9-22, 1998*

THE INDUSTRY MINISTRY HAS STRIPPED THE DISINVESTMENT COMMISSION OF MOST OF ITS POWERS

Put in its place

... The truncated terms of reference clearly state that, apart from advising the Government on disinvestment in public sectors units (PSUs), the Commission should comment only on matters specifically referred to it by the Government. This will take away, among other things, the Commission's right to monitor the progress of the disinvestment process and comment on it, an option exercised by the Commission in some of its earlier reports. The

Contd. ...

...Contd. ...

new notification reiterates that the final decision on the recommendation of the Disinvestment Commission will be vested with the Government, but it removes an earlier provision which specifically says that the Government will take a final decision on disinvestment basis of advice given by the Commission. Another important aspect left out of the new terms of reference is that the PSUs will have to implement the disinvestment decisions of the Government under the overall supervision of the Disinvestment Commission.

The response to the Government move to curtail the terms of reference has generally been hostile. The Standing Committee on Public Enterprises (SCOPE) has already come out strongly against the move. "The Commission had taken a holistic approach on disinvestment and we would like it to be continued," says M.A. Hakeem, secretary general of SCOPE. Other feel that the taking away of the supervisory powers of the Commission is not a good development. "An independent commission exercising jurisdiction on the process of disinvestment had reduced the scope for arbitrariness and helped to give it more credibility," points out O.P. Vaish, president of the PHD Chamber of Commerce. ...

... "The very wide ranging and comprehensive disinvestment measures recommended by the Commission often ignore ground realities and create hurdles in implementing the disinvestment programme," says a senior MoI official. ...

... The scope of activities of the Commission was so broadly laid out that it could even advice the Government on capital restructuring of PSUs, which would make that PSU a more attractive candidate for disinvestment. There was no doubt even in the earlier notification that the final decision was the Government's. ...

... In its first paper on the strategy and issues of disinvestment, the Commission had discussed in detail the overall working of the PSUs and their problems, the global experience of disinvestment and the issues of disinvestment in the Indian context. The board-based approach had given the disinvestment programme a semblance of a long term perspective for tackling many of the problems faced by the PSUs.

The Government's decision to curtail the working of the Disinvestment Commission is not very surprising, given the long standing hostility between the Commission and the MoI. Though the Commission's job is to advice the MoI, which is in charge of the disinvestment programme, it still functions from North Block under wings of the ministry of finance, apparently because of the MoI's disinterest in providing basic facilities.

In its third report it had pointed out the need for speedy implementation of the recommendations as any delays will have an impact on the working of the PSUs on which the recommendations were made. ...

... It complained of the lack of formal communications from the Government and its inability to take decisions on the recommendations already made by the Commission. It also noted that the government decisions till date would not help solve any of the larger objectives of disinvestment and warned that the credibility of the disinvestment process will suffer if the Government continued in this way:

Contd. ...

...Contd. ...

"The Commission would once again urge the Government to address the recommendations of the commission fully and in a co-ordinated manner so as to establish the credibility of the disinvestment process and maximise the receipts from it." In its fifth report, which was completed at the end of November 1997, the Commission had suggested a "disinvestment audit" by the Comptroller and Auditor General, to make sure that disinvestment is "implemented in the best interests of the public". It had also threatened to monitor the disinvestment process as provided under its terms to reference.

The dilution of the terms of reference show that the strong approach taken by the disinvestment commission have only served to widen the gap between the MoI and the Commission. MoI officials say that the decision to water down the terms of the reference had received cabinet sanctions three months back. But if that is the case, it is not clear why the notification had to be issued now. The Congress, in its manifesto, has proposed conferring statutory status on the Commission. The BJP has supported the disinvestment process all along. The Left parties would scrap the commission given half a chance – though in private they admit the commission has done a commendable job. The fate of the Commission will ultimately depend on the next Government.

< List of 58 PSUs, DC >

Disinvestment Modalities Recommended in Report 1 to XII

Modalities of Disinvestment	*No.*	*Name of PSUs*
Trade Sale	8	ITDC, MFIL, HCIL, R-Ashok, U-Ashok, PHL, SIIL, MSTC
Strategic Sale	28	HTL, ITI, BALCO, BRPL, KIOCL, MFL, EIL, HPL, IBP, NEPA, HZL, PPCL, NFL, FACT, IPCL, HCL, SCI, HLL, AI, HSCL, STC, HIL, RINL, MMTC, PPL, HOCL, MOECON, RCF
Offer of Shares	6	GAIL, CONCOR, MTNL, NALCO, NMDC, BHEL
No Disinvestment	1	RITES
Disinvestment Deferred*	11	OIL, ONGC, MOIL, NTPC, NHPC, NLC, POWERGRID, SAIL, CEL, PEC, MECL
Closure/Sale of assets	4	EPIL, ET&T, HVOC, RICL
Total	**58**	

*: Pending fulfillment of certain specified conditions

ITDC - India Tourism Development Corporation

MFIL - Modern Food Industries India Ltd.

HCIL - Hotel Corporation of India Ltd.

R-Ashok - Ranchi Ashok Bihar Hotel Corporation

U-Ashok - Utkal Ashok Hotel Corporation Ltd.

PHL - Pawan Hans Helicopters Ltd.

SIIL - Sponge Iron India Ltd.

MSTC - MSTC Ltd.

HTL - HTL Limited

ITI - ITI Limited

BALCO - Bharat Aluminium Company Limited

BRPL - Bongaigaon Refineries and Petrochemicals Ltd.

Contd. ...

...Contd. ...

KIOCL	–	Kudremukh Iron Ore Company Limited
MFL	–	Madras Fertilizers Ltd.
EIL	–	Engineers India Ltd.
HPL	–	Hindustan Prefab Ltd.
IBP	–	IBP Ltd.
NEPA	–	NEPA Ltd.
HZL	–	Hindustan Zinc Ltd.
PPCL	–	Pyrites Phosphates & Chemicals Ltd.
NFL	–	National Fertilizer Ltd.
FACT	–	Fertilizer & Chemical (Travancore) Limited
IPCL	–	Indian Petrochemical Corporation Limited
HCL	–	Hindustan Copper Limited
SCI	–	Shipping Corporation of India Ltd.
HLL	–	Hindustan Latex Ltd.
AI	–	Air India Ltd.
HSCL	–	Hindustan Steel Works Construction Ltd.
STC	–	State Trading Corporation
HIL	–	Hindustan Insecticides Ltd.
RINL	–	Rashtriya Ispat Nigam Ltd.
MMTL	–	Mineral & Metal Trading Corporation of India Ltd.
PPL	–	Pradeep Phosphates Ltd.
HOCL	–	Hindustan Organic Chemicals Ltd.
MECON	–	MECON Ltd.
RCF	–	Rashtriya Chemicals & Fertilizers Ltd.
GAIL	–	Gas Authority of India Ltd.
CONCOR	–	Container Corpn. Of India Ltd.
MTNL	–	Mahanagar Telephone Nigam Ltd.
NALCO	–	National Aluminium Co. Ltd.
NMDC	–	National Mineral Development Corporation Ltd.
BHEL	–	Bharat Heavy Electricals Ltd.
RITES	–	Rail India Technical & Economic Services Ltd.
OIL	–	Oil India Ltd.
ONGC	–	Oil and Natural Gas Commission Ltd.
MOIL	–	Manganese Ore India Ltd.

Contd. ...

...Contd. ...

NTPC	–	National Thermal Power Corporation
NHPC	–	National Hydroelectric Power Corporation Ltd.
NLC	–	Neyveli Lignite Corporation Ltd.
POWERGRID	–	Power Grid Corporation of India Ltd.
SAIL	–	Steel Authority of India Ltd.
CEL	–	Central Electronics Ltd.
PEC	–	Project and Equipment Corporation
MECL	–	Mineral Exploration Corporation Ltd.
EPIL	–	Engineering Projects (India) Ltd.
ET&T	–	Electronics Trade and Technology Development Corporation
HVOC	–	Hindustan Vegetable Oil Corporation
RICL	–	Rehabilitation Industries Corporation Ltd.

< The Pioneer 22.11.97; Business Line 11.11.1997;
Financial Express 9.12.1997 >

THE PIONEER *New Delhi, Saturday, November 22, 1997*

Link disinvestment with poverty: GVR

New Delhi.

Disinvestment Commission Chairman G.V. Ramakrishna on Thursday called for the need to establish a link between disinvestment and poverty so that it could lead to better management of the public sector enterprises and growth of the economy. ...

... The linkage between social objectives to disinvestment would lead to better utilisation of people's money, he observed, and added that this would require political will. PSUs should be mustered to work on commercial lines to make them accountable, he said. ...

FINANCIAL EXPRESS *New Delhi, Tuesday, December 9, 1997*

'Disinvestment should be delinked from the Budget'

Rupali Mukherjee

New Delhi, Dec 8.

India's ambitious disinvestment programme should not be linked to the Budget as it does not help to build a good negotiation process. These views were expressed by Michael R Traem, vice-president, A T Kearney, in an interview to *The Financial Express*.

He said, "for privatisation, the Government or organisation should netotiate from a stronger position for getting the best possible returns. ...

BUSINESS LINE *New Delhi, Tuesday, November 11, 1997*

'Delink disinvestment process from budgetary exercise'

Our Special Correspondent

New Delhi, Nov. 10

The Disinvestment Commission has called upon the Government to delink the disinvestment process from the annual budgetary exercise.

In its fifth report released here on Monday, the Commission has said that "Budget-driven disinvestment will have to be made under compulsion of the budgetary time-frame and may not allow the sales to be timed to suit favourable market conditions." ...

... Addressing a Press conference at the release of the report, the Commission's Chairman, Mr. G.V. Ramakrishna, said that selling under the compulsion of the budgetary time-frame would encourage the investor to bid at lower prices for the PSU shares.

The separation of disinvestment proceeds from the other non-debt capital receipts in the Budget will prevent the short-term budgetary compulsions from obscuring the long-term benefits of disinvestment in loss-making PSUs and will help in highlighting the seriousness of the fiscal and revenue deficits and can compel actions to deal with them in the context of raising current revenues or curtailing current expenditure," the Commission said.

It has instead suggested "an early and clear decision on the structure and utilisation of the Disinvestment Fund on lines recommended in the First Report". ...

... The panel has said that the establishment of the Fund is also vital to the credibility and social acceptability of the disinvestment process and would also help in building up a general consensus in the country in its favour. ...

< Presentation of DoD 21.11.2000 p 30 >

Budgetary Support to Public Sector Enterprises (Excluding provisions for Voluntary Retirement Scheme)

As the table below shows, despite huge investment in the public sector, the Government is required to provide more funds every year. The public sector equity base of about Rs. 40,000 cr. (up to March 1990) yielded Rs. 17,983 cr. for the Government as dividend in nine years. However, the Government had to invest a further sum of Rs. 61,211 cr. during this period in the form of equity (Rs. 24,829 cr.), plan loans (Rs. 26,185 cr.), non-plan loans (Rs. 10,197 cr.), besides providing for the Voluntary Retirement Scheme. The average rate of return on the Government investment for these years works out to between 1 per cent to 6.5 per cent.

(Rs. in crores)

Year	*Plan*		*Non-Plan Loans*	*Total support*	*Dividend paid*
	Equity	*Loan*			
1990-91 (RE)	3531	2477	1067	7075	413
1991-92 (RE)	2491	2735	759	5985	687
1992-93 (RE)	2238	2403	600	5241	792
1993-94 (RE)	2419	4072	780	7271	1028
1994-95 (RE)	3442	3613	911	7966	1436
1995-96 (RE)	2050	3218	1184	6452	2205
1996-97 (RE)	2439	2956	1459	6854	2836
1997-98 (RE)	3004	2550	1583	7137	3609
1998-99 (RE)	3215	2161	1854	7230	4932
Total	**24829**	**26185**	**10197**	**61211**	**17938**

Paid-up capital of all CPSUs as on 31.3.90 About **40000**

Paid-up capital of all CPSUs as on 31.3.99 **77066**

(as per DPE Survey 1998-99)

< *The View from No. 11*, Nigel Lawson, p 238 >

THE VIEW FROM NO. 11 *Nigel Lawson p. 238*

Privatization – 3 : The Programme Reaches a Climax

> The objective of raising money for the Exchequer by these disposals, which later became an important by-product of the privatization programme, played no part in the Conservatives' hostility to nationalization, and little or no part in the gathering impetus of its drive for privatization. . . The prime motives for privatization were not Exchequer gain but an ideological belief in free markets and a wider distribution of private ownership of property.

Wider share ownership was an important policy objective and we were prepared to pay a price for it – although this price declined as our techniques developed over time. ...

... Yet another criticism, which was very much in vogue at one time with the Treasury Selected Committee and other less august commentators, is that the Government, in classifying privatization receipts as 'negative expenditure', was in effect cooking the books and – perhaps even more seriously – deceiving itself in this way to an extent that adversely affected the conduct of macroeconomic policy. Despite Harold Macmillan's jibe about making ends meet by selling the family silver. ...

< *The View from No. 11*, Nigel Lawson, p 205-207 >

THE VIEW FROM NO. 11 Nigel Lawson p. 205-207

Privatization – 1 : The Jewel in the Crown

... I was subsequently driven to write a note on Nicholas Ridley in March 1989, in connection with water privatization, summarizing the case in terms which applied beyond water:

1. All experience shows that businesses are more efficient and successful in the private than the public sector.
2. The water and sewerage industry is a business like any other.
3. A quarter of the industry is already in the private sector.
4. Of course it will need regulation – to project the consumer as it is a natural monopoly and for environmental reasons (purity of water etc.) – but it is far better for the State's responsibility to be clearly confined to that of regulator rather than to have the existing clash of interest when it is both regulator and producer.
5. Even though water is a natural monopoly, the privatized water industry will still face (a) competition for capital in the private sector and (b) a published daily share price – a comment on performance and a powerful spur to management.
6. Privatization not only widens share ownership (desirable in itself) but increases employee share ownership, which previous privatizations show leads to further improved performance. ...

... Institutional investors are certainly powerful. But I give away few political secrets when I say that Governments are likely to be more concerned by the prospect of alienating a mass of individual shareholders than they are by the lobbying of half a dozen investment managers.

The Thatcher Government introduced a number of measures to encourage share ownership. During the time of Lib-Lab pact, the Liberals had obliged Denis Healey to provide incentives for employee shareholding in his 1978 Budget, and these were extended by Geoffery Howe in 1980 and further improved in subsequent Budgets. In 1982 Geoffery indexed Capital Gains Tax to eliminate the taxation of future inflationary gains. In my 1984 Budget I greatly improved the tax treatment of share options and halved the Stamp Duty on share purchase, halving it again in 1986, prior to the eventual abolition promised by John Major in his 1990 Budget. And in my 1986 Budget I introduced Personal Equity Plans (PEPs). ...

< *Ibid.* 224 >

Privatization – 2 : The Birth of Popular Capitalism

... 'People's capitalism' was my own coinage. Margaret Thatcher liked the idea but not the precise formulation, which she thought sounded Communist, reminding her of expressions like 'people's republic'. She amended it to 'popular capitalism', and thus modified, it became part of the stock-in-trade of Conservative speechmaking from that moment on.

< DoD Presentation p 37-40 >

Privatisation Across the Globe : A Few Examples

Western Europe ...

... 2. France

Phase I (1986-87)

- 8 large groups and 3 medium size banks privatised.
- Shares divested to domestic public (about 50%), large shareholders (about 25%), employees (about 10%) & foreign investors (about 15%).

Phase II (Post 1993)

- 21 companies privatised, including 2 of the largest banks and 3 largest insurance companies.
- Shares divested to domestic public, large shareholders, employees & foreign investors in, more or less, the same proportion as in Phase I.

3. Germany

Phase I (1959-65)

... • Shares sold at discount to public; upper income group excluded from sales. ...

... *Phase III (Post 1990)* ...

... • Privatisation done through public sale, sale by auction, trade sale, Management / employee buy-outs. ...

4. Italy

Phase I (1984-89) ...

... • Shares sold to private parties. ...

< 'Get the Govt. out' Indian Express 23.10.2002 >

THE INDIAN EXPRESS *Wednesday, October 23, 2002*

Get the Government out

... Now in the case of the public sector oil companies, the shareholding of Government is 51 per cent in the case of HPCL and 66 per cent in the case of BPCL. If the IPO is for 2 per cent in the case of HPCL and 16 per cent in BPCL, Government shareholding will go down below 50 per cent and the companies will cease to be Government or public sector companies and will be like any public limited company in the private sector. This will mean that the companies will not be subject to the checks and balances of a PSU. There will be no parliamentary review, no public enterprises selection board, no CAG, no CVC, no CBI. The Government shareholding, though not majority, will remain in the hands of the ministry, as the largest single holder.

This will mean that the ministry can recruit anyone on any salary as the chief executive or functional directors and no one can question him except the shareholders, and the Ministry being the largest single shareholder will prevail. All contracts awarded by the PSU will be controlled by the Minister. The chief executive, having been selected by the Minister, will be beholden to him and will do his bidding (pun unintended) in awarding contracts. ...

... The same situation will arise if instead of the company raising resources by sale of shares, the Government sells its share and its shareholding comes down to less than 51 per cent. ...

... The IPO or the rights issues route or the secondary sale of Government held shares for taking PSUs out of the public sector, is full of portents for rampant corruption in the running of these large companies in a strategic sector. The Government may be seen to be following this route and abdicating its responsibility to protect public interest. The obfuscation about IPO seems to have arisen because of the inability or unwillingness to understand the process of disinvestment. The essence of disinvestment is for the Government to give up control over the PSUs and thereby raise the maximum possible resources which should be used primarily for the creation of tangible assets for the poor people in rural areas. The IPO route will not achieve either of these objectives.

There are two ways of giving up control. One is by transferring it to private parties through the strategic sale route. The other, which will apply in the case of a few blue chip companies in strategic sectors and in monopolies, will be through the route of the share holding trust which had been suggested by the Disinvestment Commission in 1998. This will mean converting the PSUs to publicly owned, professionally managed and profitable companies, which can then grow into globally competitive entities without

Contd. ...

...*Contd.* ...

Government control. The legal validity was certified by Additional Solicitor General, Kirit Raval in 1998. This involved a three-step process. First, converting the companies to non government companies by selling 2 per cent in the case of HPCL and 16 per cent in BPCL. Second, transfer the rest of the Government holding of just below 51 per cent of the National Shareholding Trust (NST) through a trust deed. The trust will be managed by six or seven eminent persons of proven integrity, experience in business, law, capital market and administration including one or two Government representatives. Third, the NST will appoint the best talent at market rates of compensation and ensure the growth-oriented management of the companies. With this, the share values will go up and the NST will sell the shares to the public in suitable lots at the right time, keeping in view market sentiment. The sale proceeds will be transferred to the Government which may then place them in a separate fund to be used for the benefit of the poor. The NST will retain 26 per cent of shares as a safeguard against clandestine takeover by private parties purchasing significant shares in the market.

This arrangement will resolve the conflict between those who want disinvestment through the strategic sale route and those who want the IPO route. When this is resolved, the disinvestment in smaller companies can go through the strategic route. Reforms by way of Government getting out of business can then go forward keeping in view the public interest.

< NST, Seven Press Reports >

(1 of 7)

THE ECONOMIC TIMES *New Delhi, Saturday, September 12, 1998*

Core group, oil cos set face against SPV for PSU selloff

Jaideep Lahiri

New Delhi, 11 September

The finance ministry's proposal to set up a special purpose vehicle to hold and sell shares of blue chip public sector companies appears to have run into trouble with the core group, investment bankers and oil giants expressing reservations about it. Sensing their mood, the finance ministry is understood to have sought SEBI's support. ...

(2 of 7)

THE FINANCIAL EXPRESS *New Delhi, Friday, February 28, 1997*

Accept PSU report at the earliest : SCOPE

Press Trust of India

New Delhi, Feb. 27

... Stating that high powered Commission, constituted by the United Front Government to advise it on PSU disinvestment, had vindicated the SCOPE's stand on PSU reforms, Hakeem told PTI that SCOPE had demanded earlier that disinvestment proceeds be primarily used for restructuring and revitalising this sector.

Maintaining that Government had so far gone very slow on lossening its controls on PSUs, he said, "It seems reluctant to change the interface between PSUs and Government," but added his hopes about acceptance of recommendations of the panel headed by former Planning Commission member, G.V. Ramarishna, were based on the Finance Minister's repeated assertions on this. ...

(3 of 7)

THE HINDUSTAN TIMES *Sunday, September 27, 1998*

Disinvestment through National Shareholding Trust

The Government hopes to raise Rs. 5,000 crore through disinvestment of PSU shares in the current fiscal 1998-99. However, the market has not been responsive to ensure a good price. The committee of secretaries suggested that Special Purpose Vehicles (SPVs) could be put in position to handle disinvestment. Early this week, the Finance Minister Yashwant Sinha said the Government may even offer the PSU shares at a discount. Now the Disinvestment Commission headed by Mr. G.V. Ramakrishna has suggested the setting up of a National Shareholding Trust to handle the sale of PSU shares. Given below is the text of the document on the Trust prepared by the Disinvestment Commission.

Various proposals are being made with the avowed objectives of raising quick resources for the Government and for giving autonomy for the blue chip companies. One proposal seeks to raise resources through the Government and the PSUs providing resources to the SPV for the purchase of shares in excess of 49 per cent, thereby converting these companies in non-Government companies and taking them outside the purview of several constitutional and statutory bodies set up to safeguard public monies and public interest. Another proposal relates to selling shares to newly-created Mutual Fund which could buy blocks of shares of PSUs for quick realisation of

Contd. ...

...Contd. ...

money by Government and thereafter sell the shares in the market. The mechanism for price fixation is not clear.

With the background, it is now necessary to take a more comprehensive view of the policy parameters for PSUs in such a manner that the objectives of raising resources, fair pricing, transparency and autonomy could be harmonised.

It would be necessary for the Government to take a decision to identify categories of PSUs as:

- Strategic units in which Government will have full ownership.
- Units from which Government can exit and bring in new ownership, new management and additional resources for development of the enterprise through the process of strategic sales in a transparent manner as already recommended by Disinvestment Commission. All cases not included in category 3 can be referred to the DC for making recommendations and implementing Government decisions thereon.
- Identify those blue chip PSUs in which Government need not keep majority holding and yet would not prima facie like to pass them on to private ownership and management.

While the decisions in the first two categories would be relatively simple, the third category needs some further examinations.

In the third category would fall the blue chip companies such as the major oil companies, NTPC, NHPC, BHEL and NALCO. This list is only illustrative. In the case of units in this category, it would be necessary to devise a scheme by which autonomy can be given to the units by bringing down Government shareholding below 51 per cent, while ensuring a fair price for the sale of the remaining shares. It would also be necessary for Government to be the largest single shareholder in these units as long as they are not classified in category 2 for strategic sale and transfer of management. These objectives can be achieved by dealing with category 3 blue chip PSUs in the following manner:

- Transfer the entire shareholding of Government to a Trust which may be called the National Shareholding Trust as a non-profit trust. The Trust can be set up under the Societies Registration Act or as a Statutory Body or as a Company under the Companies Act. The Trust will be holding beneficial interest in the Government shares transferred into it. The Trust will make a declaration to the Public Trustee under Section 153-B, Companies Act. The shares will be registered in the name of the Trust in the register of the Company. The Government could consider at a later date exempting the Trust from Sections 153-B and 187-B by inclusion in 153-B(4) Companies Act as in the case of Mutual Fund Trusts.
- The sale of shares may be arranged by the Trust after getting advice from the Disinvestment Commission on the quantity and modalities and after Government approval for the sale price and thereafter the proceeds will be transferred to Government. It may be stipulated that the shares held in the Trust will not at any time go below 26 per cent

Contd. ...

...Contd. ...

of the equity of each of the PSUs entrusted to the Trust. Various mechanisms can be worked out by the Disinvestment Commission for ensuring transparency in block sales to Mutual Funds, banks and institutions and by providing for Government sharing in the realisation of profits when the mutual funds and institutions later unload the shares in the market. In some cases where the shares to be sold are not substantial, the Trust can also sell shares directly to retail investors by engaging underwriters and brokers for the purpose as advised by the Commission. The Commission has already recommended in some cases sale by book building among institutions in India to establish a bench mark price and later sale of additional shares to retail investors at a discount.

- The management of the Trust would be entrusted to a group of five eminent persons with experience of the market and corporate finance and could also have one representative from the Finance Ministry.
- Institutions and PSUs in which Government shareholding is sought to be divested could be excluded from the Trust. Illustratively the Trust could include the Chairman of one leading public sector bank, an eminent management expert and the Chairman of a public sector insurance company apart from the Chairman, DC and the Finance Secretary. The Trust will have to ensure that in the sale of shares, there is wide distribution among institutions and small investors so that Government with 26 per cent holding will remain the largest single shareholder and no group can take over the company. The exercise of voting rights in the Government shares entrusted to the Trust will be by the governing body of the Trust if there is abstention by the public trustee or in accordance with a proxy of the public trustee under Section 187-B Companies Act and without reference to Government and in the best interest of the stake-holders in the PSUs. The Trust would also ensure that the Articles of Association of PSUs are amended and amplifed to provide for objective selection of Board level appointees to be elected to the board and to provide effective autonomy to the board with adequate safeguards such as internal audit committees with non-executive directors, internal vigilance and disciplinary action in appropriate cases.
- If the Trust could initially be set up as proposed above under the Companies Act and shares in selected PSUs transferred to it within a month, then the trustee company in consultation with the Disinvestment Commission can work out modalities from the sale of shares to institutions, mutual funds and others so as to get perhaps more than Rs. 5,000 crore during this financial year.

These proposals can be discussed within Government to arrive at a quick decision.

(4 of 7)

THE STATESMAN *Monday, October 14, 1996*

Disinvestment Commission proposes to help small investors

Statesman News Service

Madras, Oct. 13

The Disinvestment Commission proposes to help the small investors by giving them a chunk of the shares of blue chip public sector undertakings as and when they hit the market, according to Mr. G.V. Ramakrishna, chairman of the Commission. ...

... The Commission, he said, should not be accused of underselling the "family silver". According to him, the small investor had been taken for a ride in the past and if the Commission did grant him this benefit, it should not be criticized. ...

"If you (the public) say that there is nothing wrong in providing this benefit to the small investors, then we can think of doing so in small lots. This would be a gesture towards redressing the wrongs suffered by them," he maintained. ...

(5 of 7)

THE TIMES OF INDIA *Thursday, September 10, 1998*

Disinvestment panel's views on SPV sought

New Delhi Sept. 9

The Finance Ministry has sought the Disinvestment Commission's views on its proposal to float a non-government company for privatisation of top public sector undertakings, banks and financial institutions, reports PTI. ...

... When contacted the commission's Chairman, Mr. G.V. Ramakrishna said that "we received yesterday a communication from the Finance Ministry for our comments on SPV. But before this we had communicated our views to group of ministers on disinvestment including the finance and industry ministers." While the Finance Secretary, Mr. Vijay Kelkar had suggested that the disinvestment panel chief should head the SPV, a company to be created with equity base of just Rs. 10,000 to expedite privatisation programme, Mr. Ramakrishna has opposed the move saying it was against 'public policy.' Asked if he would reply to the Finance Ministry's communication, Mr. Ramakrishna said, "I have already written to a group of ministers." The Commission has communicated to the ministers that creation of SPV was an inefficient way of privatising PSUs and would have serious consequence on public policies, according to sources. The panel said selling 49 per cent through SPV would lead to administrative ministries retaining control of PSUs without being accountable to Parliament and other statutory bodies. The panel is also believed to have questioned the rationale behind selling only 49 per cent in the 'crown jewels' since the Government has already announced its intention to bring down its stake in non-strategic PSUs to 26 per cent. ...

(6 of 7)

THE INDIAN EXPRESS *Sunday, September 09, 1998*

Kelkar may help ministers tighten grip on PSUs

Sunil Jain

New Delhi, Sept. 5

The proposal made by Finance Secretary, Vijay Kelkar to speed up the privatisation process, may actually end up by allowing politicians and bureaucrats to exercise far more control over the public sector units (PSUs) currently under their administrative jurisdiction. ...

... The crux of Kelkar's proposal is that, once the Government divests its stake to the SPV– the Government will retain 49 per cent – then the PSUs will be freed from the control of Parliament, from CAG, etc. The point however, is that once the PSUs cease to be under Government control, who will be in charge of them till the time that they become genuinely private sector companies? The answer is: The company's boards, like say in the case of Maruti Udyog. ...

... While Kelkar's proposal was discussed by the core group of secretaries yesterday, no conclusion was reached, and the matter has been referred to the Group of Ministers. It appears that the Head of the Disinvestment Commission, G.V. Ramakrishna has written to the Cabinet Secretary protesting that he was given the proposal just the day before and has not even been asked to give his comments on the proposal. ...

Highlights of Kelkar's Proposal

- Government will retain 49% equity in select PSUs, and transfer the rest of a company, a Special Purpose Vehicle (SPV), which will be owned by it and the PSUs/others.
- The Govt. and PSUs will lend money to the SPV – initially, Rs. 4,000 crore – and this will be paid by the SPV to the Govt which will then be able to meet its disinvestment target.
- When the stock market improves, the SPV will sell these shares in the market, and the profits will be divided between the Government and the PSUs/other partners.

Advantages

- Allows disinvestment even when the markets are depressed.
- Allow govt to benefit from future hike in prices of PSU shares.
- Frees PSUs from onerous controls such as those of Parliament as govt equity below 49%.
- Since shares will be placed with SPV, Govt. may find it politically easier to lower stake in PSUs to 49%.

Disadvantages

- High interest burden to be borne by PSUs and Govt. who will lend money to SPV initially.
- PSUs will be free from Parliament etc, but since their boards will still be Govt-nominated, bureaucratic-ministry control will increase.
- Since the SPV will not have enough shares of the PSUs, no 'strategic' sale possible – essential for getting high price for shares, and revamping PSU boards for genuine autonomy.

BUSINESS LINE *New Delhi, Wednesday, September 9, 1998*

Disinvestment panel opposes move on SPV

Press Trust of India

New Delhi, Sep. 08

The disinvestment panel has opposed the proposal to create a special purpose vehicle (SPV) for privatisation of top public sector undertakings (PSUs) and banks, saying it was an attempt to control them by Government without being accountable to Parliament and statutory authorities. ...

< Nigel Lawson, p 778-779 >

The BP Affair - 2 : Dénouement and Aftermath

... The Judgement of the MMC

By early March, by which time the KIO holding in BP was well above the 20 per cent limit to which I had sought to get Ali Khalifa to agree – indeed it was not far short of 22 per cent – I told Margaret that I thought there was nothing for it but to refer the matter to the MMC. With some reluctance, she agreed. As soon as they had got wind of this, the Kuwaitis responded by halting KIO purchase of BP stock. Claiming that the shares were now overvalued, they announced that they would not take shareholding above 22.5 per cent. If they hoped this would halt the process of law, they were mistaken. On 3 May, David Young, referred the KIO shareholding in BP to the MMC. He explained that 'the implication of BP coming under the influence or control of a Government with substantial oil interests, and which is a member of OPEC, raises issues of public interest which warrant investigation by the MMC. The decision to make a reference to the Commission does not in any way prejudge the question whether or not the Kuwaiti shareholding is against the public interest.' The Kuwaitis undertook not to buy any further shares in BP, pending the outcome of the investigation.

The MMC referral clearly unsettled the Kuwaitis. On 8 August, the KIO executed a formal deed specifying that it intended to reduce its stake in BP to 20 per cent, not to seek board representation, and voluntarily to limit its voting rights to no more than 14.9 per cent of BP's share capital. It hoped that this would reassure the MMC that the BP shareholding was merely a portfolio investment without implications for the future of the company. It even offered to ensure its shareholding rose no further, by undertaking to opt always for cash rather than scrip dividends, and not to take up its shares in any rights issue. But the Kuwaitis had left it too late. What would have

Contd. ...

...Contd. ...

been an acceptable offer in February, before the referral to the MMC, was acceptable no longer. David Young rightly declined to sign the deed, on the grounds that he could not pre-empt the findings of the MMC.

To my relief and some surprise, the MMC reported in September 1988 that the KOI should be required to reduce its shareholding in BP to below 10 per cent within twelve months. It was a much tougher ruling than I had expected. ...

< *Ibid* p 206, 237 >

THE VIEW FROM NO. 11 Nigel Lawson p. 206-237

Wider Ownership

Although the primary aim of the privatization programme was to improve the performance of the former State-owned industries, there was a substantial spill-over benefit in the opportunities it provided for widening share ownership.

The references in Geoffrey Howe's first Budget Speech to 'the widest possible participation by the people in the ownership of British industry' was, of course, an extension of the Tory theme, central at least since Anthony Eden's day, of the creation of a property-owning democracy – which had hitherto been interpreted almost exclusively in terms of home-ownership.

I spelt out some of the reasons at the first Maurice Macmillan Memorial Lecture which I gave in June 1985:

> Those who, in the nineteenth century, argued the dangers of a mass democracy in which a majority of the voters would have no stake in the country at all, had reason to be fearful. But the remedy is not to restrict the franchise to those who own property: it is to extend the ownership of property to the largest possible majority of those who have the vote. The widespread ownership of private property is crucial to the survival of freedom and democracy. It gives the citizen a vital sense of identification with the society of which he is a part. It gives him a stake in the future – and indeed, equally important, in the present. It creates a society with an inbuilt resistance to revolutionary change....

An Assessment of Privatization

The success of the Conservative Government's pioneering privatization programme is accepted throughout the world. But it is only right to note some of the criticisms that have been levelled closer to home.

The first and least central criticism is that the fees paid to the Government's professional advisers and to the financial institutions and underwriters have been too high – and that where shares were firmly placed with the institutions

Contd. ...

...Contd. ...

in advance of the public offer, the terms on which this was done were too generous. To the extent that this is valid, and it became progressively less true as we gained in experience, we developed new techniques – one of which, 'clawback', under which the more successful an issue was, the more the institutions had to surrender their allotments to the general public, I can claim to have devised myself. Privatization was an exercise in which Government found itself a financial innovator to an extent which is rare indeed.

A second criticism is that shares were offered to the public at prices that were less than could have been secured, in order to promote widespread share ownership. To this I would reply: 'Yes, and quite right too.' While the interests of the taxpayer had to be given adequate weight, the maximization of proceeds, despite what many commentators said, was never the main objective. ...

< 'Statics and Dynamics of DCF' Financial Express August 2002 >

FINANCIAL EXPRESS *August, 2002*

The statics and dynamics of DCF

The other day I was talking to a small business entrepreneur friend of mine. He was running a van for hire to deliver raw material from the source to a factory about 20 kilometers away. His vehicle was reasonably new but he had an old driver with a defective vision who was working for half the salary of a regular driver. He could do only 4 trips a day going 80 kilometers to and fro. My friend's income was not adequate for his survival and for his son's college education. He could not even maintain his vehicle properly and it was frequently breaking down. He said he wanted to sell off his vehicle and pay his son's college entrance fees and maintain his family by selling his wife's jewels. I asked him how he would value his vehicle and fix a price. He said that he would take the earning from the vehicle for the next few years, back out the cost of running it and calculate the Net Present Value (NPV) by discounting each year's earnings at around 10 per cent. He said he was adopting this method as the Disinvestment of PSUs is also done this way by fixing the reserve price on the basis of the NPV.

I pondered for a while and found there was some flaw in this method of valuation. I spoke to my friend the next day and made a suggestion. Give your driver a month's leave and hire a competent driver and pay him the going rate and ask him to do 8 trips a day going 160 km to and fro and also get your engine tuned for better petrol consumption.

My friend took my advice and after a fortnight he met me and said that his earnings had gone up by 2 to 3 times because of more trips and fewer breakdowns. The vehicle was the same but was operated differently. I asked him to work out the NPV on the basis of the new earnings but with the same

Contd. ...

...Contd. ...

discount rate as before. He got the value 3 times higher. If he had sold it on his earlier calculations the clever buyer would have got a bargain and would have benefited by the faulty calculation of the owner.

After he sold the vehicle at the higher price based on the dynamic NPV, my friend was able to pay for his son's admission and also pay off some of his past debts.

What is the moral of this story for PSU disinvestments. The investment advisers calculate the NPV on a static basis on the assumption of current working conditions of underpaid, unimaginative, demotivated, badly selected management and with back seat driving by the Ministries. No wonder the PSU does not perform well like my friend's vehicle. And the calculations on this static basis give a low NPV and a low reserve price is fixed and bids are also low.

When the PSU is sold what happens? As in the case of my friend's vehicle, with new, motivated well paid managements without any Government interference the company with the same assets produces more by better incentives for productivity, better management, cost cutting and therefore higher profits. And the buyer who got the company on the static NPV goes laughing all the way to the bank.

Is it not possible to have a dynamic concept of NPV? But on what basis? Why not try out the full earning potential of the PSUs by total government withdrawal and converting them into non PSUs? The taxpayer will get a lot more for the shares of such a company. He is now paying a heavy price, not the buyer, for selling the enterprise as a Government company. The solution to this problem was given about 4 years ago when the Disinvestment Commission made a detailed and legally valid proposal for setting up a National Shareholder Trust which would hold the shares of the twenty odd blue chip companies after they are technically made a non Government company by bringing down the shareholding of Government to 50 per cent by sale to the public. In many cases Government holding is already close to 60 per cent. The fact that the company will go out of the Government control will itself put up market prices. The NST can consist of 5 or 6 eminent persons of competence and integrity and will act as the holding company of all the blue chip companies. This cannot be worse than handing over the company to a single strategic buyer without realizing the full value on the basis of the dynamic concept of NPV. The NST will ensure that the full potential of the company can be realized by getting the best people to manage at market rates of salary and incentives and giving them freedom to operate and show results without any Government interference. When the results are obvious the further sale of shares of Government will fetch a much higher price for the benefit of the taxpayer and Government can use the funds to discharge debt, build houses, schools and health centres for the rural poor. Then we would have polished the family silver, sold it for the best price and used the proceeds wisely, not for paying the cook's salary but for acquiring other assets for the family like an apartment or a car.

The Disinvestment Commission had also made the proposal that shares in the blue chip companies need not be sold to strategic buyers but to the people and can thus be converted into professionally managed publicly held and profitable companies which can grow to their full potential and even become global competitors. The snag was that Government was not prepared to let go the control over these companies. It should be realized that

Contd. ...

...Contd. ...

the price of the control is very heavy and amounts to depriving the tax payer of his rightful dues from assets created out of his money.

The work of the various ministries will then be confined to policy making and even this can be reduced by setting up Statutory Regulatory Bodies. Expenditure on the Ministries can be reduced. No one has taken up this matter for a discussion and clarification by Government. It is not too late yet as some of the "big ticket" companies are coming up for disinvestments. It is no use wringing one's hands and complaining after the deed is done.

G.V. Ramakrishna
21.08.2002

< HPCL, BPCL : four news reports >

(1 of 4)

THE TIMES OF INDIA *New Delhi, Tuesday, April 15, 2003*

Notice to Centre on BPCL, HPCL

Times News Network

New Delhi

The Supreme Court on Monday issued notice to the Centre on a public interest petition (PIL) challenging the planned privatisation of the Bharat Petroleum Corporation Ltd. and the Hindustan Petroleum Corporation Ltd.

Centre for Public Interest Litigation (CPIL) counsel, Rajinder Sachar and Prashant Bhushan said the Government's decision did not have Parliamentary approval.

Earlier on March 24, a Bench of Chief Justice V N Khare and Justice S B Sinha agreed to hear a similar petition filed by the Federation of All India Petro Traders and others. It clarified that "this order shall not be construed as any stay of disinvestment of HPCL and BPCL".

HPCL and BPCL, which together command a 40 per cent petro market share, were nationalised through an Act of Parliament in the 1970s and CPIL contends that disinvestment in these two companies could be done either by repealing or amending the acquisition Acts concerned. There was no other way of going about it.

Market blues

- Order should not be viewed as a stay on disinvestment of HPCL and BPCL
- HPCL and BPCL together command a 40 per cent petro market share
- The cabinet panel approved disinvestment of 38.2 per cent of the equity shares in BPCL and 34.01 per cent in HPCL

(2 of 4)

THE TIMES OF INDIA New Delhi, Tuesday, March 11, 2003

Jurists flay oil PSUs selloff

Times News Network

New Delhi

Five of India's most eminent jurists have severely criticised the Vajpayee Government's decision to privatise HPCL or BPCL without parliamentary approval. In a joint statement issued on Monday, Justices V.R. Krishna Iyer, O. Chinnapa Reddy, P.B. Sawant, Rajinder Sachar and advocate Shanti Bhushan said the move to sell the two oil PSUs without amending the Esso (and Burmah Shell) Acquisition of Undertakings Act was unconstitutional.

"The Government's decision to bypass Parliament on a matter of such public importance also militates against Constitutional propriety and the supremacy of Parliament. It shows an unhealthy contempt for Parliament and constitutional norms," they said.

The Government says it is acting on the advice of the Attorney General, who held that there is no need to refer the matter to Parliament. The jurists have referred to the preamble of the parliamentary enactments by which these oil companies were nationalised in the 1970s.

Word of law

- Such a decision amounts to unhealthy contempt for Parliament
- The Act is grossly unconstitutional
- HPCL, BPCL can be privatised by means of express Parliamentary enactments

According to them, the reason for nationalsation was to ensure that ownership and control of the companies – and indeed the distribution of petroleum products in India – must be "vested in the State and thereby so distributed as best to subserve the common good."

Another section of these Acts, they say, provides that after having taken over the assets of these oil companies, the Central Government could direct that these assets shall "instead of continuing to vest in the Central Government, vest in a Government company."

Despite the express mandate of the acquisition Acts — i.e. the assets of the nationalised oil companies could only be vested in a Government company – the Government appears to have decided that it can divest it shareholding without Parliamentary approval.

The former judges said it would be absurd to suggest that the Government could undo the Parliamentary mandate by just selling the shares of the two companies and thus privatising them.

Instead, they have suggested that these companies could only be privatised by means of express parliamentary enactments by either amending the Acts or bringing in a new Act and repealing the earlier enactments.

THE FINANCIAL EXPRESS *Tuesday, March 4, 2003*

BOTTOMLINE: NO LIGHT YET ON HPCL, BPCL DISINVESTMENT ISSUE

A Rebuttal of AG's Opinion

G.V. Ramakrishna

On the first page of the opinion expressed by the Attorney General of India on disinvestment, he has admitted that the Government has by notification vested the right, title and interest of Esso in a Government company. However, later on page 3, he says that the Memorandum and Articles of Association of HPCL and BPCL do not impose any requirement of Parliamentary approval for sale of shares.

It is well understood that the company is different from the shareholders and the Articles cannot impose fetters on the rights of shareholders to sell shares they hold in the company. Hence this is an invalid proposition not supported by law. In any case there was no need for the Articles to impose fetters on the Government when the Parliamentary enactment imposed such a restriction by stating that the assets should be vested in a Government company as defined by the Companies Act i.e., Government shareholding should not be less than 51 per cent. This is the crux of the matter.

On page 3, it is stated that the Board of Directors may take a decision on merger or amalgamation. The Parliamentary fetters are on the Government as shareholder and not on the Board of Directors.

In quoting a specific prohibition imposed by Parliament, the AG, on page 4, quotes the Banking Cos Act 1970 to the effect that 'Govt shall at all times hold not less then 51 per cent of the paid up capital of each bank'. In the Oil Cos Acquisition Act the corresponding stipulation has been put in different language viz; the assets will be vested in a Government company as defined in the Cos Act, which defines a Government co as one in which Government holds not less than 51 per cent of the equity capital. If the stipulation is valid in the case of the banks, why is it not valid in the case of the oil companies? How the learned AG considers one as valid is not clear.

It is reported that a few days ago the finance minister said in the Rajya Sabha that the Banking Act 1970 will be amended to modify the 51 per cent Government holding to 33 per cent to enable Government to sell shares but without privatisation. Thus the finance minister has accepted the need to amend the Banking Act to bring the Government holdings below 51 per cent. The same principle should apply to other ministries/departments dealing with disinvestment.

The Government has tried to confuse matters by stating that only shares will be transferred and not assets in HPCL and BPCL.

Contd. ...

...Contd. ...

The requirement of the Oil Cos Acquisition Acts is that the assets should be with a Government company which is defined with reference to percentage of shareholding and not asset transfer. How is this stipulation met by stating that only shares will be sold to bring down Government shareholding below 51 per cent and assets will not be transferred?

In fact, selling shares to bring down Government shareholding below 51 per cent is a direct violation of the fetters placed by Parliament on the Executive.

On page 5, there is reference to an 'in principle decision'. This is an obfuscation of facts. The Cabinet Committee on Disinvestment had taken a decision to sell the shares of Government to private parties through a strategic sale in HPCL. There was nothing in principle about this. In fact, the DoD has now gone ahead without further reference to the CCD and appointed the advisers to the sale. The implementation is on. The reference to Balco on page 6 is also irrelevant. Balco was registered by Government but without any acquisition of assets of private parties or Parliamentary legislation. The case of HPCL is quite different. HPCL came into existence after, and on the basis of Acquisition Acts passed by Parliament. All Government companies are not the same. Those created out of acquired assets by Parliamentary legislation are subject to the condition imposed by the acquiring Acts. Other Government companies are directly registered and are not subject to any Parliamentary fetters as in the case of acquired cos. Shareholder rights can be restricted by law or by contract. In this case there are Parliamentary fetters on the rights of Government as shareholder. Restriction b7 contract arises when the shareholders agreement between the disinvestment department and the buyer stipulates that the shares bought shall not be transferred within a stipulated period.

On page 6 it is stated that the legal merits of the ultimate decision will depend on the shareholder's agreement etc. But the basic decision to bring down Government shareholding below 51 per cent is itself violative of the Parliamentary condition irrespective of any conditions in the shareholders agreement. What is the AGs opinion on this? On the same page AG makes a statement that his opinion is sought on the limited question whether Parliamentary approval is a must to effectuate the in-principle policy decision. Effectuate means implementation. Then why add riders to his opinion about in-principle policy decisions? Or add clarification in the last para as dealt with below?

On page 7 it is stated that the crux of the matter is whether there is a requirement of Parliamentary approval for the decision or action of disinvestment in HPCL and BPCL which would result in change of management. Here again there is confusion introduced between disinvestment and change in management and "effectuating in principle policy decision". This is merely a way of avoiding the question. Management transfer follows the sale. Government cannot transfer management while keeping it in the public sector as a Government company. What is sought to be done is to sell shares to bring down Government shareholding below 51 per cent and then hand over management to the buyer. The Parliamentary stipulation is that the company should be a Government company. Its management thereafter determined by the provision of the Cos Act and its Articles of Association.

Contd. ...

...Contd. ...

All the Checks and balances applicable to a public sector company will apply. Merely to say that in-principle policy decision resulting in change of management may not require Parliamentary approval does not answer the question of retaining the oil companies in question as Government companies. It is not realised that in the case of HPCL sale of even 1 per cent of shares will bring down Government shareholding below 51 per cent and the company will become a non-government company and the Parliamentary requirement will not be met. The last paragraph of the opinion is confined to the sole question whether there is necessity of Parliamentary approval for 'in principle' policy decision of disinvestment and not about the form and content of the actual ultimate decision of disinvestment in HPCL and BPCL. If the learned AG thinks that he needs a way out he has actually painted himself into a corner. It would appear the queries were not framed in a clear manner by talking of policy decision in principle and the opinion is equally equivocating.

Opinion wants to please the Government by appearing to satisfy it and yet keep a semblance of respectability and validity for the AG. It may have satisfied those in Government who want to go through with the sale. It has failed in its second objective. The opinion is not likely to satisfy those interested in maintaining the integrity of the Constitution. Is it now difficult to see why DoD does not want to lay the opinion on the Table of the Houses of Parliament. The Emperor has no clothes. The issues that arise in this case go beyond the present sale of shares in the two oil companies.

The real issues are whether the executive can overcome or bypass a Parliamentary stipulation requiring the companies to be in public sector as Government companies and whether the principle of Separation of Power enshrined in our Constitution is being violated.

The only authority to adjudicate on this legal and Constitution matter of great public importance is the Supreme Court of India.

(The author is former chairman, Disinvestment Commission)

FRONTLINE *Friday, February 28, 2003*

Sell-off or sell-out?

The Attorney-General's legal opinion that the Government could go ahead with the disinvestment of public sector oil companies HPCL and BPCL without Parliamentary approval goes against the object of 'common good' that is set out in the preamble to the Acts that facilitated their creation.

Prashant Bhushan

The Attorney-General, Soli Sorabjee's opinion on the disinvestment of the oil public sector undertakings (PSUs) – Hindustan Petroleum Corporation Limited and Bharat Petroleum Corporation Limited – comes as no surprise. For more than a month, many people, particularly operators of the stock market, have been held in suspense awaiting his opinion, on which hanged the sale of the oil PSUs with assets worth ten of thousands of crores. His opinion, as reported in the newspapers, that the sell-off can proceed without the approval of Parliament, bring to memory his earlier opinions. Having been a student of the AG's opinions, and having written at least two earlier articles on them, I consider myself to be somewhat of an expert on the subject.

But first let us examine his present opinion. The occasion for this opinion arose when the Government was confronted by the Opposition in Parliament some months ago about the sell-off of the huge profit-making oil PSUs, on the basis that they were created by Acts of Parliament and that, therefore, they cannot be sold without parliamentary approval. The AG has now given an opinion that the parliamentary enactments by which the original private companies had been nationalised impose no impediment upon the Government if it wants to sell off the companies or their shares to private hands. Thus, according to the AG, the Government can privatise the oil PSUs without Parliamentary approval.

Both the Parliamentary enactments (The Esso Acquisition of Undertakings in India Act, 1974, and the Burmah Shell Acquisition Act, 1976) by which these private oil companies were nationalised, begin with a preamble, which says: "And whereas it is expedient in the public interest that the undertakings in India of Esso Eastern Inc. (Burmah Shell in the other Act) should be acquired in order to ensure that the ownership and control of the petroleum products are distributed and marketed in India by the said company are vested in the state and there by so distributed as best to subserve the common good." The Preamble clearly spells out the legislative policy of the enactments and the objective of nationalisation. It says that reason for nationalisation is to ensure that the ownership and control of the companies, and indeed the distribution of petroleum products in India, must be "vested in the state and thereby so distributed as best to subserve the common good." Yet the AG says that the Government can undo this and sell the PSUs so created by these Acts to private persons without Parliamentary approval.

Contd. ...

...*Contd.* ...

Section 7 of these Acts further provides that after having taken over the assets of these oil companies, the Central Government could direct that these assets shall "instead of continuing to vest in the Central Government, vest in a Government company". A Government company has been defined under the Companies Act as one in which the Government has at least 51 per cent ownership or shares and thus controls the management of the company. Despite the express mandate of the Acquisition Acts that the assets of the nationalised oil companies could only be vested in a Government company, the AG says that the Government could divest in shareholding in the companies so as to transfer the control of the companies to private parties. All this without parliamentary approval.

It is well settled in our constitutional scheme that all parliamentary Acts and mandates bind the executive. Any executive Act that violates any express or implied mandate of Parliament, is unconstitutional and void. The legislative mandate of the Acquisition Acts of these oil companies could not be clearer. The companies were nationalised and their assets vested in the state to ensure that their "products were so distributed as best to subserve to common good", as set out in the preamble of the Acts. Yet the AG says that since these companies are registered under the Companies Act, the Government can sell its shares to private parties just like any private owner of shares. Thus, according to the AG, the Government could have sold off the PSUs even immediately after they were nationalised by the parliamentary enactments. Or, in other words, it was always open to the Government to undo the legislative intent of the enactments by just selling back the shares of the PSUs so created even to the very same private companies whose assets were acquired. Such is the opinion on the basis of which the government proposes to sell off the controlling interest in highly profitable PSUs having public assets of ten of thousands of crores.

It has thus become necessary to remind ourselves of the controversial opinion that the same AG gave the Government just over two years ago. He gave two contradictory opinions on the legality and financial property of huge concession that the Government proposed to give to private telecom operators ("Conflicts and interests", *Frontline*, October 13, 2000). The issue there was whether the Government could legally waive the contracted licence fee payable by these operators and migrate them to a revenue-sharing arrangement. In his first opinion, he categorically stated that such a change would be an unjustified give-away to these operators, that it would be perceived as putting a premium on defaults, and that it would be vulnerable to a successful legal challenge by unsuccessful bidders. However, within five months, he gave another opinion, which completely contradicted his earlier one. In this, he justified the waiver of licence fee, and the migration of the private operators from a licence fee system to a revenue-sharing system both legally and financially by referring to the financial hardships faced by private operators. The Comptroller and Auditor-General (CAG) of India, in this report on the matter, rubbished the AG's opinion by pointing out that the actual number of subscribers of cellular licensees (who had committed the bulk of the defaults), overran the estimated number by 2-9 times in each of the four metropolitan cities in the first two years of operations. The CAG also berated the Government for having used the AG's opinion to give-away more than Rs. 3,000 crores to private operators, since the AG's opinion was

Contd. ...

...Contd. ...

more on financial issues on which he was not competent to render an opinion.

The AG's other opinions that I have had the occasion to write about (Frontline, October 10, 2000) were in respect of the Hindujas' power project at Visakhapatnam. Initially, violating a rule of the Government, which prohibited law officers from advising a party in the matter in which they may be called upon to advise the Government, he went on to give an opinion to the Hindujas in precisely these circumstances. He had said that the Hindujas, in order for the counter-guarantee to be effective, need not adhere to the conditions contained in the preamble of the guarantee issued by the Government of India. What he did thereafter at a meeting at the London office of the Hindujas' solicitors was simply shocking. This meeting was also attended by the prospective lenders to the Hinduja project who needed a certificate from the Government of India assuring them of the effectuation of the guarantee of the Government.

The AG went on to advise the Hindujas to "facilitate the request by the Ministry of Power and the Ministry of Finance for a consultation with the AG". He further advised that, "this is probably best done through the Ministry of Law who he had observed to be particularly helpful in trying to find a way of resolving the current difficulties." The minutes of this meeting show the AG to be virtually conspiring with the Hindujas about how he would use his office to get the Government to issue the required certificate, in a manner so as to avoid the Government undertaking a due diligence scrutiny of the project. The minutes recorded that the AG "went on to explain that one of the problems the GoI (Government of India) is having is that they are concerned that the various attempts at clarifying this issue would result in them having to carry out a detailed due diligence on the underlying project. It was confirmed to him (AG) that this was not the intention and indeed, from the sponsors perspective, was also undesirable." The minutes further recorded that the AG "said that he would then consider these and form an opinion as to whether any of the certificates could be provided by the Ministry of Power without placing themselves in a position of needing to carry out due diligence. He would then advise the MoP accordingly, and he would hope that they would follow his advice and issue the certificate required."

The AG thus advised the private party in a matter where he knew that he would be called upon to give advice to the Government. He in fact went on to advise them to facilitate a request from the Government to issue the certificate required by the private party, by avoiding a due diligence scrutiny of the project by the Government. There cannot be a more serious case of breach of trust by the top law officer of the Government, who is supposed to be an independent constitutional authority.

It is in the light of this background that the AG's latest opinion is in tune with the line taken by Disinvestment Minister, Arun Shourie, who has been arguing that since the oil PSUs are companies registered under the Companies Act, the sale of their shares to private companies would not need parliamentary approval. There are powerful forces at work pushing the "big ticket privatisation" as the sell-off of the oil PSUs is being called. Most of the big operators of the stock market are also greedily eyeing the huge public

Contd. ...

...Contd. ...

assets set to fall in private laps. The mood of the entire stock market seems to depend on whether these "reforms" would go through. It is in these circumstances that we need to remind ourselves of what Joseph Stiglitz (former Chief Economist to the World Bank and the Clinton Administration and winner of the Nobel Prize for Economics in 2001) had said in his recent book *Globalisation and its Discontents* (Penguin Books, 2002). Stiglitz points out how privatisation has helped create private monopolies, increased corruption and destroyed the economies of most countries where it was taken up in a big way. He says, "perhaps the most serious concern with privatisation, as it has so often been practiced, is corruption. The rhetoric of market fundamentalism asserts that privatisation will reduce what economists call the "rent-seeking" activity of government officials who either skim off the profits of Government enterprises or award contracts and jobs to their friends. But in contrast to what it was supposed to do, privatisation has made matters so much worse that in many countries today privatisation jokingly referred to as 'briberisation'.

If a Government is corrupt, there is little evidence that privatisation will solve the problem. After all, the same corrupt Government that mismanaged the firm will also handle the privatisation. In country after country, Government officials have realised that privatisation meant that they could get a significant chunk of the asset value for themselves rather then leaving it for subsequent officeholders. In effect, they could steal today much of what would have been skimmed off by future politicians. Not surprisingly, the rigged privatisation process was designed to maximise the amount that the Government Ministers could appropriate for themselves, not the amount that would accrue to the Government's treasury, let alone the overall efficiency of the economy. As we will see, Russia provides a devastating case study of the harm of "privatisation at all costs." It is the significant chunk of the huge asset value of these oil companies that is being greedily eyed by the private sector and those who control this Government. That is why the resort to the tested stratagem – "Get the opinion of the AG". Such being the state of out polity and its institutions, only an awakened and proactive citizenry can save this country.

(Prashant Bhushan is a lawyer practising in the Supreme Court of India.)

14

Construction Industry Development Council

MY last official assignment was to set up the Construction Industry Development Council (CIDC). In March 1996, I was nominated by the Deputy Chairman, Planning Commission, Pranab Mukherjee, as Chairman of CIDC for a three year term. Subsequently, Deputy Chairman K.C. Pant extended my term till 30th June 2003. At the end of this period, I was designated as Chairman Emeritus. The new Chairman is Dr. Uddesh Kohli, who was former Chairman, Oiwer Finance Corporation and Vice Chairman CIDC.

The Indian Construction Industry covers a wide range of activities from roads, bridges and houses to power stations, airports etc. As a number of Ministries were concerned with these activities it was difficult to coordinate the problems of the Construction Industry. In the meanwhile, after globalization began, the need to upgrade and modernize the industry became an important objective. As I was a member of the Planning Commission dealing with most of the infrastructure areas, the task of organizing the Construction Industry related issues, and an arrangement for modernizing the industry was taken up by me.

The Construction Industry is very large. It employs about 31 million persons — second only to agriculture in terms of employment. It takes up the 40 per cent of plan expenditure and contributes 20 per cent of GDP. For all its size, the industry is not keeping pace with the needs of modernization. Firstly, in the absence of any training, employed workforce is largly unskilled. Secondly, while there are a few large contractors, mostly in the private sector, there are thousands of small contractors. The major clients were mostly in the public sector. Tendering procedures and contract terms were archaic.

My first task was to bring together the public and private sector players at one table. A number of meetings had been arranged with the participation of the largest private sector companies, the public sector entities like the CPWD, the defence, the railways, the financing companies like HUDCO, research institutions like building materials testing BMPTC and others. After several meetings spread over six months, there was general agreement on the need for a body including contractors and clients in the private and public sector. It was agreed that the new body would be jointly formed as an autonomous institution with equal contribution of corpus funds from the Planning Commission and the private sector. CIDC was registered as a society with a corpus of Rs. 5 crores, in March 1996. All the major participants were founding members; CIDC now has 80 members. While I was nominated as the Chairman by the Deputy Chairman Planning Commission who was the Patron, we had one Vice Chairman from the public sector and another from the private sector. The Board of Governors also has equal representation from the public and private sectors selected through elections every two years.

Dr. Uddesh Kohli, Chairman of Power Finance Corporation and Dr. A. Ramakrishna, President ECC of Larsen and Toubro were the first two Vice Chairmen. The Council was fortunate to find in P.R. Swarup an able and enthusiastic Director (now Director General) who has made a valuable contribution for promoting the work of the Council. After the minimum period of settling down the Council undertook a number of tasks through expert committees. It has also established useful contacts with similar bodies in other countries. Some of these activities are as following.

1. HRD in Construction Industry

Construction workers are seasonal, migrant and itinerant. Their place of work, project and their employers keep changing. They are in an unorganized sector. Employers seldom invest in training workers, who cannot sacrifice their earning time for attending courses; training centres were non-existent. Recognising these problems, CIDC has initiated an ambitious project jointly with IGNOU (Indira Gandhi National Open University).

The CIDC – IGNOU Scheme

Salient Features

a) On-the-job training, minimum loss of earning.
b) Conveniently packaged programmes and credit systems.

Contd...

c) Uniform syllabi and standards of competence as per construction industry requirements.

d) Modern "delivery technology" being designed by IGNOU.

e) Objective testing by a Board which includes practising professionals as well as trainers/ educators.

f) Training and Testing logistics provided by existing institutions/industry. They may become regional Constituent Institutions (CIs) or their Partner Institutions (PIs) under the scheme.

g) Employers are persuaded to meet the testing and certification expenses and also assure increments and/or promotion to certified tradesmen. They can also use them as instructors or demonstrators for improving the skills of other tradesmen of the same category who work alongside.

h) IGNOU certifications.

i) Scope for further education (diploma/degree level) for willing candidates who possess or acquire the basic education level.

CIDC has also tied up with Dr. B. R. Ambedkar Open University (BRAOU), Hyderabad and Thapar Institute of Engineering and Technology (TIET), Patiala (Punjab) to provide academic support for its HRD Project.

CIDC has established about 12 institutes, throughout the country, for training and certification of construction workers in various trades. A separate institute has been set up for women workers in Gujarat. Regular examinations are being held in these institutes and certificates are being awarded to the successful candidates.

Recognizing the need to boost the training programs in the country, especially those being conducted by CIDC, National Highway Authority of India (NHAI) has made it mandatory for contractors to employ 5 per cent of trained and certified workers out of the total manpower engaged for its projects. Similar encouragement by other Government Departments will give a big boost to the training programs.

2. Rationalisation and Standardization of Contract Conditions for Domestic Bidding Documents

Considering the long felt need for a review of Contract Clauses incorporated by the Governmental Agencies in their prescribed Standard Bidding Documents for construction works, I set up a Committee in July 1996 for Standardisation and Rationalisation of Contract Documents for Domestic Bidding Contracts. The Committee, chaired by Shri Harish Chandra, former DG, CPWD, and Member UPSC, with senior level representation from the Ministry of Finance, all major construction departments of the Government, important PSUs and an equal number of private sector agencies, deliberated and reached a consensus and laid down twelve Core Clauses in Standard Contracts. Based on these Core clauses, a model contract document was prepared and termed as "Standard General Conditions for Domestic Contracts".

The Ministry of Statistics & Programme Implementation, Government of India, has approved the documents and has recommended that it should be used as a model guideline for preparing and awarding contracts for civil engineering works all over the country.

3. Construction Cost Indices (CCI)

The Construction Industry represents different sectors of operations and geographical regions. Each of the sectors and regions is unique in itself and therefore, a need for comprehensive price indices encompassing the diversities was strongly felt for a long time. CIDC, therefore, commissioned a study by National Institute of Construction Management and Research (NICMAR) and formed a Committee of Experts to deliberate on the report. Finally a methodology for computation of CCI was devised. CIDC has been periodically publishing CCI for the following sectors of the Construction Industry and regions; the base year being January 1998.

Sectors	*Regions*
(1) Building	(1) Delhi
(2) Bridges	(2) Mumbai
(3) Dams	(3) Kolkata
(4) Medium Industry	(4) Chennai
(5) Maintenance	(5) Hyderabad
(6) Road	
(7) Mineral Plant	
(8) Urban Infrastructure	
(9) Power Plants	
(10) Railways	
(11) Transmission Lines	

4. Construction Financing

Financing of Construction Projects and rendering financial support to the development of construction agencies is entirely different from financing the manufacturing sector. The large construction sector remains in need of financial support while sizable funds available with Banks/Financial Institutions remain unutilised. Lenders do not have a reasonably sound and reliable system for risk assessment in the construction sector.

To address the concerns of the lenders, CIDC commenced a series of initiatives, most of which have already been implemented. The CIDC-ICRA grading system provides accurate assessment of the risk profiles of the projects and the agencies. Lender's Engineer Panel provides a pool of specialised agencies/personnel for monitoring funds application and on-going assessment during the lifetime of the projects. Insurance products, developed by CIDC are to be marketed by Insurance Companies to cover risks which are specific to Construction Industry.

5. Grading of Construction Entities

This has a direct relationship with the selection of contractors and also with construction financing. Banks and Financial Institutions have been in search of a reliable, objective and comprehensive methodology for their computation of lending risks. Other Construction entities (Owners, Consultants, Contractors) also require a comprehensive, objective and reliable instrument for assessing and forecasting the chances of success of a project. Insurance companies too will find a reliable risk assessment system very useful for designing new types of risk covers for the construction industry.

In order to develop such an instrument, CIDC has joined hands with Investment Information and Credit Rating Agency (ICRA).

The new system is comprehensive and elaborate. It takes into account every major factor that has a bearing on the success of a construction venture. The system also covers all entities concerned, viz., the contractor, the owner, the consultant and the project itself.

Twenty one construction entities have been graded so far and two more have applied. With the introduction of grading as one of the requirements in the new Standard Bidding Documents and with grading being incorporated in the Indian Bank's Association (IBA) lending norms, this number is expected to go up substantially.

6. Lender's Engineers

One of the requirements identified to faciliate financing of construction and infrastructure projects by the Bankers/ Financial Institutions (FIs), was to have an adequate quality of on-line surveillance during the project construction stage. CIDC examined a number of such systems across the world and developed the "Lender's Engineer" system. The system has now been put into place and is operating. Lender's Engineers shall provide techno-commercial-legal feedback to the Bankers/FIs for projects financed by them and oversee and monitor the application of the financial support provided to the borrower.

After a rigorous screening process by the CIDC Screening Committee, twenty one Lender's Engineers, from all over the country, specializing in the various sectors of the Construction Industry were empanelled by CIDC.

The Bankers and FIs now have a service provider, who can identify and evaluate risks and monitor application of funds on an on-going basis, in projects. CIDC has recommended to the Banks and financial institutions to make use of the services of the empanelled Lender's Engineers, and thereby promote confidence to step-up financing in construction projects. Some of them have begun to implement this system.

7. Construction Equipment Bank

A major chunk of construction equipment owned by companies remains unutilised for large parts of the year. The idle equipment requires maintenance. Depreciation adds further to the unproductive costs of the company.

With total equipment stock of over Rs. 75,000 crores in the country and with additional requirements of Rs. 9,000 crores every year, efficient utilization of construction equipment will result in huge saving for a capital starved economy.

CIDC developed a concept model for Construction Equipment Bank, which was taken up by one of its members to form the first such Bank in the country. This Bank is now going ahead full stream with financial participation of multilateral funding agencies like IFC Washington of the World Bank Group.

8. AsiaConstruct

AsiaConstruct is the regional group of the apex bodies of their respective nation from Asian & Australian Continents. AsiaConstruct promotes co-operation among the apex bodies, representing construction industries of respective member countries, through exchange and sharing of information.

India was proud to host the 7th AsiaConstruct Conference for the year 2001. The conference was organized from 3rd to 6th October 2001 at New Delhi. With the active support of the Industry, CIDC organized an Exhibition along with a conference at Pragati Maidan, New Delhi.

The theme of the Conference was "Build India with International Cooperation". Country Reports were presented by the member countries of Asia as well as guest countries like US and Canada. The Technical Sessions had detailed discussions on current global and national issues related to the economy and construction industry. About 600 delegates, out of whom 110 were foreign nationals, attended the conference.

9. Workshop on "Emerging Technology Systems & Resources for the Construction Industry"

CIDC in association with Indian Society for Trenchless Technology (INDSTT) and Consultancy Development Centre (CDC) had organized the first of the series of workshops on "Emerging Technologies Systems & Resources for the Construction Industry." The workshop was organized on 5th July 2002 at New Delhi. At present laying of pipelines, communication and power cables results in digging up the roads causing inconveneience to the road users. By this technology digging along the road can be avoided by digging under the road at two points and making a tunnel through which the cable can be drawn. This has been used in Delhi and Bangalore and is expected to catch on if the municipal authorities impose the necessary conditions on the contractors.

10. SAARC Construction Industry Group

For sometime, there has been a construction group in SAARC. With renewed interest being shown by the members, the work of this committee has picked up. The previous Chairman of this group was a Sri Lankan member. The new Chairman from the 29th January 2004 will be the Director General of CIDC.

5th National Conference on Construction Industry — New Delhi, 2002;
with Vice-President of India Shri Bhairon Singh Shekhawat (centre, both the photographs) and Shri K.C. Pant, Dy. Chairman, Planning Commission (seen above to the right of the Vice President)

15

Epilogue

A great deal has been written about the evolution of Indian polity, the public services, the public and the institutions. I would like to add some of my observations based on my personal experience of half a century in Government and offer a few suggestions.

We face many problems. One can take a pessimistic or an optimistic view of the present situation. I am trying to take a balanced view. As the prayer goes 'O God give me, the strength to change what I can, the patience to accept what I cannot change and the wisdom to know the difference.' I hope, I have a modicum of wisdom granted by the Almighty.

Problems in some cases will go away by themselves, but in many cases they can be solved by concerted effort. In a democracy, the people will be the ultimate judges of the efforts made by Government to solve their problems. They are judges, with powers to punish at the polls. But their choices are limited and very often they are silent sufferers of the system.

Issues relating to basic needs have to be given the highest priority. The worsening water situation, not only for agriculture, but also for human consumption, has been known for sometime; many solutions have been suggested, but the result is there for all to see. It is true that when the rains fail there will be widespread distress; however, it is also known that in our country with two monsoons spread over six months in the year, about 70 per cent of the rainfall goes into the sea and, after the monsoon seasons, and between the monsoons, there is shortage of water. Can't efforts be made to store the rainfall water for future use? There are experiments and pilot projects, which have been certified as successful. The Farm Pond Scheme that was successfully implemented in Tamil Nadu in 1988, which showed that farmers' income could be augmented by 60 per cent, as certified by NABARD, needs to be revived. This and other such projects should be followed up with a sense of urgency.

Urban decay in terms of sanitation, waste disposal and roads should also be considered, within the limitations of finance.

In fact lack of finance is very often given as an excuse for lack of action. But there are ways in which efficiency in the use of resources can be greatly improved, particularly by reducing corruption.

The biggest erosion of resources occurs due to corruption. This blot is not merely a moral question. It is a question of draining resources, which should be used for improving the lot of the poor people of this country. Because of leakage of funds through corruption, the same amount of government money gets less work, and poorer quality work or goods. In this sense corruption is anti-people and anti-development.

Corruption can be collusive or compulsive. Collusive corruption arises when a party wants an undue favour from a government functionary, contrary to the rules, and offers him a bribe for getting that favour. High-level corruption is mostly, but not only, of this kind. Compulsive corruption arises when a citizen is compelled to pay a bribe for getting what is due to him under the rules. Most of the cutting edge corruption is of this type.

There are three broad categories of corruption. The cutting edge corruption of the police inspector or the sub registrar calls for citizen activism along with computerization and transparency. First Information Reports (FIRs), applications for registration and copies of documents should be computerized and receipts given to the parties. The inspecting authorities should then follow up the action taken.

The second type is the high level corruption at the level of senior officers in the Government and the public sector, politicians and ministers who have a fiduciary duty to protect the resources of the State. This takes as many forms as human ingenuity can devise. Books have been written about this. Lectures have been delivered. Seminars have been held. The Central Vigilance Commission (CVC) has been entrusted with the task of dealing with this type of corruption. How effective this body has been, with its limitations, is for others to judge.

The third is the more subtle intellectual corruption of giving a wrong opinion with the dishonest intention of pleasing the minister, for favours by way of postings and transfers apart from sharing the illegal gains. In this chapter, I shall deal with the second and third types of corruption.

I believe that high-level corruption generally trickles down from the top. People in Government see a great deal more than those outside. They see, how certain decisions are taken, in a seemingly normal manner, but really to favour certain individuals or groups. They also know that there is always a *quid pro quo* in these matters. The compulsions of personal greed and electoral expenditure are well known. In the early days both were under some check. Of late, both are boundless. Earlier, there was a stigma attached to the mere allegation of corruption in high places. Now corruption has become compulsive, addictive, open, bold and shameless. This is because of the lack of accountability and the ineffectiveness of our investigative agencies and the judicial system. I have dealt with this in some of the chapters of this book.

Even with a change in Government, the contagion of corruption persists. There is only a change in style and perhaps in scale. It is also a fact that corruption has ceased to be a factor in deciding the electoral fortunes of parties and individuals. The choice before the electorate is between tweedledum and tweedledee.

If corruption by politicians is accepted as a fact of life, it invariably leads a number of officials, who are so inclined, to join the bandwagon, either in association with their political bosses, or on their own, and succumb to temptation. If a senior officer is known to be corrupt there is strong encouragement for the juniors to follow. Senior corrupt people who live in glass houses cannot afford to throw stones at the juniors. In some cases the phenomenon of leapfrogging also occurs. A minister with an obstinate Secretary, who tries to keep him on the straight and narrow path, will send pheromonal signals to an amenable junior officer or a public sector executive, and the Secretary is cleverly bypassed. In one case a minister is reported to have told the Secretary that the stronger his opposition to a favour that the minister wants to bestow, the easier it is for him (the minister) to quote a higher price for overruling the Secretary!

The evolution of corruption over the last fifty years clearly brings out these new trends. In the sixties, K. D. Malaviya lost his job as Panditji thought taking Rs. 10 lakhs for elections was a crime. Today taking even Rs. 10 crores may not invite the same reaction.

Corruption is actually a way of transferring resources from the taxpayer and the common man to greedy businessmen, unscrupulous politician and venal officials. Stock market shenanigans offer a good example. The honest official who opposes corrupt actions is easily transferred and a more pliant officer is brought in his place. Many suggestions have been made for providing protection for honest officers. The system of giving a minimum tenure in a post and for transfers to be made on the advice of a group of senior officers has not been accepted as yet. In some cases, policies are framed in such a way that particular groups are helped at the expense of the exchequer, and in others, contracts are given to individuals.

I have come to believe that while corruption in all forms is bad, intellectual corruption of officials is worse and relatively, more damaging to the country than financial corruption. In this context, it is worth quoting the eminent jurist and savant, the late Nani Palkhivala who said in his Convocation address at the University of Bangalore in January 1972:

> In India today there are shortages of many commodities but nothing is so scarce as intellectual integrity. Closer contact with the world will convince you that intellectual integrity is a much rarer quality than financial integrity. The treason of the intellectual consists in his not speaking out loud and clear for the values that he, by his vision and by the very nature of his personality, holds sacred.
>
> —*We the People*

Recommendations for policy changes, made apparently in the normal course of business, can favour particular groups or individuals in a manner that is not easily discernible. An officer's motivation is to secure favours by way of posting, transfers and post retirement benefits. It may appear strange that I should be saying this after having got successive Government appointments for over fourteen years after retirement. I have tried to explain the circumstances under which I was offered these posts by Prime Ministers belonging to different political parties. The average civil servant, and perhaps the public, knows the distinction between an intellectually and financially corrupt senior officer and an honest officer.

So what is the solution? There are a few ways in which corruption in public life could be checked or mitigated.

The present activism of the Supreme Court about the electoral law requiring candidates to declare their criminal antecedents and assets has to be widely supported. It is typical of our political mores that the same parties that passed the law are now disagreeing with the Supreme Court. However, there is still some hope that the Supreme Court's opinion will be allowed to prevail.

Till a few years ago, the practice at the Centre and in the States, after a change of Government, was to shift a few key persons in official positions to make way for the confidantes of the Prime Minister or the Chief Minister. All other officers were left to complete their normal term. This encouraged the officials to give impartial advice to the Government of the day and strengthened the independence of the civil services.

In the last ten years the situation has changed largely in the States and to some extent at the Centre.

It has become a vicious circle. When a Government transfers dozens of Secretaries, District Magistrates and top police officers in one sweep and appoints political favourites in key positions and expects them to implement all kinds of orders, legal and illegal (and they are complied with) the integrity and independence of the civil services is compromised. Non obedience attracts harassment. The compliant officers get identified with the Government of the day. Later when a new Government comes into power all the favourites of the earlier Government and even others are suspect. Another round of wholesale transfer follows.

The solution is to first break the vicious circle. The new Government should take the advice of recently retired officers and senior serving officers of known integrity, make minimum changes and leave the bureaucrats to do their job for a normal term of three to five years. Mid term transfers should be avoided unless there are special reasons which should be non political and recommended by the senior officers group. If the procedure is followed a new Government cannot have the excuse that all the officers were favourites of the previous Government.

Another major problem of governance today is the wholly unjustified and illegal use of the police to serve political ends. The Dharma Vira Commission had recommended, decades ago, several steps to promote the independence and impartiality of the police. The Government should implement these and pass legislation to protect the independence of the police. The habit of using the police to harass political opponents should stop. Politicians should stop directing the investigation of major cases. Corruption of police grows if the politician in power involves the officers in promoting and tacitly encouraging criminal activities. An example of such collusion is seen in the recent Telgi stamp case.

With regard to criminal antecedents, it is necessary to distinguish between a police charge sheet and charges framed by a court of law. The former can be engineered by ruling parties against a political opponent. The latter comes if a judicial officer so decides on the *prima facie* assessment of the evidence in the case. There are a number of corruption cases and also criminal cases where delay and temptation leads to witnesses turning hostile. Today, arrest and publicity have, unfortunately, become the substitutes of judicial conviction. Many cases painstakingly investigated by the police fail in court because of key witnesses turning hostile due to financial inducements. The provisions of Section 164 of the Criminal Procedure Code (CrPC) should be used more widely to record sworn statements of witnesses before a magistrate. This will act as a deterrent to witnesses turning hostile, as they will then run the risk of a perjury charge.

It is a well known fact that the number of cases of political corruption that have led to conviction since Independence can be counted on the fingers of one hand. When S.A. Venkataraman, a competent senior officer, was convicted and sentenced to two years imprisonment for accepting air tickets and liquor, (trivial by today's standards), we thought that it was beginning of the end of corruption. Today bribes of crores of rupees are common, as seen from the number of cases being investigated by the CBI. In order expedite trials and convictions, one solution would be to record the statements of key witnesses under Section 164 of the CrPC. The second solution is to a fix time limit for investigative and judicial processes and to publicise unwarranted delays. Even after the court frames charges, there are inordinate delays in proceeding with the case. In such cases daily hearings should be the order of the day, rather than the exception. The expense of setting up a greater number of special courts with hand picked judges would be well worth it.

The Ombudsman Bill needs to be expedited with necessary provisions in various matters dealing with corruption. The salutary effect of the Karnataka Ombudsman in reducing corruption has been well documented and other States can take a leaf from the Karnataka experience, provided they can find a person like Justice Venkatachala to head the Ombudsman.

One administrative solution would be to give greater freedom to the Government to use the provision for premature retirement of officers with a dubious reputation. To prevent misuse there could be a quasi-judicial body to determine who is to go. This could also be built in to the Ombudsman Bill.

It is generally accepted that for every bribe taker there is a giver. Companies that are found to have given bribes should be answerable. Rarely are they prosecuted under the Prevention of Corruption Act. If corporate officials are also arrested and paraded in the media in the same way in which officials are treated, it would have some effect. Politicians will perhaps hesitate to be seen with them in public functions.

We have many strengths. The scientific temper of our young people, our high quality technical, scientific, and medical institutions, and our hardworking farmers hold promise for the future. The backbone of India is formed by the integrity of its middle class. This should be fostered by giving a clean Government at all levels. Training in ethics from the kindugarten level onwards will help in character building and reduce corruption in the long run.

We have a number of weaknesses that need to be addressed. The draining of national resources from the needs of the poorer sections, lack of accountability in public office which permits corruption at all levels with impunity, a slow judicial system, an electoral process that does not screen out criminal elements, the interest that is shown in the development of the rural areas only in the context of elections, urban decay and the lack of basic needs like water, power, sewerage etc. need to be tackled vigorously.

In today's world, national security should take precedence over everything else. In these matters, political parties should realize that electoral politics should yield to national interest. There should be a bi-partisan policy that goes beyond elections.

In order to make more rapid progress in development, it is essential that there is a stable Government for the full term of five years. The fragmentation of parties in the Lok Sabha leads to forced and artificial coalitions of expediency. A single party with a strength of two or three members can swing the balance. Such coalitions do not help in getting a stable Government or sustainable policies. The solution, though difficult, lies in going back to the founding fathers of the Constitution. The scheme of the Basic Law is that there should be a House of the People (Lok Sabha) and the Council of States (Rajya Sabha). If only national parties are allowed to put up candidates for the Lok Sabha, and regional parties are able to send their representatives to the Rajya Sabha, the fragmentation of parties in the Lok Sabha could be minimized. The annexed paper on 'How to avoid a hung Parliament', which I have been trying to propogate for the last eighteen years gives a solution. The solution does not require any legislation but can be achieved through action by the Election Commission under the Allotment of Symbol Order.

The role of the civil servant in the liberalized economy has to change, and I have annexed an article on the subject.

There is hope for the future, but it has to be tempered by the reality of today's situation. May be we will overcome our weaknesses and build on our strengths.

Appended Articles

I

"Why Not Kill the Cow?"

The question is often raised by knowledgeable, and not so knowledgeable people, as to why India does not solve her food problem by the simple expedient of eating all her cows. To be fair to the question, this should be interpreted to mean not merely the so-called 'sacred cow' but generally all species of bovine animals classified as cattle. This question arises out of the sophisticated writings on India where cows 'roam the streets' and also from the observations of 'experts', who have in the course of brief visits to India, seen large numbers of cattle 'roaming the countryside.' To the western mind conditioned by the economies of the industrialised world, the question is obvious as to why Indians continue to hold on to their age-old belief in the sacred cow and thereby forego a large valuable source of nutrition in the form of beef. The question is strange to others who are equally used to different eastern ways of thinking and the realities of economic conditions in that part of the world. The unstated assumption in the question is that it is the religious sentiment of the majority of Indian against killing the cow that stands in the way of the country's emancipation on the food front. This assumption greatly over emphasises the religious aspect of the matter and totally ignores the economic rationale for "not killing the cow". This paper attempts to provide a simple rationale and economic answer as to why it is uneconomic and even disastrous for Indian to consider cattle as a major source of food.

The role of cattle in the Indian economy is radically different from the role of cattle in developed countries. If it is strange for some westerners to find cattle roaming the countryside while there is standing crop on agricultural fields, it is just as strange for simple visitors from developing countries to see tractors and mechanical contraptions garaged in farm houses during the winter in the US. Just a tractors cannot plough the land during the winter when there is snow on the ground, cattle cannot go to work on crop lands when the crop is growing. It seems as facetious to tell the Indian farmer to eat his cattle as to tell a US farmer in Iowa to sell his idle tractor and go for a winter vacation to Florida.

The uses to which cattle are put in the Indian agricultural economy are :-

(a) As a draft animal for agricultural operations.

(b) As a source of energy for shallow irrigation.

(c) As a means of transportation for fertilizers, seeds and agricultural inputs from the markets to the field and of agricultural produce from the villages to the markets.

(d) As a source of milk for human consumption.

(e) As a source of energy for domestic cooking in areas where dung continues to be used as domestic fuel.

(f) As a source of fertiliser.

(g) As a means of producing biogas by mixing dung with vegetable waste.

(h) As a source of animal meat for human consumption.

(i) Other uses such as leather and medicinal products from the viscera are also quite obvious.

India has a total cattle population of about 245 million animals including buffaloes, cows and bullocks. Of these 160 million animals are used for draft and other purposes as a direct energy source. The draft animals are an essential source of energy for ploughing, levelling, puddling and other agricultural operations. 160 million animals with an average of ½ HP per animal represent a 80 million HP source. A substitute for this horse power would mean the equivalent of one million small tractors in terms of capital and maintenance expenditure.

In India, with each animal having ½ HP capacity and working on an average for 1,000 hours per year, the useful energy output per animal is about 1.2 million BTU per year at 5 per cent efficiency of utilising energy from feed. One tonne of oil yields 7.5 million BTU at 20 per cent efficiency of 38 million BTU per tonne of oil used in a machine. The output per animal of 1.2 million BTU per year corresponds to the energy output from 0.15 tonne of oil. The output from 160 million animal will be equivalent to about 23 million tonnes of oil. This will approximately cost $ 4.9 billion (Rs. 3900 crores) per year at current oil prices close to the value of the entire oil imports of India.

With a cultivated area of about 135 million hectares, the distribution of 160 million draft animals is quite thin and gives an average of about 0.6 horse power per hectare. As the optimum requirement of energy for efficient agricultural operations over 1 hectare varies form 1 to 1.5 horse power, draft cattle in India provide less than half the desirable energy and almost the entire available energy need of agriculture.

The pattern of land holdings in India also has particular significance in relation to the use of animal power on the farm. Out of a total of 50 million holdings nearly 75 per cent are two hectares or less. With the small size of holdings the use of even small tractors becomes uneconomic apart from other disadvantages of providing fuel and other maintenance needs of these tractors.

While animal power substitutes for imported oil, the main source of energy for the animals comes from grass on uncultivated hill sites in the countryside with supplement of fodder and vegetable wastes. In the summer season it is difficult for the cattle to find all the grass within the areas nearby and therefore they wander into distant areas and generally subsist at sub-standard levels of nutrition. The farmer also feeds his cattle selectively with greater attention being given to the animals that are of immediate use by making the limited fodder go as far as possible. There is a case therefore for increasing fodder production for feeding a larger number of animal to increase the availability of power for better agriculture in India.

It is therefore obvious that Indian agriculture is deficient in total energy input and gets most of its energy input for farm operations from animal power and it would be a great folly to deplete this source of energy when alternatives would mean so much additional investment and current expenditure of the kind which the western world is now trying to minimise.

While draft animals are used mainly for agricultural operations they are also a useful source of energy for shallow irrigation through Persian wheels and other ways of lifting water from dug wells. In the present state of roads linking villages to market places and with the consequences of higher oil imports, the obvious means of transportation for men and materials in large parts of the country still continues to be the animal driven cart.

The 85 million cattle which give milk comprises of about 53 million cows and 32 million buffaloes. Total milk production in the country which was about 17.5 million tonnes in 1951 has gone up to about 28 million tonnes. The continuous effort to improve the milk yielding capacity of milch animals by crossbreeding with exotic breeds has encouraged the setting up of 190 dairy plants and the expansion of milk production and distribution in smaller cities and towns. The average Indian diet which is low even in purely calorific terms is particularly deficient in proteins. And milk and milk-products are a valuable supplement to the Indian diet along with fish and eggs and poultry.

The use of dried dung as a source of energy has also to be taken into account in evaluating the overall contribution of cattle to the economy. Out of a total availability of about 320 million tonnes of dried dung per year only 80 million tonnes is at present collected and used as fuel in the rural areas. Calculations given in the attached Annex I show that the energy value from the use of this quantity of dried dung for domestic cooking and heating purposes is the equivalent of over 21 million tonnes of petroleum which at today's prices would cost about $ 4.6 billion (Rs. 3680 crores) per year. Another alternative way of using dung for generation of energy is by bio-gasification. Calculations in Annex II show that if the same quantity of 80 million tonnes of dried dung is used for generating gas the energy equivalent would be about 23.4 million tonnes of oil with a value of about $ 5.5 billion (Rs. 4400 crores). In addition to this the biogasification process yields an effluent with a nitrogen content of about 3 to 4 per cent which would be a valuable addition to our fertilizer supply. There is therefore a case for a greater use of dung for biogasification and as a fertilizer. Some idea of the value of dung as a fertiliser can be obtained if it is realised that 75 million tonnes will yield the equivalent of about 3 million tonnes of nutrient nitrogen which at today's prices will be valued at about $ 1.2 billion (950 crores). Apart from these potential uses, we may say that the current actual use of cattle as animal power for agriculture and for domestic energy alone results in a saving of over $ 10 billion (Rs. 8000 crores) per year in terms of an equivalent amount of oil required to yield the same amount of energy.

It is not true that Indians by and large are averse to eating meat. The simple fact is that many of them do not have access to meat of any kind. The country's 75 million goats provide not only milk and leather but also 1,72,000 tonnes of meat a year. The sheep population of 42 million provides apart from wool, 1,20,750 tonnes of meat. The so-called religious sentiment against killing the cow is really an over-simplification of the ancient practice of presenting economic, medicinal and health precepts in simple homespun language at it is some times the practice in western countries to present good politics as good economics. The Indian approach to the cow which symbolises all cattle is to emphasise the great economic value of the animal in an agrarian society. The fact that there is no rigid and fanatical resistance to killing cattle can be seen from the fact that over 5,80,000 buffaloes are killed annually for meat.

There is also the category of the aged, diseased, maimed and emaciated cattle, including cows. These are scattered all over the countryside and do not live in any single place. Such animals by their very condition do not offer a satisfactory source of edible meat – they are mostly skin and bones. Such animals are to the extent possible, collected and taken to slaughter houses for recovery of meat and medicinal products. The common impression that the slaughter of cattle in India will solve the food problem is based on the wrong assumption that they are very numerous and are available in large concentrations. These assumptions are incorrect. Perhaps to the average western eye a normal bullock or buffalo already appears emaciated in comparison with the cattle in the West. But these are the normal cattle which are so vital for agriculture in India. There is no doubt a case for better care of cattle with a view of improving their utility.

It will also be easy to appreciate, in terms of a free market economy, the value of any commodity in terms of its monetary exchange rate. The average price of a pair of useful draft animals varies from $ 150 to $ 300 (Rs. 2400) or more in some cases. The market price of a milch animal of the crossbred variety is even higher. This itself should show the economic value of these animals.

The question also arises as to why India should not develop a beef industry patterned on the model of industrial countries. The basic features of the industry are to breed and specially feed the animals to add to their weight and to recover the maximum quantity of meat in the shortest possible time. It is now generally recognised that it takes 8 to 10 times the amount of grain to produce a given quantity of animal meat, particularly beef. The uneconomic and wasteful means of producing animal meat even in western countries has been commented upon. Land, water, fertilizers and other resources required to produce foodgrains are economically used to produce grain for direct human consumption rather than for indirect human consumption in the form of animal meat. In a country like India, with its large population in relation to land resources and with present levels of nutrition well below desirable standards, it would be the nadir of ignorance to divert scarce resources to produce animal meat in an organised meat industry. Even in western countries the suggestion has been made to feed animals on grasslands rather than with feedgrains and the Indian situation offers no other alternative to the use of resources for maximum food grain production for direct human consumption.

It is not as if there is not enough scope for the diversification of the Indian diet. With a large coastal line of over 3500 miles the prospect for increased fishing production is very considerable in India. The present level of production of about 2.8 million tonnes can be increased several fold. Similarly in a poultry population of 150 million and an annual level of egg production of about 12 billion only a beginning has been made for the large scale expansion of this source of protein.

The suggestion for 'killing the cow' is very often made with the best of motives as an easy and obvious solution for solving the food problem. What is not obvious is that a careful and serious study of a country's economic background is necessary in order to understand the context in which certain customs and practices are followed.

---

* Written in 1975, updated upto 1980.

Annex I

• 2.5 tonnes of dry cow dung	=	1 tonnes of coal on replacement basis@
• 75 million tonnes of dry cow dung	=	30 million tonnes of coal on replacement basis.
• 1 tonne of coal	=	26 million BTUs.
• 30 million tonnes of dry cow dung	=	7,80,000 billion BTUs
• 38 million BTUs	=	1 tonne of oil
• 75 million tonnes of dry cow dung	=	20.5 million tonnes of oil.

Annex II

• 1 Kg of dry cow dung	=	550 litres of bio-gas
• Total dry dung in India	=	320 million tonnes#
• Actual consumption of dry cow dung for fuel in 1975-76	=	75 million tonnes (Estimated)*
• Total biogas from 75 million tonnes of dry cow dung	=	41,250 billion liters of gas
• 1,000 Litres	=	1 Cubic Meter
• 41,250 billion litres of gas	=	41.250 billion Cubic Meters.
• 1 Cubic Meter of bio-gas	=	20,000 BTUs
• 41.250 billion cubic meters	=	8,25,000 billion BTUs
• 38 million BTUs	=	1 tonnes of Oil
• 8,25,000 billion BTUs	=	21.7 million tonnes of oil

@ Converted from Table on page 27 of World Bank report on Energy Sector in India.

Para 7.10 of Fuel Policy Report.

* In 1970-71 the consumption was 68 million tonnes (page 27 of World bank Report on Energy Section in India.) For 1975-76 the consumption has been estimated at 75 million tonnes.

II

A Solution to the Problem of Hung Parliaments

During the last few years, elections to the Lok Sabha have not provided a simple majority for any one party. It has, therefore, been necessary to run minority governments or coalition governments. The problem has become more acute after the general elections of 1996 and 1998. After the 1996 election, a United Front of about ten political parties formed the Government with the 'outside support' of the second largest party in the Lok Sabha. This arrangement did not last long, as the supporting party withdrew outside support on two successive occasions, finally leading to fresh general elections within two years.

In 1998, general elections again resulted in a hung Parliament with two major national parties having 323 seats, five other national parties with 64 seats and the remaining 156 seats distributed among 20 state parties (105 seats), 10 unrecognised parties varying in size from 20 members to one member (49 seats) and six independents. A coalition government with the single largest party and the support of 12 other parties came to an end within a year after one of the coalition partners withdrew support and opposition parties were unable to form an alternative coalition government. A fresh general election had to take place, the second in 16 months.

The lack of stability in the Central Government has serious implications for the country. Economic policies and the associated parliamentary legislation get disrupted, investment sentiment gets adversely affected and international negotiations on important trade and financial matters cannot be pursued with any credibility. National defence, security matters and bilateral negotiations with various countries become discontinuous.

One of the main causes of unstable governments is generally recognized to be the multiplicity of small parties, with membership in one and two digits, being represented in the Lok Sabha. After the 1998 general elections, there were, apart from the seven national parties, 20 smaller parties recognized as State parties. In fact, the last government fell as a result of one adverse vote which can be attributed to any one of the several smaller parties.

Several suggestions have been made for 'reform of the electoral system' and almost all of them require amendment to the electoral laws or even the constitutional amendment. These measures are almost impossible under the present conditions with the smaller parties having developed strong vested interests in acquiring political leverage in a hung Parliament.

It is nevertheless necessary urgently to look for other solutions in the national interest.

There is one way out, which does not require parliamentary legislation but only action by the Election Commission of India, which may largely mitigate the problem of hung Parliaments, but may not eliminate it.

The Election Symbols (Reservation and Allotment) Orders, 1968 have been made by the Election Commission of India in exercise of powers conferred under Article 324 of the Constitution, the Representation of People Act, 1951 and Conduct of Elections Rules. In this Order, political parties have been defined and classified in different ways, as follows:

1. Political party means an association or body of individual citizens of India registered with the Election of India under Section 29-A of the Representation of People Act, 1951.
2. Political parties are either recognised or unrecognised political parties.
3. A political party should be treated as a recognized political party in the State only if it fulfills any of the following three conditions:

    (1)(a) has to be engaged in political activity for a continuous period of five years and

    (1)(b) should have returned at least one member of the Lok Sabha for every 25 members of a fraction thereof, elected from that State, i.e., if a State has 54 seats in the Lok Sabha, a party should have at least 3 members elected to the Lok Sabha or

(2) has at least one member to the legislative assembly seat for every 30 members of that Assembly or fraction thereof.

(3) that the total number of valid votes obtained by all the contesting candidates of such party in the elections to the Lok Sabha or Assembly is not less than four per cent of the total number of valid votes polled by all the contesting candidates. (Details of calculating the percentage of votes given in Clause 6 of the Order are not relevant for the present purpose). Having defined recognised political parties in the above manner, the Order classifies national parties and state parties, as follows:

- If a political party is treated as a recognised party in four or more states, it can have the status of a national party throughout the whole of India.
- If it is a recognised party in less than four states, it shall have the status of a state party.

The classification of national and state parties is relevant for the reservation of symbols. In the case of a national party, its contestants in elections in any constituency in India will have a symbol reserved for the party. In the case of a state party, reservation of symbols will be available in any constituency in a State where it is recognised as a state party.

An important point to be noted is that this reservation of symbols for a state party will be available at the elections in any constituency in the state. 'Any constituency' implies both Parliamentary and Assembly constituencies in the state. A state party being a single state party in most cases, may not have interest in getting a reserved symbol for Lok Sabha elections from any other state. However, in a single state, it will be at par with a national party, as the reserved symbol will be available for all the Lok Sabha constituencies in the state. In fact, a state party will be at an advantage *vis-à-vis* a national party as it can concentrate its efforts and exploit local sentiments within the state, while a national party has to contest elections in several states.

The Election Symbols Allotment Orders lay down stringent criteria for determining the national and state parties. However, in practice, both are treated equally in Lok Sabha elections. As far as Lok Sabha elections in any state are concerned, state parties which are treated as recognised state parties even in one state are entitled to get a reserved symbol for Lok Sabha elections from that state. This is the main reason for several single State parties puting up several candidates for Lok Sabha elections in the State with each having a common reserved symbol. There are at present over 30 such state parties who contested and got 101 seats in the last Lok Sabha which resulted in a hung Parliament.

National parties will be concerned with broader national issues related to economic, defence, foreign policies, etc.

State parties will be concerned essentially with local issues, such as meeting the basic needs of the people, food, water, housing education, etc. within the framework of the broad economic issues discussed in the National Development Council.

It is essential to ensure that the Lok Sabha is not fragmented by the representation of state and other local parties, and thereby deprived of a clear mandate from the people for the pursuit of clear cut national policies.

The situation can be substantially remedied if the Election Commission amends the Symbol Orders to the effect that only national parties will have reserved symbols for elections to Lok Sabha and state parties can have reserved symbols only for Assembly elections. State parties will not be deprived of their presence in Parliament as they can come to the Council of State (Rajya Sabha) through the State Assemblies.

If state parties are not given common reserved symbols, their candidates can contest on the same basis as candidates of unrecognised parties and independent candidates, with different unreserved symbols under Rule 10(4) of the Conduct of Election Rules, 1961. They may not have the same advantage as national party candidates in terms of funding, electioneering, etc. Moreover, Section 33 of Representation of People Act, 1951 makes a distinction between party candidates and others by stipulating that individual candidates should have ten proposers. This is intended to dissuade such candidates from contesting elections based on the party system. A similar distinction between national party and state party candidates in the matter of allotment of common reserved symbols for election to the Lok Sabha would be a valid differentiation in national interest.

The justification for this distinction can be that elections to the Lok Sabha should enable people to make a choice among the national parties and to enable a stable Government to be formed at the Centre on the basis of a clear mandate of the people in the national interest. The scheme of the Constitution appears to provide for regional and state parties to come to the Rajya Sabha, which is called 'Council of States', and to participate decisively at the national level in all legislative matters (other than money bills). The constitutional right under Article 19 to form an association is not affected. There is also no constitutional right for a political party to be recognised. There is also no constitutional right for state parties to get a common symbol for Lok Sabha elections. The Election Commission has been given the powers under the Constitution and the Representation of People Act, 1951 to notify the Symbols Order 1968.

The Election Commission can now amend, before the next general elections, paragraph 8 of the Symbols Order to the effect that the reserved symbols for a state party can be allotted to a candidate set up by a state party only at an election to the State Assembly.

The Election Commission can also make the conditions for the recognition of parties more stringent by amending para 6 of the Symbols Order by stipulating that at the last general elections to the Lok Sabha, a party should have returned at least one member for every 20 members of the House (instead of 25 members) or any fraction of that number or at least one member to the Legislative Assembly of that State for every 20 members (instead of 30 members) of the Assembly or any fraction of that number. This will also reduce the number of recognised parties which can claim to be State parties with presence only in one state, as specified in para 7 of the Symbols Order.

Consistent with the above proposals, it should also be examined whether independent candidates for the Lok Sabha elections should be required to have a higher deposit and the largest number of proposers, as already recommended by the Election Commission a few years ago.

III

A Tale of Two Friends

The other day I was sitting behind two persons in a long distance bus. After the bus left the city and entered the highway the passengers settled down to chat or to snooze. Since I was not sleepy I could not help overhearing the conversation up front. This is how it went.

A: You must be thinking of contesting the forthcoming elections?

B: Yes but I was only worried about the Supreme Court and the Election Commission's directives.

A: You have probably not seen the Draft Bill that the Government has prepared as desired by all the parties.

B: No, What does it say? If all parties want it then it should suit us.

A: Yes, of course they have not disappointed us. After all they all know which side of their electoral bread is buttered.

B: What does the Bill say?

A: It says that you can contest elections if you have committed only one offence of murder, rape robbery etc. and the court has framed charges.

B: Then it is okay for me, I have one murder and one rape case against me, but the court has not yet framed charges. There is however one robbery case where charges have been framed, but that was quite sometime ago.

A: Good for you. The charges should not be more than six months old for you to be disqualified.

B: My charge is more than six month old and so I am free to contest, am I ?

A: Yes and you can even commit one more heinous crime within six months of the elections. After all, you may have to prepare for the elections and let your supporters know who the boss is.

B: That is great! Our leaders really know the realities and how we can be helpful to them in the legislature when it comes to throwing mikes and chairs.

A: That is not all. Even if you have committed two heinous crimes and the court has not framed charges in both cases within six months, you are okay.

B: I have a fourth case of murder where the police have filed a charge sheet. What happens then?

A: You don't have to worry as long as the court has not framed charges, I am sure you can see to it.

B: Well, that is not too difficult. We can pass the word that heinous crimes are okay and if two of them are committed within six months of the polls, they should see to it that no charges are framed at least in one of the cases till the election dates are announced. We have good lawyers - real experts in getting adjournment, and in any case the judiciary, bless their souls, is overworked with so many cases.

A: So how do you think your party will fare?

B: Well, we have a number of potential candidates with various combinations of cases – some with murder charges, some with rape cases and even some so-called terrorists. (reflects for some time) May be we can always find right candidates who have only one charge framed by the court or those who have an old case of more than six months or even those with two charges. So the draft bill will suit us fine and we need not care for the Supreme Court or the Election Commission. But tell me, there was some talk about disclosing assets.

A: Oh that is all forgotten, who can afford to disclose all these financial matters at any rate before the elections. Everyone knows that only those with vast resources of black money can contest elections. The recent study of the Election Commission confirms what has been a well known fact. In any case why are the voters concerned with your assets before you get elected. If you get elected you can give the details to your leaders in any way you want and who is to scrutinize it.

B: What is all this talk about educational qualifications?

A: That is clearly against adult suffrage. Nehru dealt with it at the time of the framing of Constitution. Also, who can say that an educated man will be less corrupt. See what is happening in the financial world.

Only educated people are involved in scams. Even the draft bill has presumably been framed by educated people and the political leaders are highly educated.

B: So with all these loopholes wide and inviting, what do they mean by clean and fair elections?

A: You seem to be very simple-minded. Who really believes in all that?

B: I am happy with the present situation and the way our leaders are handling the Supreme Court and the Election Commission. Do you think the Election Commission can say that with so many loopholes they cannot conduct elections in a fair manner of 'keep out' so called criminals from the polls?

A: Yes, they can make their point only by resigning *en masse.*

B: Will they really do it?

A: Don't be silly. Who gives up a post these days on any matter of principle?

B: Tell me, what prompted the Government to bring these proposals now, after all these years.

A: It is only to plug a recently discovered loophole that as long as the Parliament does not frame laws in this regard, the Election Commission can issue directives by notification which will have the force of law.

B: It is really not for me to say it but sometimes I wonder whether we are a corrupt elitist democracy based on vote banks of caste, crime and money.

A: Well, I cannot honestly disagree with you. After all, laws are made by people who are beneficiaries of the present system and we have a democracy.

B: Is there a solution?

A: Better education and better electoral laws, not the sham law now being touted, may help matters, perhaps!

B: Here is the bus stop. For all the good news you have given me, I shall stand you tiffin and good coffee.

This may be considered an imaginary conversation but it is not so far fetched as people may wish to believe. After, all laws are made by the elected persons and who can question their wisdom in a democracy.

IV

The Civil Servant in a Deregulated Economy

The bureaucracy has come in for much discussion and some criticism in the last few years, post liberalisation and globalisation. In India liberalisation is an important aspect of implementing globalisation. In the new context of large companies going global and the new uses of information technology, worldwide attention has also been focussed on the role of the management in private companies.

The general impression is that the civil service is not equipped to deal with specialised areas of the economy and that it is unwilling to let go of its traditional control. While partly true, this impression is already changing with many technical bodies playing an active role in policy making.

In the new deregulated environment, the civil servant will have to rise to many challenges and be prepared to essay many roles:

- A clear understanding of the policy objectives of the Government is necessary. However, this is more easily said than done, as in many cases there is no clear thinking within the Government and in these days of coalition governments, the lowest common multiple operates in policy making. Several mid course corrections are made, partly to rectify past mistakes and sometimes to meet the compulsions of coalition politics. Nevertheless, the civil servant has to be quick enough to keep pace with the changing situation.
- Advising the minister frankly and after a full understanding of all the pros and cons of a given situation. The civil servant has to have a measure of understanding and humility to know what he does not know and be receptive to different points of view from technical and non-technical persons. Assembling diverse opinions and analysing and assessing them within the

framework of policy making is an important part of the civil servant's role. It is in this role that his/her intellectual integrity is really tested. S/he has to withstand pressure to tailor his advice according to the preference of various influential groups within and without the Government. The temptation of choice posting during service or after retirement has to be resisted. At the same time, it should not be assumed that every posting given after retirement is a reward for pliant conduct. The fairly common tendency to block out views divergent from one's own or anticipate the minister's wishes must be guarded against. In fact it is the duty of the civil servant to place before the minister the different views and then give his preference on the basis of his own analysis. In a deregulated economy, the areas of policy making will diminish, but will not vanish altogether.

- The new civil servant has to make a special effort to get acquainted with the latest developments round the world. The experiences of other countries which have traversed the same ground, have to be taken into account with appropriate adjustments for the Indian situation.
- A fair degree of familiarity, with the use of the amenities provided by new technology, such as the computer at the very least, will be necessary if the civil servant has to network with other agencies, technical or otherwise, and to keep his/her own data in order.
- Attitudinal change towards technical persons and bodies is essential to treat them with the respect that they deserve and to encourage them to express themselves freely. This valuable input in policy making should not be choked off.
- However good a policy may be, it needs to be presented both inside and outside the Government by the minister after adequately preparing his colleagues and other to understand and appreciate its significance. In this also, the advice of the civil servant will be valuable. Many good policies like the disinvestment policy, have floundered because of inadequate preparation and education of various interested groups.

- Learning to let go of old prerogatives and allow autonomous bodies, particularly public sector boards, to function is necessary.
- Implementing government policies, even if they go against personal preferences, diligently and imaginatively.
- It is necessary in these days of deregulation to act with transparency, not by rushing to the media with the suggestions one has made in the official papers, but by keeping paper work in order, by recording the process of evolution of policy accurately. This is a good way of watching one's own back when it comes to enquiries and fixing responsibility.

There are other problems and issues that arise in the course of a civil servant's career.

How does one deal with criminalisation in politics? In the first place, what is a criminal background? There are a number of stages in a criminal case. The First Information Report, the investigation, followed by the charge sheet to be filed in court if the investigating agency is convinced there is evidence. After going through the evidence and examining witnesses, the court will either discharge the accused or frame charges for regular trial. It is only when the court frames changes that there is a judicial opinion of a prima facie case against the accused, but there is no conviction as yet. At what stage in this process is the person deemed to have a criminal background for the purpose of getting party tickets or for occupying any public position? Civil servants should seek a clear legal opinion on this matter. Someone with court charges but not a police charge sheet, can get elected as an MP or MLA and even become a minister. If the law permits all this what should or can a civil servant do while dealing with him?

As a country we have the reputation of being corrupt at various levels. Corruption could be either coercive or collusive. The first is where a party is forced to pay a bribe to a civil servant for doing something that is normally due to it or for not doing anything against its interests. Delays in dealing with a case or registering a document or registering a case are some examples. The other is where the party pays a bribe to a civil servant for favouring it with something against the law. This is applicable in the award of contracts, revenue assessments of various kinds, for closing investigations or giving a weak report and so on. Civil servants could also be guilty of intellectual dishonesty in giving advice or in implementing policies, by favouring certain classes or groups of individuals or companies, thus causing loss to the exchequer or the public. Often superior officers and ministers expect subordinates to act as rubberstamps.

It is generally said that corruption, like growth, trickles down from the top. It is within the capacity of the civil service, if it so wants, to device systems which will reduce the lower level cutting-edge corruption which affects the common man. In all these grey and difficult areas of higher level corruption, what should an honest officer do? The simple answer is do your duty fearlessly and be prepared to face the consequences. I am aware that it is also an easy answer. Perhaps civil servants should debate this amongst themselves.

Thus, there should be reorientation of the role of the bureaucracy to meet the changing needs of the Government in keeping with its own changing role in the new global environment.

V

Scheme for Women's Welfare

The Family Planning Programme

Our Family Planning Programme has so far been aimed mainly at the upper age groups in the fertility range. It is time to see if we can also place emphasis on the lower age groups, particularly women. The planning and implementation of a Family Planning Programme that lays greater attention on the younger age group of women calls for bold initiatives to bring about major social transformations which will also have significant economic benefits.

Women's Welfare Scheme

A Women's Welfare Scheme, broad-based to include maternity, child care, nutrition, education, employment, and contraceptive facilities, needs immediate attention. There is considerable evidence correlating fertility among women with levels of education and employment and with delayed marriages. It has not been possible to identify any one of these causes as contributing to lower fertility but if we deal with these factors as an integrated package, it is easy to see their undoubted effect on fertility. The following facts will be useful for an appreciation of the proposal:

- There are in India about 130 million couples in the reproductive age between 17 and 45 years, which means there are over 110 million married women in the reproductive age group.
- Of these 100 million married women, nearly 50 million are in the age group of 17 to 24 years. With the average age of marriage of women being about 17 years, this number would include all women above the age of 17 years.
- The total number of crude births in India is about 24 million per year. Married women in the age group of 17 to 24 years account for over 15 million of these births.

The figure are outdated but the concept is valid.

- It has been observed that upto the age of 45 years for a women, the average number of children is 5.5 if the women is married at the age of 17; 3.8 if she is married between the ages of 21 to 24 and 2.3 if she marries at the age of 25 or later.
- It is, therefore, obvious that a major impact on our population growth can be made by directing a Programme towards reducing the fertility of women in the age groups of 17 to 24. In order to achieve this, the proposal is aimed at women in the younger age group of 15-20.

The Proposal

In view of the close correlation between fertility and education, employment, and delayed marriage, the scheme is intended to achieve the latter set of conditions by a system of incentives and disincentives for three categories of young women *viz.*

- Unmarried girls for postponing marriage.
- Young married women for postponing the first child.
- Young mother for spacing children.

Unmarried Girls

Special training institutions should be started for girls above the age of fifteen where they will be given basic education in nutrition, sanitation, homecare, and also vocational training in the crafts. As an incentive, they will be given employment in simple crafts for part of the time to convince parents that there is economic advantage in sending these girls to school. Payment for the work done at school will be partly in cash and partly in the form of interest bearing bonds which will be accumulated and cashed in lumpsum after a minimum period of three or four years of the girl's marriage. If an unmarried girl wishes to get married after she joins school, she will be eligible for the cash bonus earned upto the time of marriage, together with the delayed maternity bonus if she postpones child bearing by three years after marriage.

In this way, we can provide an incentive for a girl to get useful education, to earn cash while being educated and to be assured of a lumpsum bonus (the delayed marriage bonus) at the time of her marriage so long as it is put off by at least three years beyond the age of 15. The three year period will ensure the full benefit of education and also provide for delayed marriages, making a real contribution to lowering the birth rate. The further advantage is that even after the girl gets married after the three year period, she will be a better educated and economically useful wife and mother and will be more receptive to the idea of a small and well planned family.

For Young Married Women

Since it would also be useful to take into account currently married women in the younger age group of 15 to 20 and also the possibility of future marriages in this age group, it would be necessary to provide for the inclusion of such women in these educational and employment-oriented institutions but with slightly different incentives. For them, the cash bonus in a somewhat smaller amount (the delayed maternity bonus) will be given on the birth of the first child so long as it is delayed by three years. In the meanwhile, they will continue to get monthly cash payments for employment in these schools.

For Young Mothers

For young women, who have a child within three years of joining the scheme and for young mothers with one child who are willing to postpone the second child by three years, the scheme will provide similar incentives by way of child spacing bonus or cash at the end of the three year period. The advantage of having in the institutions, young unmarried women side by side with young married women and mothers motivated towards postponing and spacing child-bearing will have a salutary demonstration effect and will reinforce all the three aspects of the scheme.

Other Benefits

Since these institutions will employ exclusively women teachers, they will also provide useful employment for a number of educated women which will itself reduce fertility in this category. By far the most important benefit, apart from lowering fertility, will be the evolution of a new generation of educated, emancipated and enlightened young women.

Financial

In view of the financial and administrative implications, it would be obviously not possible to start this scheme to cover all the 50 million women between the age of 15 to 20 years in one stage. Initially, the scheme could be a pilot scheme in selected areas covering about 2.5 million. The estimates of working costs are given in the attached statement in the Annex. If the economic and social costs to the country of addition to population are considered, the costs of the scheme for reducing the total fertility of women will be fully justified.

Annexure*

Estimate of Expenditure on the Pilot Women's Welfare Scheme for Family Planning.

A. Expenditure on a special school for 100 girls in all the three categories:	
1. Teachers - 3 @ Rs. 400/- per month	Rs. 14,400/- per year
2. Training Materials and Capital Equipment @ Rs. 500/- per month	Rs. 6,000/- per year
3. Cash Stipend @ Rs. 45/- per month per student	Rs. 54,000/- per year
4. Deposit towards marriage bonus @ Rs. 25/- per month per student (Rs. 2,500/-)	Rs. 30,000 per year
[A pupil will get Rs. 300/- per year or Rs. 900/- in three years or Rs. 1,200/- with interest at the end of three years.]	
Total Expenditure	Rs. 1,05,000/- per year
Or	
B. Expenditure for 2 million young women	Rs. 210 crores per year
C. Likely number of births prevented or postponed per year	One million
D. Cost of preventing or postponing per birth	Rs. 2,100/-

Note: Conservatively, no credit has been taken for the value added in any economically useful goods produced in three schools. It is, however, likely that after the first year or two the students will begin to produce useful goods which will provide an economic return and reduce the financial burden on Government in later years.

* The figure are outdated but the concept is valid.

VI

The Truth About CNG

CNG or Compressed Natural Gas is **not** a clean fuel. It no doubt reduces visible smoke emission in vehicles, but it's emission in vehicles contains carbon monoxide (CO), unburnt hydrocarbons (HC) which are highly dangerous. They are invisible and cause heart disease, cancer and genetic changes. This has been proved in studies by the California Air Resources Board. The study compared emissions from a bus fuelled by CNG with those of a bus powered by a conventional diesel engine equipped with advanced pollution controls. The report of the results released on April 18th, 2002 states *inter alia* that the "CNG bus emitted higher level of aldehydes, toxic hydrocarbons and mutagens than the diesel bus". In 1996, the prestigious Society of Automotive Engineers (SAE) published in its conference proceedings two important papers by the South West Research Institute, Houston and the National Renewal Energy Lab. Paper No. 961089.

The results showed that for the five fuels compared for emissions the total hydrocarbon emissions were highest for CNG followed by LPG. It also showed that fuel consumption was also highest in CNG followed by LPG. The CO emissions were also the highest for CNG.

Why then is CNG being forced on the people of Delhi. The various parties who went before the Courts did not mention the above facts.

Why is this so? Because a new CNG bus chassis costs Rs. 12 lakhs while a diesel chassis costs Rs. 6 lakhs. There is a lot of money to be made in new CNG buses!

Are there not emission standards for CNG vehicles? Yes there are standards for CO, HC, Nox (Nitrogen oxides) and SPM (Suspended Particulate Matter) but only on paper. Have any of the CNG buses, taxis and autos been tested for HC emissions.

Cannot hydrocarbon emissions be measured in CNG buses and taxis? Yes they can be measured in pollution control centers along with Carbon Monoxide. The Central Pollution Control Board, for reasons best known to it, has directed these centers to indicate the hydrocarbon value. They only indicate the CO value. The media which carries news about pollution in metros does not indicate the hydrocarbon pollution. At least now they will ask for this measurement and report it!

What about the new Euro-II and Bharat-II vehicles. Are they pollution free?

There are two interesting facts, which are little known.

First, before certifying them, government-approved test centers use so-called test fuels which are pure Iso Octane (for petrol) and N-hexa decane (for diesel) which cause much less pollution. But these are only laboratory fuels and no-where are these fuel available on a commercial basis. If the same "certified" vehicles start using commercial petrol they will fail the Euro standards. Then they insisted that post-1996 vehicles use an exhaust catalytic converter. This can be used only with unleaded fuel. However, with unleaded fuel being freely available, there is no move to prescribe the same standards and use of cat converter for pre-1996 vehicles. Even unleaded petrol causes CO and HC emission and need other devices.

Moreover, diesel vehicles which consume six times the consumption of petrol in the country and pollute heavily with smoke and Nox, have not been prescribed any anti-pollution measures except total replacement with more polluting CNG vehicles.

What is the best and cheapest way of reducing vehicular pollution in cities?

There is an Indian invention called Hydrodrive developed by an engineer who has 29 years of experience. It is the first of its type in the world as it works on a new principle of pre treating the fuel before combustion using microwave synthesis. It has won the Asian Gold Award for the best Asian invention in 2001. It has been used over 2000 vehicles by private vehicle owners in Chennai, Bangalore and Coimbatore, who are very satisfied as it also improves fuel consumption. The device reformulates the fuel, both diesel and petrol on board the vehicle, before combustion by microwave-induced ionization and electron catalytic action leading to cleaner combustion and less pollutants. It costs only Rs. 6,000 for a car and Rs. 12,000 for a bus or truck. It brings down emissions in old vehicles to Euro II standards and new vehicles to Euro III standards. It has also been exported to Asian countries. It is much cheaper than other alternatives like CNG and more effective in controlling emissions. Its use with low sulphur diesel available in Mathura refinery in existing buses and trucks will be the cheapest way of reducing pollution in Delhi.

Its use will save the taxpayer thousands of crores and bus commuters will be charged less for tickets.

Why is this not being tried more extensively? Are there strong vested interests in promoting the expensive and dangerously polluting CNG?

VII

New Dimensions in Disinvestment

It has been stated, though in low key, that disinvestment or privatisation, can, if not properly handled, lead to corruption, overt or covert.

The classic example of privatisation with overtones of corruption was the Russian experience. The voucher system and private placement of government shares led to business tycoons cornering shares and acquiring control over major undertakings at well below their true value and stripping the assets of the companies at the expense of the people and the country.

In India we have now reached a stage where privatisation is about to take off. But we should be careful that we are not on the wrong runway.

Questions have been raised about the valuation of the companies before they are offered to bidders. The Disinvestment Commission, while recommending transparent procedure, had also said that a reserve price should be available to the Government before deciding on accepting the highest bid so that unduly low bids and collusive bids are identified. Here one should distinguish between valuation of assets and valuation of an enterprise taking into account several factors such as the cash and other assets of the company, the condition of the assets, the need for additional investments to modernise it, the product range of the facilities, existing competition within the country, the domestic and international market, the level of import duties and the entry barriers for new units in the same line of manufacture. Government should not only have competent financial advisers but also its own consultants to give it a second opinion on the advice given by the global financial adviser.

In regard to the blue chip companies, the Disinvestment Commission had not recommended privatisation but the placement of minority government shares in a National Shareholding Trust. These companies will become non-public sector, non-private sector, publicly held companies which are professionally managed. This proposal which was made in 1998 has not been accepted though it was fully supported by the top management of the blue chip companies. The idea of the NST was proposed because merely taking them out of the public sector will be fraught with hazards. The minority shareholding of 26 per cent in the hands of politicians and bureaucrats without any of the checks and balances of public accountability can lend itself to charges of corrupt action in whatever they do rightly or wrongly.

A current case in point is VSNL which has substantial cash reserves of Rs. 1,200 crores. It has been proposed that the Government share be brought down to 49 per cent by divesting only 4 per cent. 49 per cent shareholding in the hands of ministers and bureaucrats will give virtual control and the power to do what they want with the assets of the company and its future activities. Parliament will have no role, the CAG and CVC will be kept out of jurisdiction by virtue of the company being technically converted into a non-public sector company. Future disinvestment will also be in the hands of the new management with defacto control of some Government functionaries. The appointments of the top manatement will also not be PSEB recommendations. If subservient persons are hand-picked, every contract and every transaction of the company will be subject to approval by the powers that be. The scope for mischief can easily be imagined. VSNL has recently been privatised by selling a 25 per cent share with transfer of management control.

Apart from this, the proposed arrangement will make it difficult for the company to raise funds in the market. Further disinvestment will also not get the required response from the public.

These are the reasons that led to the suggestion of the NST and it is for these reasons that the proposal was supported by the blue chip companies.

This is one more example of how an innocuous proposal can have seeds of corruption in very large enterprises. One wonders whether the same proposal for keeping 49 per cent shares would have been made in the case of a loss making company.

Unless the Government is alive to these pitfalls of privatisation, our own privatisation can go the way of the Russian experience.

VIII

The Zero Sum Game

It starts with nature's balance of elements. When matter gets transformed into different elements or compounds like the burning of coal or petroleum, the overall balance in the Universe is restored. The sum total of all the elements, in whichever configuration they may occur, remains the same.

The same principle can be applied to different situations in life. Economists call it the zero sum game when one party gains an amount equal to the loss of the other party. Sometimes when both parties gain by any arrangement, it is called a non-zero sum game.

In the Indian situation, zero sum game is played in a three-cornered way, the parties being, the tax payers, the Government and the corrupt beneficiaries of various scams.

Take the case of the stock market scams. The small investor loses either directly or through institutions like the UTI to unscrupulous beneficiaries in various kinds of market manipulation and shady deals. The institution, being a creature of the Government, seeks government support on the ground that it was after all carrying out various transactions at the behest of the Government. Market manipulation by Stock brokers and others was facilitated by these institutions. So when the scam surfaces, the small investor is left high and dry. Based on the recommendation of the Deepak Parekh Committee, the Government paid out about Rs. 5,000 crores to support the UTI. The bill for the latest scam in UTI has not yet been settled. The small investor in US 64 has already taken a beating but further government support is not ruled out.

The same situation arises when banks lend recklessly or knowingly to shady companies and lose their capital. Again the Government as the putative party is asked to step in to save the banks and inject fresh capital. The Government of India has paid over Rs. 20,000 crores to such Banks to recapitalise them. The recent budget adds a further sum of Rs. 1,300 crores to recapitalise the Indian Bank, for the third time.

When government companies incur huge losses year after year by paying non-working workers salaries every month, the first port of call for the distressed management is the Government. The losses of the loss making government companies have gone up from Rs. 5,183 crores in 1995-96 to Rs. 10,600 crores in 1999-2000. During this five year period, total losses amount to Rs. 37,189 crores.

The total losses of these three categories alone amount to Rs. 62,000 crores during the last five years.

Where does this money come from? Accounts have to be squared to meet the natural law of zero sum game. The answer is that the money comes from the tax payer in the guise of patriotic surcharges and also in higher prices for essential items like kerosene etc.

We have not yet squared the equation. We have quantified the total draft on the budget on account of these three categories which have been passed onto the tax payer. In fact, a lot more is passed onto the tax payer for various purposes like staff salaries of bureaucrats, Ministers MPs, etc., some of which may not be justified but at least the tax payer knows where his money is going for openly certified uses. In the case of Rs. 62,000, crores the tax payer would like to know why he should be asked to pay for the illegal gains of unscrupulous functionaries, corporates and market players. He would like to know what the Government and its agencies have done to stop this. In the case of the UTI, they would like to know why Government has refused to allow the SEBI to inspect the largest Mutual Fund inspite of several requests from the then Chairman in 1992 and 1993 till the first scam in 1998. Who were the persons responsible for shielding the UTI from the regulatory body when all other mutual funds came under SEBI.

In the case of loss making PSUs, disinvestment was not seriously attempted. In fact, many of them have to be closed with the workers given VRS. In fact, the corpus of VRS at about Rs. 5 lakhs on an average, giving a return of eight per cent risk free, amounts to Rs. 40,000 per year. This is the income from six hectares of dry land which a land owner will get after toiling day and night, after taking the risk of the monsoon and incurring debt for seeds fertilisers and pesticides. The VRS employee can get this by sitting at home and having free time to pursue any other vocation to augment his income.

Even the VRS payment will have to be borne by the tax payer but it will not be a recurring draft like the losses of PSUs. The disinvestments process should not take the relatively easy route of selling profit making companies but should make a serious effort to restructure where necessary and sell loss-making PSUs or close them down.

Another point that the tax payers should know is that the proceeds of disinvestments during the 10 years from 1991 amount to about Rs. 20,000 crores. This money has been merged in the general resources of the Government. Its impact on lowering the fiscal deficit on the average is only 0.02 per cent. In other words the average fiscal deficit would have gone up from 5.7 per cent to 5.72 per cent. On the other hand, if the amount had been spent for creating assets for rural people, 40 lakh houses and one lakh schools could have been built and Rs. 5,000 crores given as VRS before closing down the loss making companies. This would be creating assets after selling other assets in the form of shares of good companies. What has happened is that the assets have been sold and the proceeds used for revenue purpose. That is why there is skepticism among the public not about the process of disinvestments but about the use of the money. After all, these assets were created out of the tax payers money and he should be satisfied that the sale of these assets will either create other assets or reduce the future draft on him on account of the loss making companies. It is the duty of the Government to deal with this responsibly to the satisfaction of the tax payer.

Name Index

N

P

Q

R

S